The
Way of Interior Peace

The Way of Interior Peace

Dedicated to Our Lady of Peace

BY

REV. FATHER DE LEHEN, S.J.

TRANSLATED FROM THE GERMAN VERSION OF
REV. JAMES BRUCKER, S.J.
BY A RELIGIOUS

WITH A PREFACE BY
HIS EMINENCE, CARDINAL GIBBONS

Original Copyright
1888 by Benziger Bros.

Copyright © 2014 by Refuge of Sinners Publishing, Inc.
Pekin, Indiana.

The typography of this book is the property of Refuge of Sinners Publishing, Inc., and may not be reproduced, in whole, or in part, without written permission from the publisher.

Printed and bound in the United States of America.

Published by

Refuge of Sinners Publishing, Inc.
5271 E Mann Rd - Pekin, IN. 47165
www.JoyfulCatholic.com
1-800-451-3993

PREFACE.

THE WAY OF INTERIOR PEACE, by Father de Lehen, S.J., is regarded as an excellent book for priests, religious, and the laity who wish to serve God in peace of heart and mind. In it directors of souls can thoroughly learn how to conduct their penitents through the devious ways of casuistic troubles and difficulties. Many persons of good will, but of a scrupulous, doubtful, or erroneous conscience, will find a true guide and consoler in this book, so calculated to impart tranquillity, contentment, and love of God to hearts agitated by anxieties of conscience. Appropriate quotations of Holy Scripture, principles and opinions of notable theologians, of experienced directors of souls, of prominent saints and doctors of the Church, are so well arranged and linked together that the book commends itself both in form and substance.

It is attractive by its clear, simple, concise style, adapted to the capacity of the learned and the unlearned.

The work was originally written by a holy, learned, and experienced director of souls. It has, besides, been recommended by the venerable and zealous Bishop A. Räss, of Strasburg, lately deceased. The book has not only been highly appreciated ever since its appearance in French, but also since its translation into German. The fact of its having reached ten editions in German since 1870, and that at a time in which thousands of religious were exiled from their fatherland by the Kulturkampf, and thousands of priests deprived of their salaries by unjust laws, is of itself sufficient proof of its intrinsic worth and usefulness.

The English translation from the German, which is an improved arrangement of the French original, commends itself by its fidelity to the original text, as well as by its idiomatic and easy style.

J. CARD. GIBBONS,
Abp. Balto.

APPROBATION TO THE ENGLISH EDITION.

The great St. Teresa experienced sadly the want of knowledge and skill in several who had attempted to be her guide in the paths of perfection.

In her valuable writings, this great saint speaks of the damage that is done to souls by such indiscreet and incapable guides. In the remarkable wisdom and prudence which so eminently characterized St. Teresa, she most earnestly recommends that only those be chosen as directors of souls who will be found well trained in the science of that "*ars artium.*"

We gladly welcome, therefore, the publication of "The Way of Interior Peace," a work eminently qualified for this object. It has been greatly appreciated in France and Germany, and has the hearty approbation of our illustrious Cardinal and of many other Prelates. We wish it a wide circulation.

W. H. Gross, C.SS.R.,
Abp. Oregon.

Portland, August 24, 1888.

APPROBATION TO THE GERMAN EDITION.

The instructive and edifying book of Rev. Father de Lehen, S.J., is a reliable guide on the way of salvation. Its being placed within the reach of the German Catholic public merits approval and warm commendation.

✠ Andreas,
Bishop of Strasburg.

Strasburg, April 3, 1872.

AUTHOR'S PREFACE.

THIS book is intended to put into the hands of Christian souls the proper means of preserving interior peace, or, if lost, of regaining it. Its highest recommendation is, that in one volume it contains many salutary instructions compiled from various excellent works, the special aim of which is to secure interior peace. This is that high good which Our Lord announced at His entrance into the world, and which is an almost indispensable condition to progress in virtue or the spiritual life: "Peace to men of good-will."[1]

But since the preservation of interior peace is for us of so great importance, it is easily explained why the Evil One makes so many exertions to rob us of this blessing.

Unfortunately, he succeeds only too well; for in human nature itself, in the errors of the mind and disorderly inclinations, already lies more than the germ of interior trouble and disquiet. In fostering these evil propensities, by permitting the mind to stray and the will to turn from God, it is easy to understand into what misery the human heart is plunged. The first condition of interior peace is the removal of all hindrances known to man; the second is simple, child-like abandonment to the Divine Will in all the mutable events of this life. For both of these we have need of a twofold knowledge: that of our duty, and that of the way in which God leads us to sanctity. The lack of this knowledge is the source, above all others, whence innumerable interior anxieties and troubles spring.

[1] Luke ii. 14.

But such an explanation does not include everything. On the way of perfection we meet a thousand unforeseen events that may easily throw us off our guard. Sometimes it is faults into which we unexpectedly fall; sometimes, the thought of the frailty and misery of our nature; again, it may be temptations, or passions that powerfully stir our heart; finally, it may be our neighbor's faults that put our patience to the test. All this quickly discourages us; and discouragement is the most dangerous snare for souls that have a good-will but are yet weak and inexperienced. That, therefore, this work should perfectly attain its end, we must touch upon all those occurrences that give rise to interior trouble, and try to meet each with a corresponding remedy.

To accomplish this task with order and clearness, we have divided the book into four parts, each of which, in one way or another, refers to the subject.

Part First treats of resignation to God's will and the dispensations of His providence, and is particularly rich in consolation for all whom God tries by suffering. The last three chapters of this part are chiefly taken from the works of Fénelon and Father de la Colombière.

Part Second is intended to give a clear and comprehensive idea, first, of true devotion as the surest foundation of interior peace; secondly, of the principal deceits that endanger this peace; thirdly, of the necessary conditions for true and solid progress in virtue; and fourthly, of the way in which God usually leads souls to perfection. The writings of St. Francis de Sales and of Fénelon have been taken as guides in working out this part. Besides this, we have culled many beautiful thoughts from the manuscripts of a certain spiritual director as enlightened as he was experienced.

Part Third is addressed more particularly to individuals. It treats of the various means by which, in all the temptations and spiritual infirmities inevitable here below, peace of soul and confidence in God may be preserved.

This part contains extracts from different works; for instance, from the "Spiritual Combat;" the "Treatise on Christian Hope," by Father Gaud ; and the "Treatise on Discouragement and Temptation," by Father Michel. From Fénelon are culled the pages that treat more especially of prayer.

Finally, Part Fourth deals with scruples. It enlightens the scrupulous upon what they must do to regain lost peace ; and it is also to be hoped that it will afford souls not suffering from that dangerous malady much that will prove useful and consoling. This extract or fourth part is based (the necessary changes being made) on Duguet's precious work on the source of scruples. Numerous additions taken from reliable sources complete the whole. All additions and changes are designated by quotation-marks, and may thus be distinguished from Duguet's text.

This same method we have observed throughout the other parts of the book, enclosing in quotation-marks extracts or passages taken from other works than the chapter itself.

Timid or fearful souls may give all the more credence to Duguet's teaching, as he belonged to a school justly accused of extreme severity.

At the conclusion of the book will be found different methods of prayer, which experience has taught will contribute much to facilitate the spiritual exercises.

The compilation of so many portions from various sources naturally proved injurious to unity of style and caused frequent repetitions, which would have been unpardonable if our aim had been literary perfection. But as the end in view is to be preferred, precedence has been given it.

The portions extracted from other writers have been inserted in their original wording, in order to insure to them full authority. This accuracy will cause literary imperfection to be overlooked.

If we have in any way contributed to the consolation of a soul in distress, we shall cheerfully embrace the opprobrium of literary enormities, confidently hoping that they to whom this book may prove useful will not fail to pray for the soul of him whose words have brought them light and consolation.

We place it in the hands of St. Joseph, begging him to commend it to the patronage of Mary, Mother of God. May the comfortress of the afflicted obtain peace of heart for all who read these lines!

TRANSLATOR'S PREFACE

TO THE FIRST GERMAN EDITION.

The book which we now present to the pious souls of Germany has in France, and in a very short time, reached four editions. It justly merited so wide-spread a circulation; for it would be difficult to find another ascetical work suited to so many and various needs of the soul, or which sets forth so fully and practically the interior life.

The author, Father de Lehen, S.J., was one of those men to whom God gives the requisite qualifications for directing others. In him were combined the experience of an enlightened man of the world, together with the cultured piety of a religious. Of a noble, old Breton family, trained from early years to esteem honor and justice, he devoted the first period of his youth to the study of law. But God had other designs upon him. He directed the steps of the pious youth into the sanctuary, where only could his soul find the nourishment it desired. After perfecting himself in the sciences and finishing his juridical studies, having received in both branches the degree of Doctor, he entered the Society of Jesus. At that time this Order was not legally recognized in France. The greater part of the French Jesuits had, therefore, to seek elsewhere their religious and scientific training. Accordingly, de Lehen was sent to Savoy, to finish his studies. Here he was acknowledged, in every respect, the model of a perfect religious. What called for particular admiration in him was his great love for the interior life. Those that knew him best saw in him the future skilful master of novices. And, in reality, soon after his profession the responsible office of training the novices of the Society was confided to him for a number of years, both in Alsace and Amiens.

This position afforded him an opportunity not only of putting to profit his knowledge of the spiritual life, but also of daily increasing his own experience in it. The result he has confided to the readers of his "Way of Interior Peace." From this book may be conjectured with what insight, prudence, and care the author devoted himself to the difficult task of directing souls. He himself acknowledged one day, in confidential intercourse, that he sometimes searched through entire volumes to find a single line corresponding to the wants of a soul confided to him. This he did not only because in his charity he wished to give what was best and most suited to instruct, but also because, for the sake of security, he desired to support his decisions on the authority of approved spiritual writers.

Father de Lehen died at Angers in the sixty-second year of his age.

He had long desired to see his work translated into German, that it might in Germany, also, be of use to many souls interested in their own salvation. But as the book was in its first form rather crude, on account of its numerous repetitions and literary defects, it would have been but poorly received in Germany. We have, therefore, not only translated, but also endeavored to give it a more pleasing style, by abridging and uniting its several parts.

May it, in its new garb, effect as much good as it has done in the old!

PREFACE TO THE THIRD GERMAN EDITION.

ABOUT two years have elapsed since this unpretending little book made its first appearance in German. The fact that a third edition has so soon become a necessity is proof sufficient of the welcome everywhere accorded it. Although

Preface to the Third German Edition.

similar works have had equal success, yet the sale of this has been more rapid than recent political events would have allowed us to hope.

It is, assuredly, pleasant and consoling to know that, in the midst of the tumult of the world and the sounding of the war tocsin, a voice was heard proclaiming the way to interior peace; and that far from being stifled by the bustle around it, it made itself heard and gained the attention it demanded.

Many of the daily papers noticed the book favorably, and not a few were the congratulations received by the editor on his success.

What is most generally praised is Father de Lehen's ability in demonstrating the theory of asceticism and the solidity with which he works out its practice. These are two advantages not possessed by all ascetic writers; for whilst one leaves his reader in ignorance of what constitutes true piety, another presents it in so radiant a light that poor human nature seems altogether incapable of attaining it.

Now, the author, Rev. Father de Lehen, S.J., combines these two merits with that of not requiring from all souls the same degree of perfection. He knows how to meet human weakness, and how to distinguish in piety the essential from the non-essential. In this way he infuses courage into the weakest. He urges them to approach the fountain of grace, and taste how sweet it is to serve the Lord.

May the God of peace grant to this new edition, as to those that have preceded it, His blessing, that all who seek the "Way of Interior Peace" may, by its aid, find it and walk therein!

FEAST OF THE SEVEN DOLORS, March, 1872.

CONTENTS.

	PAGE
Preface,	3
Approbation to the English Edition,	4
Approbation to the German Edition,	4
Author's Preface,	5
Translator's Preface to the First German Edition,	9
Preface to the Third German Edition,	10

PART I.

Of Resignation to the Dispensations of Divine Providence.

CHAPTER I.—Of the Loving Dispensations of Divine Providence toward Men, and of the Happiness of those that wholly submit to Its Decrees, ... 21
CHAPTER II.—In what we should submit to the Ordinances of Divine Providence, ... 38
CHAPTER III.—Why and How we should Resign Ourselves to God's Will, ... 59
CHAPTER IV.—Of the Utility of Sufferings for the Just.—Of their Necessity for the Sinner, ... 68
CHAPTER V.—Of the Good Use of Sufferings, ... 75

PART II.

True Piety the Indispensable Foundation of Interior Peace.—The Way in which God leads Souls to Peace and Perfection.

CHAPTER I.—The Foundation of True Piety.—Points in which we should Imitate the Example of the Saints, . . . 83
CHAPTER II.—We must Serve God according to His Will and not for the Gratification of our own Inclinations, . . 92

Contents.

PAGE

CHAPTER III.—Of the Sacrament of Penance, and of the Peace and Comfort found in its Reception, ... 96
CHAPTER IV.—Of Holy Communion.—What is required to receive worthily, and the Reason that It is for so many a Subject of Fear, ... 106
CHAPTER V.—Of Prayer and the Manner of Fulfilling this Duty. —Of the False Ideas often formed of this Exercise, . . 115
CHAPTER VI.—The Knowledge of God and of One's Self the First Condition of Solid Virtue and True Peace, . . 122
CHAPTER VII.—Patience with Self the Second Requisite of True Piety and Peace of Soul, ... 129
CHAPTER VIII.—We should Courageously Labor at our Advancement, and thereby, without losing Interior Peace, draw Spiritual Benefit from our Faults and Miseries, . 137
CHAPTER IX.—Of the Transition from a state of Sensible Devotion to that of Pure Faith and Spoliation, . . . 148
CHAPTER X.—Of Self Renunciation and the Total Surrender of Self to God, the Last Condition for Obtaining Constant Interior Peace, ... 154

PART III.

Of the Means for Preserving Peace Amid Spiritual Weaknesses.

CHAPTER I.—Various Instructions on these Means, . . . 164
First Point. Fundamental Maxims on Liberty of Spirit, . . 164
Second Point. Of the Snares by which the Fiend seeks to rob us of Peace, and of the Means by which to Defend Ourselves against him, ... 165
Third Point. The Soul when Disturbed should strive to Regain her Calm as soon as possible, ... 167
Fourth Point. Of Watchfulness over Self, ... 168
Fifth Point. Of Mistrust of Self, ... 169
Sixth Point. Of Confidence in God, ... 171
Seventh Point. A Mark of True Confidence in God and Mistrust of Self, ... 172
Eighth Point. How greatly Diffidence and Mistrust offend the Lord and Injure the Soul, ... 174
CHAPTER II.—Of Faults Springing from Weakness, . . 177
First Point. One should without Disquiet or without Mistrust Return to God when he has Fallen into Venial Sin, . . 177
Second Point. Frequent Relapses into Venial Sins are not always a Sign of Insufficient Sorrow for them, . . . 182

Contents.

	PAGE
Third Point. How God Permits the Venial Sins of the Just and all their other Imperfections to Redound to their Greatest Good,	184
Fourth Point. Of Bearing with Self and our Daily Faults and Weaknesses,	191
Fifth Point. The Faults of our Neighbor should Disturb our Peace as Little as the Imperfections Found in every Human Virtue,	193
CHAPTER III.—Of Discouragement,	197
First Point. Evil Consequences of Discouragement,	197
Second Point. Why Discouragement occasions so much Harm,	200
Third Point. The True Foundation of Christian Hope the same for All Men,	202
Fourth Point. The Passions and Merits of Christ a new Foundation for Confidence,	204
Fifth Point. To be Wanting in Confidence, is to be Wanting in Faith,	206
Sixth Point. No Victory without Combat; No Combat without Labor,	208
Seventh Point. He who Anticipates Future Combats and Sufferings Tempts both God and Man,	212
Eighth Point. Aversion, Disgust, and Weariness in God's Service are not Unfrequently the Sources of Unreasonable Discouragement,	214
Ninth Point. We should not Pray God to Free us from our Sufferings and Combats.—Should we do so, we must not desire to have such Petitions Immediately Granted,	217
CHAPTER IV.—Of Temptations,	221
First Point. Temptations are no Proof that God has forsaken a Soul,	221
Second Point. Temptations are no Evidence of a Bad State of Soul,	223
Third Point. In Temptation we should Turn to God.—He sustains us in the Combat without our Perceiving it,	225
Fourth Point. How one may Know whether or not he has Consented to Temptation,	226
Fifth Point. Passing Temptations,	229
Sixth Point. Lasting Temptations, and those that Powerfully Affect the Senses,	230
Seventh Point. On Temptations that Retard us in the Practice of Virtue,	232
Eighth Point. One should not Parley with the Tempter.—Means by which we may Turn from the Temptation,	234

	PAGE
Ninth Point. How Temptations proceeding from the Imagination are to be Combated,	238
Tenth Point. Of Frequently Recurring Temptations.—In Time of Peace Prepare for War,	243
Eleventh Point. Of the Advantages of Temptation,	245
Twelfth Point. Devotion to the ever-Blessed Virgin Mary is an Excellent Remedy against Temptations and a Means of Preserving Interior Peace,	247
Thirteenth Point. Means Against Sadness,	250
CHAPTER V.—On Prayer,	252
First Point. For What we should Pray.—We must Persevere in Prayer,	252
Second Point. Various Instructions on Prayer and on the Dryness often Experienced in it,	259

PART IV.

Of Scruples.

CHAPTER I.—What is to be Understood by Scruples.—The Difference between the Scrupulous and the Truly Pious.—Certain Characteristics by which Scruples may be recognized,	265
CHAPTER II.—General Causes of Scruples,	268
1. Weakmindedness,	268
2. A Perplexed Brain,	268
3. An Unbridled Imagination,	269
4. Ideal Perfection,	270
5. Imperfect Knowledge of Religious Principles,	271
6. Too many Reflections upon Self and One's own Intentions,	274
7. How Difficult it is to Judge One's Self Justly,	274
8. The Difficulty in Distinguishing the Thought from Impressions, and the Impressions from Consent,	275
9. A Tender, Timorous Conscience,	277
10. The Malice of the Devil,	278
CHAPTER III.—Dangerous Consequences of Scruples,	280
CHAPTER IV.—Universal Remedies for Scruples,	282
1. Occupation,	282
2. Cheerfulness,	282
3. Humility and Child-like Simplicity,	283
4. Conscience Considered in the True Light,	285
5. The Necessity of Depending upon Another, and of following his Advice,	287

Contents.

	PAGE
6. Sacrifice of One's own Doubts,	289
CHAPTER V.—Various Kinds of Scruples, and their Remedy,	292
1. Scruples about Former Confessions,	292
2. Scruples of Ordinary Confessions,	293
3. Scruples on Sincerity of Contrition.—Good Resolutions,	298
4. Scruples about Devotions of Obligation,	300
5. Scruples about Motives of Well-doing,	302
6. Scruples about Duties Supposed to be Essential,	304
7. Scruples with Respect to Hope, the Soul Believing herself in a Bad State,	305
8. Scruples that Make us see in everything a Punishment from God,	308
9. Scruples that Make us Consider Little Faults an occasion for Greater Ones,	310
10. Scruples with regard to Faith.—Does One really Believe or not?	312
11. Scruples about Temptations against Faith,	314
12. Scruples about Temptations to Blasphemy,	316
13. Scruples from Ambiguous Points Suggested by the Imagination,	318
14. Scruples concerning Christian Love of the Neighbor,	319
15. Scruples on Holy Purity,	322
CHAPTER VI.—Conclusion and Summary of What has been said of Scruples and the Remedies for them,	330
CHAPTER VII.—Examples of the Danger that attends Self-Willed Persistence in Scruples,	336

APPENDIX.

Preparatory Remarks,	342
General Remarks upon each of the Various Methods of Prayer,	342
First Method of Prayer.—The Actual Meditation,	344
Second Method of Prayer.—The Contemplation,	348
Third Method of Prayer,	350
Fourth Method of Prayer,	352
Fifth Method of Prayer,	355
Sixth Method of Prayer.—Spiritual Reading in the Form of Consideration,	355
Method for Examination of Conscience,	357
Directions to Render the Exercises of the Monthly Retreat of one Day Profitable,	361

	PAGE
Meditation for the Eve of the Retreat, ...	361
Meditation for the Day of Retreat, ...	363
Reflections on the Present State of the Soul, . . .	364
Preparation for Death, ...	368
Prayer of Absolute Submission to the Law of Death, .	369
Prayer to Obtain a Happy Death, ...	370
Invocation, ...	371

PART I.

OF RESIGNATION TO THE DISPENSATIONS OF DIVINE PROVIDENCE.

CHAPTER I.

Of the Loving Dispensations of Divine Providence toward Men, and of the Happiness of those that wholly submit to Its Decrees.

NOTHING happens in this world but by the direction or permission of God. "Nothing," says St. Augustine, "occurs by chance in the whole course of our life. God overrules all." He has said by the mouth of the prophet Isaias: "I am the Lord and there is no other; I form light and create darkness, I make peace and create evil."[1] "Shall there be evil in a city, which the Lord hath not done?"[2] says Amos. "Good things and evil," adds Sirach, "life and death, poverty and riches, are from God."[3]

It may, perhaps, be said that this holds good in sickness and in death, in cold and in heat, and in all the events of inanimate nature; but not in what depends upon the free-will of man. You say, "If some one speaks evil of me, defrauds me, persecutes and ill-treats me, is that the will of God? How can I see God's will in that? Does He not forbid such actions? Consequently, I can ascribe them

[1] Isaias xlv. 7.   [2] Amos iii. 6.   [3] Ecclus. xi. 14.

only to the evil designs, to the wickedness, or to the ignorance of men." But, I answer, God Himself speaks clearly and distinctly on this point. On His own Holy Word, we must believe that even what appears to be left to the caprice of men, must be attributed to God's permission. The Jews imputed their captivity to other causes than the dispensation of Providence. The prophet Jeremias says: "Who is he that hath commanded a thing to be done, when the Lord commandeth it not? Shall not both evil and good proceed out of the mouth of the Most High?"[1]

Therefore, when we are robbed of our good name, despoiled of our wealth, abused, or otherwise wronged, we must ascribe it to the will of God. It is His hand that is visiting us; all is the work of His providence.

But, again, you object, "All such actions are sinful. How can God will them? How can He take part therein? God's essence being holiness itself, He can have nothing in common with sin." I answer: In every evil deed two things must be clearly demonstrated: namely, the action itself, or the exterior movement; and the straying of the will from the Divine Law. Does your neighbor strike you, or calumniate you? You must, on the one hand, distinguish the motion of the arm or of the tongue; and, on the other, the evil intention that directs the movement. The movement itself is not sinful; therefore God can be the Author of it. And this He really is, for no creature has life or motion of itself; all receive it from God, who works in them and by them. The evil intention, on the contrary, is entirely the work of the human will, and it alone makes the sin. In this God takes no part. He permits the evil act, in order not to do violence to the free-will of men.

Accordingly, God shares in the deeds of men only in so far as He contributes to the exterior movement. The bad intention underlying the act proceeds from our will; and in this God has no part. You have abused your honor, your riches—God wills that you should lose the one or the other;

[1] Jeremias iii 37, 38.

but He takes no part in the sin of either the robber or the calumniator. Let us illustrate by an example : The judge passes condign sentence of death upon a criminal. Now, it happens that the hangman is a personal enemy of the condemned. He executes the sentence upon the culprit, not merely because his office obliges him to do so, but because he is animated by a spirit of hatred and revenge. Evidently, the judge has no share in the sin of the executioner. The gratification of revenge formed no part of the judge's design in passing the sentence. He aimed only at seeing justice executed. In like manner, God shares not in the evil designs of the calumniator or the robber; consequently, the wicked intention is wholly confined to the latter. God wills you to be humbled and deprived of temporal goods, that thereby you may become better and more virtuous. This, in His eternal goodness, is His only intention; and this He might effect by a thousand other means if He so willed. But He in no way contributes to the sin of men, though He may make use of them as instruments for the fulfilment of His designs. It is, then, really not the sin that humbles you, that plunges you into poverty or misery; it is the blow dealt at your honor, the loss of your wealth, that produces those effects, for the sin itself hurts him only who commits it. We must always discriminate between what God accomplishes through the instrumentality of men and what their own evil will may add thereto.

St. Gregory shows us this in the following example : " A physician has ordered leeches. The little creatures are intent only on satisfying their thirst. They would for this end deprive the sick man of the very last drop of the vital fluid; but the physician seeks only to withdraw the impure blood and, by so doing, restore his patient to health. The leeches are merely his instruments. He has nothing in common with their thirst for blood. God makes use of man in precisely the same way that a physician does of leeches. As for the patient himself, he feels no anxiety.

He does not look upon the leeches as enemies; on the contrary, he endeavors to suppress the disgust aroused by the sight of them. Yes, he even does all in his power to facilitate their action, for he knows very well that it will be continued no longer than the physician considers efficacious." In like manner, should we endure those to whom God has given command over us. We should neither judge their intentions nor harbor aversion against them. We should rest satisfied that, however hostile or inimical they may be toward us, they are only instruments of salvation in the hands of an All-good, All-wise, All-powerful God. He will give them no more power over us than is for our good. Our own interest should impel us to embrace rather than to withdraw from their guidance; for they exercise over us, not their own, but the Lord's authority. Creatures can do us no harm, unless power is given them from on high.

All enlightened souls have been firmly convinced of this truth. The history of Job presents a beautiful illustration of it. Job is bereft of his children, and stripped of all his wealth; from the pinnacle of human happiness he falls to the depths of earthly misery, and what does he say? "The Lord gave, the Lord hath taken away: as it hath pleased the Lord, so is it done: blessed be the name of the Lord."[1]

"Behold," says St. Augustine, "how this holy man understood the great mystery of God's providence! He did not say: 'The Lord hath given me children and riches, and the devil hath taken them from me.' But he said: 'The Lord hath given, the Lord hath taken. As it has pleased the Lord, and not as it has pleased the devil, also is it done.'" Not less striking is the example of the Egyptian Joseph. His brothers, actuated by hatred and envy, sold him; but he ascribed all to God's providence. "God," he said, "sent me before you into Egypt for your preservation, that you may be preserved upon the earth, and may have food to live. . . . Not by your counsel was I sent hither, but by the will of God."[2]

[1] Job i. 21.   [2] Gen. xlv. 5, 7, 8.

David, pursued and insulted by Semei, sees the hand of Providence in the insolent behavior of his unruly subject. Twice did he restrain his indignant servant who wished to avenge him with the words, "Let him alone and let him curse: for the Lord hath bid him curse David."[1] And Jesus Christ Himself, the Holy of Holies, Our Lord and Saviour, who came down from heaven to teach us by His word and example, did He not say to Peter, who with inconsiderate zeal urged Him to avert His sufferings and deliver Himself from the hands of His enemies: "The chalice which My Father hath given Me, shall I not drink it?"[2] Jesus attributed the ignominy and pain of His bitter torments, not to their immediate authors; not to the Jews that accused Him; not to Judas who betrayed Him; not to Pilate who condemned Him; not to the executioners who, with most horrible treatment, dragged Him to death; not to the devil, the instigator of the shocking deed: but only to God, in whom He saw, not a cruel Judge, but a loving Father.

We must not attribute our losses, our misfortunes, our sufferings, our humiliations, to the evil spirit or to man; but to their true author, God. Let us not venture to say: "This one or that one is the cause of my misfortune, my ruin." No, our trials are not the work of man. They are God's own work. This will redound to our greater tranquillity, for all that God, the best of fathers, does is full of infinite wisdom; all is subservient to His highest and holiest purposes.

"All God's works," say the holy Fathers, "are perfect, performed with weight and measure." They are so good that they could not possibly be better. We should, as St. Basil recommends, be thoroughly convinced that we are the work of a good Master, who, with infinite foresight, is at all times occupied with us, His creatures. Under His loving protection, nothing can befall us contrary to His will. Nothing can hurt us without His permission. What-

---

[1] II. Kings xvi. 10, 11   [2] John xviii. 11.

ever happens to us is so good that nothing better can be imagined. "Great are the works of the Lord : sought out according to all His wills."[1] The most striking characteristic of God's wisdom is the perfect conformity of the means He employs to the end. And as His wisdom cannot be separated from His love, He sends us nothing that is too hard or too painful for us to bear. "Almighty Sovereign," cries out the Wise Man, "Thou judgest with tranquillity, and with great favor disposest of us."[2] Infinite is His power; nothing can withstand it. And yet God does not make us feel the absolute dominion of His sovereignty; He deals with us in mildness. He takes into consideration the natural character, the talents of each individual. He assigns to each the place in which he can best work out his salvation. Yes, we may even venture to say that He treats us with deference and respect, because He recognizes in us His living image. He commands us, not imperiously as slaves, but with forbearance and all possible consideration Is He, for our good, compelled to visit us with sickness, trouble, or other painful afflictions, He acts like a good physician who must effect a cure by using the knife. But how gently He makes the incision! With what tender care He dresses our wounds! His whole aim is to cause us no more pain than is indispensably necessary for the success of the operation. How lovingly He sweetens the bitter potion !

Ah ! God tries us only that we may attain perfection ; and this for the holiest and noblest end that can be conceived, His own honor and glory.

What God sends us is always proportioned to our strength and abilities. It is suited to our needs as the glove to the hand that wears it, or the scabbard to the sword hidden within. All things would contribute to our perfection if we corresponded to the intentions of Divine Providence.

When tribulations overwhelm us, let us not grow im-

[1] Psalm cx. 2.   [2] Wisdom xii. 18.

patient. As God sets bounds to earth and sea, as He directs the waves that threaten the land with destruction until they break on the moving sands of the shore, so does He mete out our trials and temptations. He has measured their extent, He has set limits to their duration, He watches that they should further our salvation and not our ruin. Tribulations are, indeed, an essential feature in the means that work unto salvation. "For gold and silver are tried in the fire, but acceptable men in the furnace of humiliation."[1] Temptations are necessary. In refusing to accept them, we become our own enemies. We are in the hands of God like a block of marble in the hands of the sculptor. To form a beautiful statue, the workman must use the chisel and the hammer; he must hew and hack the marble; he must make the splinters fly. God intends to fashion us to His own image; therefore, we must passively submit to His skilful hand. Every stroke is a master-touch toward our sanctification. "For this is the will of God, your sanctification," says St. Paul.[2] Yes, our sanctification is the only end God has in view in all that He sends us. O what would He not effect in us for His glory and our perfection if we allowed Him! Look at the heavenly bodies. See how unresistingly they follow established laws; admire the uninterrupted regularity of their course. Were they for one moment to deviate from these sublime laws, the whole universe would be thrown into fearful confusion. And so it is with our will. Does it yield to God's will, all in man is well-ordered; and the powers of his soul, like the members of his body, abide in perfect harmony. But let the will swerve from that of God, and confusion and disorder reign in the whole man. Perfection consists in nothing else than in conformity to the will of God. The more fully we submit to the Divine Will the more we advance; when we resist it, we go backward. St. Teresa said to her spiritual daughters: "Direct your prayer to one thing only, that is, to conform your

[1] Ecclus. li. 5.   [2] Thess. iv. 3.

will perfectly to the Divine Will. Be assured that there is no greater perfection attainable than this conformity, and that they who most earnestly strive for it will receive from God the richest graces and most quickly advance in the interior life. Believe me, this is the secret. Upon this point alone rests our sanctification." It is related that the Blessed Sancino, a very saintly religious of the Dominican Order, once saw in vision the felicity of the blessed, who were ranked according to their merits among the nine choirs of angels. In the choir of seraphim, she remarked some whom she had known upon earth. Upon inquiring how they had attained so high a degree of blessedness, she was answered: "By conformity and perfect union of will to the will of God!" But if, by this conformity, we are to arrive at the highest degree of glory in heaven, even to the rank of the seraphim, may we not conclude that the same virtue raises us on earth to the highest degree of grace, and that it is the foundation of the sublimest perfection attainable in this life?

The submission of our will is, in truth, the most pleasing sacrifice that we can make to God, and the one that honors Him most. It is the most perfect act of love, the most elevating and meritorious virtue. By it we can at every moment amass incomparable treasures of grace, and gain in a short time the richest merits for eternity. A remarkable example of this is given in the life of a certain holy religious who was not distinguished in any way from his brethren; and yet he had reached so high a degree of perfection and sanctity that the mere touch of his garments healed the sick. Once his Superior said to him: "How is it? You pray, you fast, you watch no more than any other member of this community; and yet you work so many miracles! I am surprised at this. I should like to know the cause of it." The good religious replied: "These wonders astonish me more than they do others. I know not their true cause. But if I were allowed to guess, I should say only this, that I am always most careful to will what God wills. He has given me the grace to unite my will so closely with His that, in little as well as in great things, I do nothing without His particular inspiration. Success does not elate me, nor does misfortune cast me down; for, without losing time in examining, I take the one and the other equally from the hand of God. I do not desire things to turn out as I might naturally wish, but simply and only as God wills. All my prayers tend to one end; namely, that the will of God should be perfectly accomplished in me and in all creatures."

"What!" exclaimed the astonished Superior, "were you not disturbed when an enemy set fire to our barn the other day, when our whole harvest and all our cattle were burned?"

"No, Father," replied the religious; "on the contrary, my custom is to thank God for such reverses, because I am firmly convinced that He permitted it only for His greater glory and our good. Therefore I did not concern myself as to whether much or little of our property escaped the flames; for I know that God, if we confide in Him, can feed us with a scrap of bread as well as with a whole barn full of grain. Hence, come what may, I am always peaceful and joyful."

The Superior admired his perfect conformity with the will of God, and his confidence in Divine Providence. He was no longer astonished at seeing this religious working miracles.

We see by this example that conformity to God's will makes us not only holy, but also perfectly happy. It fills us with the sweetest peace that can be tasted in this life, and makes earth a paradise. King Alfonso the Great very justly expressed this truth. When asked whom he considered the happiest on earth, he answered: "They that give themselves up entirely to the guidance of God, and accept everything, joy and sorrow, from His hand." God Himself says by the mouth of the prophet Isaias: "Oh, that thou hadst hearkened to My commandments: thy peace had been as a river!"[1] And in the same sense Eliphaz speaks to Job: "Submit thyself then to Him and be at peace. Then shalt thou abound in delights in the Almighty, and shalt lift up thy face to God."[2] Thus, also, sang the holy angels at the birth of Christ: "Glory to God in the highest, and on earth peace to men of good-will."[3] But who are those men of good-will? They whose will is perfectly conformed to the divine good-will, the will of God.

Good-will, or conformity to the will of God, is also the condition of that blessed interior peace which, according to St. Paul, "surpasseth all understanding."[4] Would we enjoy peace? Then nothing must resist our will; all must go according to our wishes. But such happiness here below is reserved for those only whose will is entirely one with the will of God. All that such a one wills shall be exactly accomplished: for he wills only what God wills.

"I firmly believe," said the eloquent Salvianus, "that no one on earth is happier than the righteous, for nothing can happen to them that they do not desire." "But shall even the righteous endure humiliation and contempt?" Yes, indeed; but they long for them. "Are they poor?" They are; but they love poverty, and consequently they are happy. For who is happier, who more at rest, than he that is what he wishes to be? Solomon says: "Whatsoever shall befall the just man, it shall not make him sad."[5] Nothing shall disturb the peace of his soul, because nothing happens to him contrary to his will.

Not that I wish in any manner to imply that man in this happy state shall experience no more sufferings. We shall assuredly feel our sorrows even after we have perfectly conformed to the will of God; but we feel them only in the inferior part of the soul. They do not disturb the superior, the nobler part, wherein dwells the peace of God. A soul truly resigned to God is like our Divine Lord, who, though scourged and fastened to the ignominious wood of the cross,

---

[1] Is. xlviii. 18.   [2] Job xxii. 21, 26.   [3] Luke ii. 14.
[4] Phil. iv. 7.   [5] Prov. xii. 21.

yet ceased not to be happy. Immersed as He was in an ocean of suffering, His Sacred Heart still overflowed with infinite joy.

Doubtless, to our nature the thought of suffering, humiliation, confusion, and poverty is directly opposed to our ideas of happiness; and only by a miracle of grace can we rejoice in the midst of such evils. But such a miracle will certainly be wrought in the souls of all that give themselves up unreservedly to the accomplishment of the Divine Will. The honor of God demands that all who generously devote themselves to His service should experience therein contentment and happiness.

Perhaps in many souls the question will arise: "If this is so, how are we to understand the words of Jesus Christ: 'If any man will come after Me, let him deny himself, and take up his cross and follow Me'?"[1] The question is not a difficult one, and may be readily answered. When our Divine Master requires, as the condition of our happiness, that we should deny ourselves, take up our cross, and follow Him, He pledges Himself to give us not only eternal life, but also a hundredfold here below over and above all that, for love of Him, we have renounced.[2] Still more, He promises to carry the cross with us, else He would not say: "My yoke is sweet and My burden light."[3] If we do not experience how sweet is the yoke of Jesus, and how light is the weight of His cross, it can only proceed from the fact of our not having rightly taken up its burden. We have not fully renounced our natural views, not yet learned to consider all things in the light of faith; for faith teaches us, in the words of the great Apostle to the Gentiles, "In all things give thanks: for this is the will of God in Christ Jesus concerning you all."[4] This faith shall be for us an exhaustless fountain of that unspeakable and lasting joy assured to us by the same Apostle: "Rejoice in the Lord always: again, I say, rejoice."[5]

[1] Matt. xvi. 24. [2] Matt. xix. 29. [3] Matt. xi. 30.
[4] Thess. v. 18. [5] Phil. iv. 4.

32 *Resignation to the Dispensations of Providence.*

A memorable example of this truth is given us by Tauler. This worthy priest ardently desired to make rapid progress in perfection; but, in his humility he feared to rely on his own judgment. For eight years he prayed fervently and humbly that God would be pleased to send him a director who would point out to him the shortest and safest way to His love. One day he felt himself more powerfully urged than ever to implore God to grant his prayer. Suddenly a voice said to him: "Go out to the church door. There you will learn what you desire." Tauler obeyed. He went out; but saw no one except a poor beggar, ragged and barefoot, who stood there apparently more calculated to excite the compassion of the passers-by than to direct them in the interior life.

Tauler, approaching, wished him good-day. "I thank you for your friendly salutation," answered the beggar, "but I cannot remember having ever had a bad day." "Good!" exclaimed Tauler. "I hope that to the good days you have had God may add every possible happiness." "Thank you," replied the beggar, "but know that I have never been unhappy, that in my whole life no disaster has ever befallen me." "God grant," said Tauler astonished, "that with all your happiness you may attain eternal blessedness! But I must admit that the sense of your words is not quite clear to me."

"You will be yet more astonished," replied the beggar, "when I assure you that I have always been happy, and that I am still so." "Indeed!" replied Tauler; "but your words are unintelligible; they astonish me. Be so good as to explain yourself." "Listen," returned the beggar. "I told you that I had never had a bad day, for our days are bad only when we do not employ them in honoring God by submission; on the contrary, they are always good when we use them to honor and glorify Him; and this, by His grace, we can always do, come what may. I am, as you see, a miserable beggar, sick, homeless, and without support. I wander alone through the world, finding misery everywhere. If I am hungry, because no one gives me to eat, I praise God. If I am exposed to rain, hail, and wind; if my poor rags are insufficient to protect my limbs benumbed by the piercing cold, I thank God. If my poverty and wretchedness draw upon me contempt, I praise and bless the Divine Majesty. In a word, no matter what happens to me hard and contrary to nature, whether men receive me with compassionate words or drive me off with harsh epithets, my will is always united with that of God, and for all I praise His holy name.

"And so, you see, every day is good for me. Not adversity, not suffering, but our own impatience brings us bad days. And why are we impatient, if it is not because our will revolts against duty instead of subjecting itself as reason requires; instead of praising and glorifying God with all our strength? I have, moreover, told you that I have never been unhappy; that in the course of my life I have never met with an accident; and you yourself may judge whether or not I have told you the truth. All esteem themselves happy when their desires are fully satisfied. Now, this happiness is always mine. You express surprise; but what I say is true, as you will soon comprehend. You know that nothing happens to us that God does not will, and that what He does will is always the best for us. Hence it follows that I should esteem myself happy, let God send me what He will. And why should I not, since I am thoroughly convinced that whatever happens to me is the best for me?"

Tauler, transported by the deep wisdom of the beggar, implored him to tell him how he had reduced these fundamental maxims to practice. "By living with God as a child with the most tender of fathers," answered the beggar. "I never forget that this All-wise, Almighty Father knows well what is best for His children, and that He always gives it to them. Things may oppose or flatter nature, may appear honorable or dishonorable in the eyes of men, sweet or bitter, conducive or prejudicial to health.

I accept them in the conviction that, at the present moment, they are the very best for me. I feel satisfied that nothing could render me happier. In this way, I have peace in all events; and for all, without exception, I thank the dear God!"

"But you told me that you were blessed," said Tauler. "Pray, explain that also." "Yes," said the beggar, "surely he is blessed whose will is never opposed, whose desires are fully satisfied. True, no man can fully attain such happiness in this life. That is reserved for the saints in heaven, whose union with God's will has reached the highest consummation. But we are called even here below to share in it by conforming our will to that of God. No obstacle crosses the path of him who wills only what God wills; all his wishes accord with the good pleasure of God and, therefore, must infallibly be fulfilled; he is, consequently, blessed. It is this blessedness that I enjoy. The will of God constitutes my whole happiness. All that God wills so rejoices me that I experience a thousand times more pleasure in its fulfilment than another would over the highest gratification of his natural inclinations." The learned Tauler was astounded at the extraordinary wisdom of the poor beggar.

"My dear child," says the Lord, "know that I am your Creator, your Saviour, and your God. Your body and soul are in My hands; I give you all that you possess, the air you breathe, the bread you eat. By My orders the elements, the planets, and even the angels serve you. I have created heaven and earth for you.[1] And, more than all that, I love you, and for love of you 'I became a worm of the earth.'[2] I willed to be born in a stable and to die on a cross, and all because of your sins. Now, can you think that I would do you any wrong? What more can you expect from Me, since I have washed you in My blood, fed you with My flesh, and given you My body and soul, My

[1] Deut. iv.   [2] Ps. xx. 7.

life and divinity? What stronger evidence could I give you of My loving designs in your regard?

"Never, then, harbor the thought that I hate you when I send you sufferings, or that I will crush you under their weight. Afflictions are a proof of My love, of that love which gave you existence. They flow to you from a hand that was once nailed to the cross for you. Do you think you could find a safer way than that of suffering when I, your Lord and your God, chose it as the path to My glory? Know you not that men must labor in the sweat of their brow, and encounter a thousand dangers in order to acquire earthly goods? See you not that earthly crowns are given only to him who fights courageously and gains the victory? If you suffer with Me you shall rejoice with Me; if you share My humiliations you shall have part in My glory, but not otherwise.

"If I knew a higher, a more precious blessing upon earth than suffering, I should have given it to you and should have chosen it for My own portion in this world. But because I know that nothing leads more quickly and securely to the highest pinnacle of happiness than the cross, I present it to you with the same love with which I embraced it Myself.

"It is I who placed those difficulties in your way; therefore, blame no one else, for I alone have so ordained it. Complain not of chance. By so doing, you would act against your conscience, as you well know nothing happens by chance. Accuse not the hostile elements of earth, nor yet the stars of heaven, for they are but weak creatures, inanimate instruments which My hand wields according to My good pleasure. Neither complain of the world, nor of the wicked spirits. Their malice can do you no harm, for their power is subject to Me; they can exercise it only in so far as I permit. To Me alone, therefore, should you ascribe whatever evil creatures do you. Your illness, your tribulations, your afflictions and contradictions are sent you from Him who created you and who has you engraven in His hands and in His Sacred Heart.[1] They are the love-tokens of My Heavenly Father, and He shares them only with His well-beloved children; they are thorns from My crown, splinters from My holy cross, which He distributes to them as to His favorites; they are the chalice from which, in obedience to His will, I, because the first-born and dearest of His children, more than any other drank, yea, to the very dregs!"

"Who would not eagerly respond to the call of Divine Love that leads him to the marriage of the cross? O my Father, my Lord and my God, be it done unto me according to Thy divine good-pleasure! To follow Thy inspirations and guidance shall henceforth be my only aim! I will suffer because Thou willest it. I will suffer what Thou willest, although other crosses might be lighter for me. Yes, Lord, I submit with perfect docility to Thy holy will. 'Yes, Father, I praise and bless Thee from my heart, for so it hath seemed good to Thee.'[2] So great is my confidence in Thy goodness and infinite love that I can value nothing more than what Thou ordainest for me. Thou hast created me that I might attain the highest degree of happiness, and I am firmly persuaded that all that Thou sendest me tends to that end. Even if Thou hadst not called me to eternal happiness, I would not follow any other will than Thine. Thy will is my whole happiness; without it I could taste no joy in heaven or on earth."

Thus do all souls speak that have wholly given themselves to the guidance of Divine Providence. They have arrived at the conviction that God's providence is the fundamental principle of all the events of this world; that it governs the seasons; that fruitfulness or sterility, sunshine or rain, depends upon it; that it directs from first to last, with unlimited power and even in the smallest particulars, all human things; that it turns and shapes at will even the slightest circumstance of our life. Could souls penetrated with these sentiments regard what comes

[1] Is. xlix. 16. [2] Matt. xi. 26.

to them from God's hand as hurtful? "God is so good," says St. Dionysius, "that He, who alone needs nothing for Himself, yet is constantly producing good for others. He is so glorious and magnificent that, through the unattainable and inexpressible fulness of His love, He conducts all things to their perfection."

And Philo, the Jew, adds yet more: "God will never weary of doing good. He allows no occasion for doing so to pass unimproved." What evil then can we apprehend? Should we not rather hope for all good?

CHAPTER II.

In what we should submit to the Ordinances of Divine Providence.

THE first question is: In what should we submit to the will of God? We answer: In all things. Of the chief points, which include all others, we shall now take a clearer view. Let us begin with the least. We should accept quietly and willingly all kinds of weather, heat and cold, rain and hail, storm and tempest.

Instead of becoming impatient and angry if the weather does not suit us, we should not only be satisfied with it, since God sent it; but even if it should particularly inconvenience us, we ought, with the three young men in the fiery furnace, exclaim: "Cold and heat, ice and snow, lightning and thunder, praise the Lord, praise and magnify Him forever." Inanimate nature honors the Lord unconsciously by fulfilling His holy will; we must glorify Him by acquiescing intelligently in all natural events. It often happens that that particular state of weather which proves so disagreeable to us is most acceptable to others. It thwarts our designs, but it may perhaps favor those of our fellow-men. And even if this were not so, do we not know that all kinds of weather contribute to the glory of God and the accomplishment of His holy will? Should not this be enough for us? In the life of St. Francis Borgia we read a beautiful example of conformity to the will of God. This saint, visiting a convent of his order, arrived late one night after all had retired and were sound asleep, so that he was kept waiting at the door in the intense cold during a heavy fall of snow. At last, some one heard him knocking and opened

Submission to the Ordinances of Providence.

the door, with excuses and a thousand apologies that he should have been kept waiting in such weather. The saint merely remarked: "Ah, it was a sweet thought to me that it was God who permitted the snow to fall so heavily upon me."

Such conformity is so agreeable to God that it often exerts a visible influence on temporal matters. This is shown by the story of the pious farmer of whom the early Fathers of the Desert make mention. His fields always yielded more than those of all others. When his neighbors questioned him as to how that was, he answered: "Do not wonder at the rich harvests of my sowing. I always have just such weather as I desire to ripen my crops." Astonished at his words, they asked for an explanation. "That is easily given," replied the good man; "I never wish for any other weather than that which God sends; and as I will only what pleases Him, He favors me with a harvest as abundant as I can desire."

In all public calamities, war, famine, pestilence, etc., we should humbly submit to the decrees of God, and in sentiments of the deepest humility adore His divine judgment. However severe the punishments of the Lord may appear to us, we must admit that an infinitely good God would not let such scourges fall upon us were it not for the greater good of His creatures. How many souls have been saved by tribulation who, by any other way, might have been lost! How many souls in the hour of affliction turn with their whole heart to God, and die in true sentiments of sorrow for their sins! It often happens that what we consider a punishment and chastisement of God is a special work of grace, an act of His infinite mercy.

What concerns us personally is, that we must be thoroughly penetrated with the consoling thought that all the hairs of our head are numbered; that not one falls except by the will of our Heavenly Father. This shows that nothing can injure us excepting by God's will or permission. In the light of this truth, we shall easily understand that, in seasons of universal dereliction and tribulation, we have no more to fear than at any other time; for God can just as well save us from harm in the midst of these trials, as He can plunge us into want and misery when we deem ourselves secure in peace and happiness. We have, then, nothing else to do than to invoke the grace and favor of God, the Almighty, and this we can best accomplish by conforming our will to His. Let us, then, be always ready to accept everything promptly and joyfully from the hand of God, for such dispositions are powerful over His Sacred Heart. Touched by our humble confidence and resignation, He will either take from us the afflictions which we so magnanimously accept, or turn them to our greater merit and sanctification. We read a remarkable example of this in the history of Attila, King of the Huns, who was rightly styled "The Scourge of God." This fierce invader had entered Gaul and vented his barbarous rage against the cities of Rheims, Cambria, Besançon, Auxerre, and Langres. He was now about to storm Troyes. The inhabitants were seized with terror, but their bishop, St. Lupus, was not dismayed. Full of confidence in the protection of Heaven, he issued forth in full pontificals, preceded by the cross and accompanied by his clergy, to meet the terrible invader. "Who art thou?" said Lupus in a tone of majesty. "I am the Scourge of God," haughtily answered Attila. To this the saintly bishop replied: "The Scourge of God is welcome," and he ordered the gates to be thrown open to the conqueror. This was done; but God, who rules the hearts of men according to His good pleasure, set a bridle upon the fierce passions of the marauding Huns, and they passed through the city leaving it and its inhabitants unharmed. And here Rodriguez remarks that although Attila was truly the Scourge of God, yet He permitted him not to prove such to those who had received him in so great submission to the ordinances of His providence.

Parents should recognize God's will both in the number and in the sex of the children He gives them, and

Submission to the Ordinances of Providence. 41

bow to it. As long as lively faith animated men, they regarded a large family as a blessing, as a gift of Heaven, and parents looked upon God as the real Father of their children. But now that faith is well-nigh extinct, when lives are spent almost without God, family cares are borne without thought of Him. Resting in themselves, and not seeking help from God, it comes to pass that even the most opulent parents dread to see their families increase; they regard their children as a plague which embitters life. O how differently would one judge were he thoroughly penetrated with the thought that God watches with fatherly solicitude over those who, with childlike confidence, remit all to His paternal providence!

Would you have a proof of this? Then, acquiesce with all your heart in His holy will, and you will experience what St. Paul says of the God of all goodness: "And God is able to make all grace abound in you: that ye always having all-sufficient in all things may abound in every good."[1]

You must be solicitous for one thing only, and that is to train your children as children of God. Let this be the aim of all your desires, all your endeavors. You must have the courage to renounce every ambitious suggestion; then can you rely with perfect confidence on the tender love of your Heavenly Father, be your offspring ever so numerous. God will Himself watch over them, conducting all things to their happiness. The more fully you renounce worldly aims for your children, remitting their future into God's hands, the more wonderfully will He provide for them, and spare you all anxiety on their account.

We should be resigned to God's will in temporal losses of money and property. In the same disposition we must pay all our debts, even when they fall heavily upon us and appear unjust; for example, if called upon to make a second payment because of our inability to prove

[1] II. Cor. ix. 8.

the first; to liquidate the debts of another whose security we are; to discharge demands of all kinds, etc. When he who is empowered to claim your money makes use of his authority, it happens by God's permission. We must say to ourselves: "God Himself demands this amount of me." And to Him in reality we give it when, in paying it, we have the intention of pleasing Him by submission to His holy will. How many graces would fall upon him who acts in this spirit! Would you have a faint idea of this? Then represent to yourself two persons: one pays, in perfect union with the Divine Will, a sum of money to him who has the power, although, perhaps, not the right to exact it; the other gives spontaneously an alms of equal value. You know how many graces and merits are attached to almsgiving, but understand that the first person has yet more merit; for he sacrifices his money, not in conferring a positive favor nor as a voluntary charity, but in a spirit of conformity to God's will. The latter is a purer offering, one more agreeable to God than even an alms, since it is devoid of self-will. If, according to Holy Writ and the experience of all ages, almsgiving has brought to charitable families the greatest blessings, we may justly hope still richer rewards for such compulsory sacrifices.

We should subject ourselves in poverty and all its inconveniences to the will of God. This will not seem hard to us if we are rightly penetrated with the thought that God watches over us as a father over his children, and that He permits us to experience privations only because they are good for us. Viewed thus, poverty appears in quite a different light. We no longer consider ourselves poor when we accept the privations which our needy circumstances impose upon us as the salutary prescriptions of our Heavenly Physician and Father.

If a powerful prince subjects his son, who is ill, to a plain and sparing diet, would the young prince think himself poor because he is served with the fare of the poor? Would he be concerned for the future? Or would an observer from that fact conceive the idea that the prince was in poverty? Certainly not. And are we not the children of the Most High, the co-heirs of Jesus Christ? What can be wanting to us? Yes, we can go farther and boldly assert that upon all that God possesses we have a claim, as soon as we, by our love and confidence, become His true children. Then everything belongs to us alone. But it is not good for us to enjoy all at once; indeed, it is often desirable to abstain from many things. Privations are necessary for us; therefore, let us conclude that we shall not suffer the want of what is really for our good. Let us believe with unswerving confidence that our Almighty Father will infallibly give us in the future all that is necessary for us, all that can be to our advantage. Has not our Divine Saviour Himself said: "If you being evil, know how to give good gifts to your children: how much more will your Father who is in heaven give good things to them that ask Him?"[1] The doctrine of God's providence is an incontestable truth of our holy faith. Doubts on this point, anxiety and vain fears for the future, if not conscientiously banished, are criminal and offensive to Jesus Christ, who has left us in several parts of the Holy Scripture most explicit promises on this head.[2] He has given us His word, and this on the single condition that we seek first the kingdom of God and His justice, and make this our greatest and most important aim. This means that all other undertakings should have but this object in view; and to attain it we should faithfully accomplish all our other duties. On this condition, God relieves us from all other care. He Himself assumes our necessities and those of our relatives. He will provide for all with so much the more liberality as we cast ourselves more confidingly into His arms, and make greater efforts to acquire this conformity.

We should, in prosperity and adversity, honor and humiliation, fame and confusion, subject ourselves to God's will, accepting everything from His hand; for, thus

[1] Matt. vii. 11. [2] Matt. vi. 24-34; Luke xii. 22-32.

received, all will contribute to His glory and the furtherance of our eternal salvation. When David fled from Jerusalem in order to escape the persecution of his son Absalom, the high-priest Sadoc had the Ark of the Covenant carried after him, that it might be to the king in his threatened danger a protection and shelter, a pledge of his happy return. But David said to Sadoc: "Carry back the Ark of God into the city: if I should find grace in the sight of the Lord, He will bring me back, and will show me both it and His tabernacle. But if He shall say to me 'Thou pleasest Me not:' I am ready, let Him do that which is good before Him."[1] And yet there was question here of the highest earthly good,—whether he should remain on the throne or lead a poor, desolate life. Like David we, also, should speak, happen what may.

We dare not excuse ourselves on the plea that we are not called to so high, so perfect resignation. God Himself effects the measure of it in us when we do not resist His grace. Cassianus tells us of a man, old in years, who had studied this truth well. In Alexandria he was once surrounded by a whole band of unbelievers, who covered him with confusion. They beat him, kicked him, and abused him in every possible way. But he remained perfectly calm, silent, and patient as a lamb. When, at last, he was insultingly asked what miracles Jesus Christ had wrought, he replied: "The miracle which Jesus Christ has just now worked is, that I, through all your ill-treatment, have not become angry; nay—not even ruffled."

Our conformity to the will of God must extend to all natural defects of body as well as of soul. For example, we must not be troubled, we must not complain, no, not even regret, that our memory is not good, our understanding dull; that we are not so accomplished, possess not so solid a judgment as others. Thus to lament would be to complain that God has endowed us with little. Have we deserved what He has given us? Is not the little we do

[1] II. Kings xv. 25, 26.

possess a free gift of His grace and mercy, for which we owe Him the greatest thanks? How have we merited that He should call us into existence? We should not only refrain from regrets that our gifts are few and small, but we should not even wish for more than God has given us. What God considers enough should be truly so for us. As the workman adapts his tools to his work, so God, according to His designs over us, has endowed us intellectually. The good use of what we have received, is the one thing necessary. We should remember that for many it is a great blessing to possess but moderate talents; with the little that God has given them they will save their soul. Had the Creator favored them more, they would perhaps have been lost; for great spiritual gifts often engender pride and vanity, and become to many the source of damnation.

"You have not so great ability as another," says Father du Sault; "consequently you are not so learned, you are not so fit for different kinds of employment. That afflicts you, troubles you, and in secret you yield to vain desires. "O if I only had what this one or that one has! If I but knew what he knows! If I were only what he is!" Ah, my dear friend! you know not for what you long. With the few talents that God has given you you will win heaven; had you more, you would precipitate yourself into hell. Therefore did God take this into consideration when He formed your body and soul, and made you what you are and not otherwise. Conform yourself with perfect submission to the will of your Heavenly Father who loves you so tenderly and so heartily, and who Himself ordains all for your greater sanctification. Tell Him how much you wish to be conformed to Him in all things, and, in union with His Divine Son, say with your whole heart: "Yes, Father; yes, my Lord and my God! because it is pleasing to Thee that I should be poor and despised, I desire to be nothing else. What Thou willest me to be, is the most perfect for me. My will has reached its centre when it is united with Thine!"

In bodily suffering also we must bow to the will of God. He sends us this or that malady; He sends it at this or that time; He allows it to continue for such or such a period; He couples it with this or that circumstance: in all which we must perfectly unite with the divine ordinance. We should wish for no change, but at the same time not neglect proper means for recovery, since God Himself wills that we should make use of such remedies. When impatient nature revolts, we must repress such emotions with the words: "What! I, a miserable creature! Foolhardy that I am, to rise up against my Lord and Creator, and to rebel against His ever just and most adorable ordinances!" St. Bonaventure tells us that a religious of the Order of St. Francis of Assisi, during one of the extraordinary and painful illnesses of the saint, said to him in all simplicity: "Dear Father, pray God to deal with you a little more gently, for it appears to me His hand lies heavily upon you." At these words the saint groaned aloud and said: "Did I not know that you have said this from simplicity, not thinking any evil, I would never look upon your face again, since you have been so audacious as to sit in judgment on the just punishments of God." Then, in spite of his weakness and violent sufferings, he cast himself from his poor couch, and, kissing the bare floor of his cell, exclaimed: "O my God! I thank Thee for all the suffering Thou sendest me. I earnestly implore Thee to give me a hundred times more if Thou findest it good. I shall be filled with joy when Thou strikest me without sparing me in anything, for the fulfilling of Thy holy will is the greatest consolation that can be given me."

St. Ephraim expresses the same sentiments when he says: "Uncivilized men know how much their beasts of burden are able to carry, and they do not tax them beyond their strength. The potter knows how long his clay must remain in the oven before it is fit for use. Would it not, then, be the greatest foolishness to say that God, infinitely loving and infinitely wise, lays too heavy a load upon us,

Submission to the Ordinances of Providence. 47

and tries us too long in the fire of tribulation? Let us, therefore, resign the care of ourselves to Him. Our body will not be baked longer or harder than is good for us."

But in order not to confound these perfect intentions of the saints with those to which all are bound, and thus create scruples in timid souls, we shall here remark that every suffering, of what kind soever, may be considered in two different ways: first, as an effect of the will or the permission of God; and secondly, as an evil for us or for our neighbor. From the first standpoint we are bound to submit our will to that of God; that is to say, to esteem good the suffering that He either sends us or permits to befall us. Whoever does not do this opposes Divine Providence, who guides and directs all with infinite wisdom. But if we regard suffering as an evil, we are not bound to desire it either for ourselves or for our neighbor. God commands us to submit to His will, which permits sufferings; but He does not require us to desire them. It is often His will that we should do all in our power to avert them. It is His will, for example, that we make use of all reasonable means to recover our health if He has sent us sickness. And if we cannot ward off suffering, we are not forbidden to grieve over it; yea, we may sometimes even wish for death to free us from our pains, if in so doing we do not yield to impatience and murmuring. Christian resignation should always govern our grief and moderate our tears. So long as this kind of submission is dominant there is no sin in wishing to die, if only to escape the sorrows of this life; or, like Elias and other saints, no longer to witness the oppression of the servants of God and the persecution of holy Church; or to be freed from spiritual infirmities, the source of so many faults; or, finally, to be the sooner admitted to the enjoyment of God.

In the matter of our death and all that relates thereto, we should submit to God's will. Die we must, according to the irrevocable decree of the Eternal Judge. We shall die on the day, at the hour, in the place and manner that God pleases. This death, and its attendant circumstances, we should accept, because they are certainly those that will best further God's glory. St. Gertrude was ascending a little hill one day with some of her religious. The saint missed her footing, slipped, and fell. Lovingly serene, she arose, exclaiming: "O my Jesus! how truly happy I should have been if, by this fall, I had been brought sooner to Thee!" Her companions, struck by her words, asked the saint whether she did not fear to die without the last Sacraments. She answered: "With all my heart. I certainly desire to receive them. But I prefer the will of God even to this consolation; for I believe that we cannot better or more securely prepare for death than by resigning ourselves in all things to God's will. Therefore, I desire no other death than that by which God may call me to Himself, and I await it with unshaken confidence, knowing that He, in His mercy, will be with me at my last hour and direct its every circumstance."

We should submit to the will of God when He removes from us the exterior helps we may have had toward our sanctification. For example, you lose a spiritual guide, or a friend who till now has directed you, urged you on to good, and encouraged you. It seems to you that without him you can no longer tread the narrow path securely. This fear has some foundation. In truth, you certainly are not in a condition to proceed alone. Help is indispensable; therefore, Providence gave you this friend and guide. But does He love you less now that He has deprived you of this support than when He gave it you? Is He not still your Father? Could such a Father abandon His children? He has called you to a certain preordained degree of perfection. You have already passed over a part of the way, and the guide whose loss is so painful to you has, indeed, led you till now happily and safely onward. But who can assure you that he would continue to receive grace to render him capable of conducting you farther on your spiritual journey? And did not Christ say to His Apostles: "It is

Submission to the Ordinances of Providence. 49

expedient to you that I go; for if I go not, the Paraclete will not come to you"?[1] Can you after these words consider the loss of your friend or guide, however excellent or holy, a spiritual disadvantage? But you answer me: "Who knows whether this loss is not in punishment of my unfaithfulness?" I will admit it to be so, but this does not change the matter; for the paternal rod of correction is raised for the good of the docile child. Would you disarm the chastising hand of God? Would you, as it were, touch the heart of your Heavenly Father and constrain Him to overwhelm you with new graces? Then accept His chastisements generously; and as a reward of your confident resignation to His holy will, this God of all goodness will give you either a more enlightened guide, or He Himself, in His infinite goodness and mercy, will be your friend and director. He will send to you, as to His Apostles, the Holy Spirit. His light will enlighten you, and the unction of His grace will invest you with wonderful strength.

Again, let us suppose that you have all your life been devoted to prayer and good works; your daily devotional exercises are the food and support of your soul. But illness forces you to interrupt them; you can no longer assist at holy Mass daily,—no, not even on Sunday; you must abstain from Holy Communion; and soon your weakness will become such that it will be impossible for you to pray. Do not complain, pious soul; you are called to the honor of eating with your Divine Master a food of which many others know not.[2] By it you will profit, and your illness will prove a sanctifying remedy. Hear what the Lord said to His disciples: "My meat is to do the will of Him that sent Me."[3] The same food is now offered to you. Ponder well that by it alone it is given us to live for heaven. Prayer itself loses its efficacy when not fructified and animated by this heavenly food. Our Divine Master has expressly said: "Not every one, that saith to Me, Lord, Lord, shall enter

[1] John xvi. 7.   [2] John iv. 32.   [3] John iv. 34.

into the kingdom of heaven: but he that doth the will of My Father who is in heaven, he shall enter into the kingdom of heaven."[1] It is God who sends you this illness. He Himself dispenses you from your spiritual exercises; or rather, He forbids you to perform them. Give yourself, then, no anxiety about them; direct your whole attention to what He now requires of you instead of them. He desires that you should in all things, renouncing your own, learn to fulfil His holy will. For the future, this should be your daily bread; hence, He gives you so many occasions for practising it. How many inconveniences, how many sacrifices, does not your illness impose upon you! It thwarts you in your plans, it increases expense, medicines are distasteful, imprudence injures you, and neglect annoys you; in short, a thousand little things give you pain. How many occasions here upon which you can say to yourself: "God so wills it!" Make it a duty to allow none of these opportunities to pass unimproved, for then your illness will unite you most intimately and closely with Him who said: "For whosoever shall do the will of God, he is My brother and My sister and mother."[2]

Again, a great feast is near. You are earnestly preparing for it. Your fervor and devotion appear to you already a foretaste of the spiritual consolations that await you on the day itself. The feast comes, but finds you no longer the same. Instead of pious feelings and holy aspirations, you experience naught but dryness the most desolating; you are not even capable of conceiving a good thought. Do not be distressed. Act in this case as in others. Make no nervous exertions to change such a state. God sends you this cross. You know that whatever comes from Him is good; and that to such as receive it like little children, it is beneficial and rich in blessings. Take quietly from His hand, also, the state of your soul. Recollect yourself as well as you can in His holy presence, submit to Him as the sick man to the physician from whom he expects his perfect cure, and

Submission to the Ordinances of Providence.

be firmly persuaded that no spiritual consolation could be so salutary to you as such dryness and desolation borne resignedly. Not our feelings, but our good-will makes our soul susceptible of God's graces. An act of the will very frequently exerts no influence upon the feelings, but that does not render it the less meritorious before God. Even were the feelings and sentiments in open opposition to the will, it does not matter so long as the latter disapproves it. Never forget, therefore, that the effect of prayer depends not upon the feelings. This applies, also, to the workings of God in the human soul. They are noiseless and almost unobserved. As the nourishment we borrow from perishable food assimilates itself to the whole body, supporting and increasing life's exhausted strength in all its members, without any interior perception of how this is done, so also does the Body of Jesus Christ act upon us. This heavenly Food, which is given to us for the nourishing and strengthening of our soul, acts secretly and imperceptibly in our interior. But we, alas! desire to *feel*. As soon as this feeling, this interior satisfaction, is wanting, we at once become discouraged. We seek to force, as it were, a return of those sweet sentiments; and for that end, with the greatest pains and spiritual exertions, we make long hours of prayer. But such a mode of proceeding does not render us more susceptible of the grace of God. On the contrary, it hinders His operations, since it agitates and occupies the soul too much. St. Catharine of Sienna once asked Our Lord why He had so freely revealed Himself to the patriarchs and prophets of the Old Law, also to the first Christians, and why He so rarely did it now. Jesus answered her: "The saints of the early ages were not absorbed in self, were not full of self-love. They came to Me as true disciples. They walked in My holy presence, and were always ready to hear and to follow My words and inspirations; they allowed themselves to be formed, to be purified like gold in the crucible; their souls were before Me like canvas under the hand of the painter. I could write freely the commandment of love on their heart. But in the present day Christians wish to say everything, do everything themselves. They speak as if I neither saw nor heard them. They are always so busy, so excited, that they will not permit me to act in their soul." In His Gospel the Lord warns us of this error when He says: "And when you are praying, speak not much, as the heathens; for they think that in their much-speaking they may be heard. Be not you therefore like to them; for your Father knoweth what is needful for you, before you ask Him."[1]

We should bear with submission to the holy will the sufferings which we have drawn upon ourselves by our sins. For example, you are, in consequence of some excessive indulgence, indisposed, or even seriously ill; or you have made some extravagant expenditures; you have squandered your money in dress and vanity; hence, you must now impose some privations upon yourself. Your negligence in the fulfilment of your duties, your imprudence, your slanders, your anger, your sulky disposition, or your rude character, bring upon you disagreeable mortifications, prejudicial losses, change of circumstances, humiliations, affronts to which are further added spiritual troubles. You reproach yourself with your conduct, you are distressed, dejected; your mind is full of troubled thoughts; you are harassed by interior disgust and anguish whose wearisome attacks you cannot shake off. God has not willed your sin; but for your own good, He does will that it should bear these painful consequences. Take them, therefore, from His hand, and be persuaded that humble submission is the surest means not only to regain the favor of God but even to increase it in your regard. Then your faults will cease to be detrimental to you. They will become, so to say, a memorial of your perseverance in the service of God. Let us suppose that you wish to make a journey on foot to Rome. But the roads are bad, you are weak, your sight is bad, or you are heedless, and you stum-

[1] Matt. vi. 7.

ble at almost every step. Yet, in spite of all this, you do not lose courage. You rise without delay and, instead of wasting time in grumbling and fruitless anxiety, you push onward, determined to continue your journey to the eternal city cost what it may. In the end you will succeed. Is not your constancy so much the greater and heroic the more obstacles you have had to overcome, and the more frequently you have had to rise? It is precisely thus in the service of God.

We should resign ourselves to God's will in interior sufferings, temptations, doubts, darkness, aridities, desolation, and in all other difficulties of the spiritual life. To whatever source we may ascribe them, God is and He ever will be their first cause. You think, for example, that these sufferings come from yourself. No; it is either the ignorance of your understanding, the sentiments of your heart, your unbridled imagination, or one of your corrupt inclinations, that is the source of them. Mount higher and behold whence this trial comes. Does not the cause lie in the will of God? He did not endow you with greater perfection. He subjected you to all such imperfections and imposed upon you for your sanctification the obligation of bearing patiently all the evil consequences thereof, until He Himself shall put an end to your sufferings. If God would enlighten your mind with only one ray of His heavenly light, if He would pour only one drop of the dew of His grace into your heart, you would immediately be strengthened and consoled. Perhaps you imagine that your interior sufferings came from the Evil One? Even so, you must regard God as the first cause of them. The history of holy Job proves that the devil can do nothing against us if God does not give him the power. When the temptation to hatred and envy raged in the heart of Saul, the Holy Scripture says he was tormented by an evil spirit from the Lord. How can this spirit be evil if it comes from the Lord? And if it is evil, how can it come from the Lord? It is evil through the malicious intention of the devil, who lies in wait for men to compass their destruction; and yet it comes from the Lord, because He permits the snares of the Evil One to tend to our salvation. But still more, our faith, as well as the teaching of the saints, tells us that God often withdraws Himself all at once from the soul. His lights, His consolations, the sensible effects of His grace cease, and this from designs that correspond to His infinite wisdom and goodness. How many lukewarm souls, negligent in the fulfilment of their duties, in the days of their interior anguish and affliction have entered into themselves, and have, in desolation and dereliction, regained their former fervor! How many others have in their interior sufferings found the occasion and the means of putting into practice the most sublime virtues! To what perfection and heroism did not the virtues of a St. Teresa, a St. Francis de Sales, a St. Ignatius attain through such trials! Wonderful ways of Divine Providence who, with infinite love and care, watches over the welfare of His children whom He appears to desert, in order to rouse some from tepidity, and preserve and strengthen others in the spirit of humility, self-denial, confidence in God, prayer, and submission! Therefore, let us not be confounded if sometimes our soul is hard pressed by interior suffering. Let us act like a sick person who consults the doctor, makes use of the remedies prescribed, and then calmly waits till it pleases God to restore his health.

Blosius tells us of a holy man who was continually harassed by temptations, desolation, and aridities, but who well understood the value of his interior pains. Once, when overwhelmed by trouble, he began to weep. Angels appeared and offered him consolation; but he declined their solace, saying: "I desire no relief. My greatest and only consolation is the fulfilment of the Divine Will!"

This same Blosius relates, also, that Jesus Christ once appeared to St. Bridget and asked the cause of her sadness and dejection. The saint said: "Lord, I am tormented by evil thoughts and I tremble at Thy judgments." The Saviour replied: "Contrary to My will, you once took pleasure in the vanities of the world; therefore it is just that you should now be tempted against your will with vain and evil thoughts. It is also right that you should tremble at My judgments; but, at the same time, you must always confide in Me, your Lord and your God. Be firmly persuaded that the evil thoughts that one resists and banishes according to his strength, serve the soul here in this life as a purgatory. They afford also ample opportunity to accumulate merits for heaven. But if you cannot banish the evil thought, despise it and wait patiently till it departs of itself."

Many persons in interior suffering applied to Tauler, and he has left us the advice which he gave them. When such a one explained to him his lamentable condition, his incessant spiritual trials, Tauler would say: "All is going on well. That of which you complain is precisely the greatest grace from God." If the penitent argued that, on the contrary, he believed his sufferings to be a punishment for his sins, the skilful director would say: "Be it on account of your sins or not, believe that this cross comes to you from God. Embrace it lovingly therefore. Thank the Lord and resign yourself wholly into His hands." If, finally, some one told him that he felt interiorly consumed by dryness and vexation, he answered: "Suffer patiently, and you will receive more grace than if you now experienced the most tender and fervent devotion."

We are now at the last and, perhaps, most difficult and sensitive point: namely, that we should desire even virtue itself, grace, and eternal glory only in the measure in which God wills to give them to us, and not wish for more than He grants. Our sole aim should be to attain by fidelity the degree of perfection for which we are destined. It is not given to all to rise to the same height of glory. For example, it is certain that, in spite of our conscientious co-operation with grace, we can never become so pure, humble, and perfect as the Blessed Virgin. Who could attain to the grace and blessedness of the Apostles? Who could reach the virtue and perfect holiness of St. Joseph? Or who could equal St. John the Baptist, him whom the Divine Saviour Himself called the greatest among the children of men? In this respect, as in all others, we must submit unreservedly to the will of God, that the word of the Lord may be verified in us: "But thou shalt be called: My pleasure in her!"[1] When we either hear or read that God led souls in a short time to the highest perfection, and endowed them with extraordinary graces, we must watch over our heart, that no violent desire for the same favors be aroused in us, and that our perfect conformity to God's will suffer no disturbance thereby. Yes, on such occasions we should all the more closely adhere to the most amiable will of the Lord and, in sentiments of unlimited resignation, say to Him: "O my God! I praise and extol Thee that Thou hast imparted Thyself, hast revealed Thyself to these chosen souls with so much love and generosity. The honor Thou dost confer upon them is so great that no man is able to estimate it worthily; but I value the fulfilment of Thy adorable will above all the illuminations, sweetnesses, and extraordinary graces of Thy saints. I prefer it to all, and therefore, I implore of Thee but one grace: viz., that I may have no will of my own, that it may be lost in Thine, entirely transformed into Thine! Others may implore a thousand graces. I shall for the future know but one prayer: Grant that I may always follow Thy direction, correspond to Thy designs, and fulfil Thy will; that I may become a perfect instrument laboring for Thy honor. Do in me and through me, for time and eternity, all that Thou dost will!"

Resignation such as this is so pleasing to God that, on account of it, He called David a man according to His own heart: "I have," says He, "found a man according to My heart who shall always do My will."[2] And in fact, David's

[1] Is. lxii. 4.   [2] I. Kings xiii. 14.

Submission to the Ordinances of Providence.

heart became in the hands of God like soft wax, which unresistingly receives whatever form is given it. "My heart is ready, O Lord! my heart is ready!"[1]

It is good to commit to memory some passages of Holy Scripture with which, from time to time, to give expression to this virtue. For instance, "Lord, what wilt Thou that I should do?"[2] Behold, I am ready to do Thy will in all things! "I am Thine,"[3] dispose of me according to Thy good pleasure. "I seek not my own will."[4] "My meat is to do the will of Him who sent me, that I may perfect His work."[5] "Yea, Father, for so hath it seemed good in Thy sight."[6] "Thy will be done on earth as it is in heaven!"[7] Our Saviour Himself once recommended to St. Catherine of Genoa to dwell particularly on this petition of the Our Father. But if on account of the revolt of our inordinate inclinations we find it difficult to fulfil God's will, let us cry out with David: "Shall not my soul be subject to God?" From Him have I received all good things. "From Him is my salvation." O I will obey His commands "for He is my God and my Lord," even if my perverse nature refuses to do what He commanded me. "He is my helper I shall not be moved."[8] Or say with Our Lord in His death agony: "Father, not my will but Thine be done."[9] Leo the Great, commenting on these words, says: "These words proceeding from the mouth of Christ, our Divine Head, are the salvation of all His members. They have instructed the faithful, animated the confessors, and crowned the martyrs. Ye children of the Church, who have been redeemed at so high a price and, without any merit on your part, have been justified, attend to these words; and when the tempter presses you hard, let them serve you as your best buckler, that you may conquer your perverse nature and endure tribulation with courage!"

[1] Ps. lvi. 8. [2] Acts ix. 6. [3] Ps. cxviii. 94.
[4] John v. 30. [5] John iv. 34. [6] Matt. xi. 26.
[7] att. vi. 10. [8] Ps. lxi. 9. [9] Luke xxii. 42.

Let us add in concluding this chapter that, in conformity with the will of God, we should also accept the interior struggles which such submission costs. The will is often firmly determined to unite itself to that of God, and it really does so; but the mind is busy with all kinds of thoughts as to what may happen. For example, one says to himself, "If I should now become ill; if I should receive that appointment, if I should be sent hence—Would this be good or not for me? Then, I must abandon this plan, I cannot carry out this design. It would be possible for me to do this or that according to my inclinations," etc. But we must cut short such reflections. We have for the love of God sacrificed to Him our will, and we no longer possess the liberty to choose or to reject. In the same spirit of love let us offer to Him our understanding, generously renouncing all useless reflections, plans, and judgments; let us leave ourselves unreservedly to Divine Providence.

But for our consolation be it said, that the struggles and opposition of our disorderly nature against all that costs it pain, is no hindrance to our perfect submission to the divine will. Let us lay to heart the words of St. Francis de Sales: "When things go not according to our liking, although we would naturally wish them to be otherwise, yet we must with our whole heart submit; for in this consists the victory."

CHAPTER III.[1]

Why and How We Should Resign Ourselves to God's Will.

THIS doctrine of Divine Providence is one of the most consoling truths of revelation; for it assures us that, sin excepted, nothing happens on earth without God's willing it. But the richest consolations are founded on this, that the sufferings and adversities which God sends us, are for our good, our salvation. We do not readily perceive this. God loves to accomplish His designs by means very different from those suggested by human prudence. This is proved by many examples which show how, in purely natural occurrences, He has allowed what seemed to be misfortunes to turn to our greatest good. Joseph is sold, dragged into slavery, and thrown into prison; he bewailed an apparent misfortune, but it proved afterward to be the foundation of his happiness. It was his sufferings that raised him to the steps of the Eygptian throne. Saul lost his father's asses; in vain did he seek them far and near, vexed, no doubt, over time lost and fruitless trouble. But who ever reproached himself so unreasonably as Saul? For, through God's wise guidance, his little vexation served to bring him to the prophet, who, by the command of God, was to anoint him king of his people. How great will our shame be, when we shall appear before the face of God and clearly recognize the loving intention with which He sent this or that cross, and for which we have been so ungrateful! "I have," says one, "so deeply mourned the death of my only son cut off in the springtime of his years." Ah! had he but lived some

[1] This and the following chapter are taken from the works of Father de la Colombière.

months, some years longer, he would have fallen by the hand of an enemy and died in mortal sin. "I cannot console myself that this matrimonial affair came to naught." But had God permitted it to take place, sorrow and misery would have been your fate. The illnesses against which you have so often repined have, perhaps, prolonged your existence thirty or forty years. You must thank that humiliation which cost you so many tears, for securing your eternal salvation. Were it not for the loss of that sum of money, your soul would, perhaps, have been irretrievably lost. Why, then, do you grieve? Why vex yourself? God has taken upon Himself the guidance of our destiny; and yet we burden ourselves with it! We confide our health and our life to a physician whom we consider very skilful. He prescribes a painful operation; he cauterizes, he amputates, and we let him do all that he will. We even thank him and reward him, for we know that he would not impose such suffering if it were not necessary. Shall we refuse to God the confidence that we place in man? Shall we doubt His wisdom or fear His leading us astray?

If we knew all that God knows, then we should certainly will all that He wills, and with burning tears implore Him for those sufferings which we now so earnestly pray Him to avert. For this reason, the Redeemer says to all in the persons of the two sons of Zebedee: "O ye blind men! I have compassion on your ignorance,—you know not what you ask."[1] Leave yourselves in My hands. I know better than you what is necessary. If I had in the past granted your petitions and yielded to your desires, you would long since have been irretrievably ruined.

But would you be convinced that, in all that God permits to happen to you, He has only your real good and eternal happiness in view? Recall, then, what He has already done for you with all its attendant circumstances. Heavy trials now afflict you—remember that He who sends you this sorrow passed His whole life in poverty and suffering, to

[1] Matt. xx. 22.

deliver you from eternal damnation. He has placed one of His angels at your side, to guide and protect you in all your ways; He prays for you upon the altar without ceasing; He offers Himself daily thousands of times for you in the Holy Sacrifice; and He knows no greater joy than to unite Himself intimately with you. What base ingratitude, after so many proofs of love, to doubt whether He visits you for your good or for your prejudice! "But His blows are hard, He inflicts deep wounds, and His hand rests so heavily upon me." What have you to fear from a hand that was pierced for you on the cross? "He leads me by steep, thorny paths." Thoughtless creature! If there is no other way by which to reach heaven, would you rather be eternally lost than tread it? Has not your Lord, for love of you, gone before you on the road of suffering? "He offers me a chalice full of bitterness." That is true, but consider that He who presents it is your Saviour. How could He, who so tenderly, so constantly, who eternally loves, determine to deal harshly with you, if it be not for your highest good and even urgent necessity? This thought alone should stimulate us not only to accept willingly the apparently insupportable dispensations of Divine Providence, but also to love them and to resign ourselves perfectly to the will of God.

A holy man once said: "Who could force me to do anything against my will? For such a step it would be necessary for my adversary to do violence to God Himself; since so long as God's will is accomplished, I am free, as I will nothing but what He wills. Is it His will that I should be sick? Then, will sickness be more agreeable to me than health. Does He will me to be poor? Then, under no consideration would I be rich. Shall I become an outcast among men? If such be God's will, I shall be satisfied, nor shall I seek celebrity excepting in the contempt of the world. Shall I live here or there? Shall I pass my days in retirement or in the turmoil of the world? Shall I die in the flower of my years or in old age? I cannot say, in truth, which of these I should prefer to do. But as soon as God makes known His choice of them, as soon as He shall signify which are according to His Heart, then shall my own heart incline to His will ; then shall I find real happiness."

But is this perfection merely an unattainable ideal, conjured up by our imagination? or can men really be found so indifferent as to look with equal calmness upon happiness or unhappiness, fortune or misfortune? Ah! yes, there are such. I myself know souls who in sickness and health, in poverty and riches, are ever contented. They even prefer indigence and suffering to abundance and happiness.

For the rest, there is nothing truer than what I have still to say: The more we conform to the will of God, the more freely God will anticipate our desires. As soon as we aim at obeying Him, He is willing to fulfil our wishes. He not only hears our prayers, but anticipates them. He penetrates the deepest recesses of our heart and discovers the hidden desires for love of Him suppressed, all of which He fulfils more richly than we could dare to hope. In a word, the happiness of a soul truly resigned to God is constant, unchanging, eternal. No fear disturbs the tranquillity that no accident can affect. I regard such a soul as a man set upon a rock in the midst of the sea of this world. Fearless he beholds the billows dashing below him; he numbers them one by one, and smiles to see them breaking harmlessly at his feet. Whether the waves dance in the bright sunshine, or leap and roar and foam in the storm; whether they rise upon his right or upon his left, he remains unshaken, for the rock upon which he stands is firm and immovable.

How can we reach this blessed conformity? The first step toward it is the constant, steady practice of it. As great opportunities are rare, the whole secret of its acquisition lies in this, that we make use of little daily occurrences. Fidelity to this, will soon put us in the way of bearing even the greatest misfortunes with unwavering firmness. Every one of us daily experiences a thousand little unwelcome vexations. Now it is something purely foreign to us, again the cause arises from ourselves or from another. Our whole life is an unbroken chain of such little annoyances. From them spring a thousand involuntary emotions of aversion, envy, impatience, and fear, a thousand passing vexations and trifling alarms, which for the moment, at least, disturb the peace of the soul. For example, some expression escapes your lips which, on the instant, you would gladly recall; a sharp, cutting word is addressed to you; you are served badly or slowly; a child allows you no rest; a troublesome visitor detains you; you are inadvertently pushed or jostled; a passing vehicle bespatters you; the weather does not suit you; your work does not succeed according to your liking; some article gets broken; your dress is torn or soiled, and so on. Certainly in such trifles you cannot practise heroic virtue; but if you wish, you can by them attain the highest perfection. A soul that is faithful and persevering to accept these little sufferings from the hand of Divine Providence and to make an offering of them, not only lays up for herself many rich merits; not only arrives at close union with God; but in a short time she will be able courageously to endure the most trying and painful events of life.

This so easy and yet so useful practice, one so pleasing to God, is the first means to arrive at union with His will. In addition to this, we may make use of another means. God does not send heavy tribulations daily, but daily we can say to Him that we are ready to accept them when it pleases Him. If God should take your husband, your son; if He permit that this lawsuit, this investment be lost, then you must summon all the strength of your soul to bear so heavy a stroke. But first of all accept His ordinances, for you know not what God has hidden therein. Resign yourself to all that He may send you; renounce in His holy presence every wish, every desire, your possessions, your health, your ambition to increase or to preserve your good name; protest to Him that you are ready to sacrifice all to Him. In the morning consider what evil may occur to you in the course of the day. Perhaps you may receive the news of a shipwreck, or a conflagration, or a bankruptcy; you may, perhaps, be insulted in an unheard of manner, brought to confusion on the most sensitive point. Death may rob you of what is nearest and dearest to you in this world; or you may yourself die a sudden, or a violent death. Prepare, then, in advance for all such possible sufferings, in case God should permit them. Force your will to unite in this offering and desist not in your efforts, till it is perfectly ready to will all that God wills and desire nothing that He does not will.

In this practice there is, however, a distinction to be made between the suffering that we can very naturally foresee, whose possibility stares us in the face, as it were, and those almost impossible ones that we conjure up of ourselves. As to what relates to the first, it is in case of necessity always good to accept it in advance. Should one at the moment not feel the courage, let him calmly say to himself: "When this trial comes upon me, I hope to receive with it from Divine Goodness the graces necessary to endure it courageously and resignedly. However weak I now feel I am resolved, with the help of grace, to submit entirely in the hour of trial to the will of my Lord and Creator."

Quite different is it with the sufferings we purposely represent to ourselves, conjure up, so to speak, in order to accustom ourselves to their acceptance. This practice is not always without danger, and is not good for all souls. It may be very useful to those who have made progress enough in conformity to God's will to look forward to heavy tribulations without fear or agitation. But for souls that do not yet possess sufficient strength firmly to gaze upon the cross, truly it is foolhardy to challenge an enemy whom they are too weak to encounter, and from whose assaults Providence has spared them. Jesus Christ warns us against disquieting cares for the future. They who, on account of their weakness and imperfection, cannot look into the future without alarm, should turn away their eyes from it and throw themselves blindly and unreservedly into the arms of Divine Providence. To them especially applies what Fénelon so beautifully says:

"The cross that we ourselves make by yielding to gloomy forebodings of the future comes not from God. On the contrary, we tempt Him when we anticipate His plans and substitute our own foresight for His Divine Providence. Our own false wisdom always bears bitter fruit. God permits it thus, in order to shame us when we withdraw from His paternal guidance. The future is not ours. Who knows whether it ever will be ours? If so, it may turn out quite differently from what we imagined. Let us, then, close our eyes to what God hides from us, and, in His unfathomable decrees, yet withholds. Let us adore without seeing, be silent, and remain in peace!"

The cross of the present moment always brings with it the grace necessary to render it more easy to bear. In it we recognize the hand of God, which is actually felt. But the cross that our anxious conjectures concerning the future construct, is not in conformity with the divine plan. When we court it, we go beyond the will of God. We see then only the cross, and not the grace that makes it light and bearable. This anxious peering into the future is an infidelity that subtracts grace. Hence it is that everything connected with such a cross is so bitter, so heavy, so dark, so hopeless; and the soul that toiled through curiosity for the forbidden fruit, finds interiorly only restlessness and death, without consolation. We come to this when we do not trust God unreservedly, when we presume to search into the mysteries of which He is so jealous. "Sufficient for the day is the evil thereof,"[1] says Our Lord Himself. Daily sufferings contribute to our sanctification when we allow God to act. Who are we, to ask Him: "Why hast Thou done this?" He is the Lord, and that suffices. He is the Lord, let Him do all that seems good to Him. He raises up or casts down, He chastises or comforts, He wounds or

[1] Matt. vi. 34.

heals, He kills or restores to life; and He is at all times the Lord. We are only the work of His power, a mere playball in His hand. What matters all else, provided He be glorified and His holy will accomplished in us? Let us give up self, renounce every selfish aspiration; then shall the will of the Lord that reveals itself in all things be our abiding consolation even when such resignation is to our own cost. The resistance of men, their inconstancy, yes, even their injustice, will then appear to us as the working of the unchangeable wisdom, justice, and goodness of God. Everywhere we shall see but God alone, since He conceals Himself under the material forms of this world, under the weakness of blind and perverse men.

Then shall the deceitful figure of this world, passing away like a shadow, be to us a mirror reflecting the splendor of God in order to His praise. But let us return to the real trials and sufferings of life.

When misfortune overtakes you, lose no time in vain complaints against creatures or destiny; but fly at once to the Divine Master. Cast yourself at His feet, and implore the grace to carry your cross bravely. A man, dangerously wounded, but still possessing consciousness, will not pursue his murderer; he will have immediate recourse to a physician who can heal his wound. And will you, in your sufferings, seek first the cause of them? If you do, you will have to turn to God, for He is the author.

Go, then, to God; but go promptly, go straight to Him. Let this be your first impulse. Carry back to Him, so to say, the dart with which He has wounded you; take Him the rod with which He has scourged you. Kiss a thousand times the hands of your crucified Saviour, those hands that have struck you, that have given you pain. Repeat often what He Himself exclaimed in the height of His Passion: "Father, not My will, but Thine be done!"[1] I praise and thank Thee a thousand times that Thy will is being fulfilled in me. Were it in my power to oppose Thee, yet would I freely submit. The sufferings Thou sendest me, I accept with all their concomitants and all their consequences. I do not complain either of the pain, of the persons who have caused it, of the place, of the time, or of the manner of their visitation. I am assured that Thou hast ordered all well, and I would rather die than oppose Thy holy will even in the least particular. Thy will be done! Yes, my God, may this will to-day and always, in time and in eternity, be fulfilled in me! Thy will be done on earth, as it is in heaven.

CHAPTER IV.

Of the Utility of Sufferings for the Just. Of their Necessity for the Sinner.

HAVE you ever seen a mother at the sickbed of her child during a surgical operation? With a thousand little endearments she tries to dry the child's tears, though she does not prevent the physician's cutting or searing. But if the mother consents that her little darling be subjected to treatment so severe, who can doubt that it is necessary for the child's well-being? Would the mother permit it if the health of the child did not depend upon it, and were it not to spare it more prolonged and more intense pain?

My thoughts run in this train when I see you suffering. You complain that some one wrongs you, insults, slanders, calumniates you, or unjustly robs you of your property. Your Saviour (in this name is contained more love and tenderness than in the name of mother)—your Saviour sees what you suffer. He bears you in His Heart, He who said so explicitly, that whoever injures you wounds the apple of His eye, He Himself, though He could so easily have averted it, permits that you should suffer. And can you still doubt that this passing trial is meant to contribute to your true happiness?

Remember all that your Saviour has done to spare you useless suffering. Suffering after death bears no merit for eternity. In hell one suffers only to suffer. What did Jesus Christ do to save us this fruitless pain!

He took upon Himself our penalty, He shed every drop of His blood, He died upon the cross. He voluntarily exposed Himself to His Father's anger and the fury of the

Jews. This He did to snatch you not only from the flames of hell, but also from the purifying fires of purgatory. His sufferings are sufficient to atone for all our failings, He left no debts for us to pay. On the contrary, He bequeathed to His Church an inexhaustible treasury of merits from which we may daily draw, in order to satisfy Divine Justice for our repeated transgressions. This divine love of God appeals to me more powerfully than any other evidence in favor of the value of suffering. Yes, though the Holy Ghost had not proclaimed them happy who suffer here below; if the Holy Scriptures did not so frequently extol the advantages of sufferings; if, finally, experience did not point to them as the common lot of the true friends of God, I should not esteem them less. And why? Because I know that our sufferings come from God, from that same God who, to spare us the least pain hereafter, willed here on earth to undergo every imaginable torture. God gives me the chalice that I must drain here on earth. This one thought will endue me with courage to raise it to my lips— He who endured so much to spare me, will not allow me to suffer merely to procure for Himself vain and cruel pleasure.

When I hear a Christian complaining in time of suffering, I say to myself: "This poor man bewails his happiness. He aspires, perhaps, to riches, and he should thank God that he is poor." I am firmly persuaded that no greater joy could be granted him than that which has rendered him so disconsolate. I have a thousand reasons for my conviction. And if I knew all that God knows, and saw the future rich blessings resulting from these sufferings, how strengthened I should become in my first convictions!

But I hear some one say: "What use to me is this sickness that hinders my spiritual exercises? or the loss of my property, which throws me into despair? or that humiliation which dejects my soul and produces in my interior confusion and disorder?" Quite true! An unforeseen accident may, at the first moment, cast the soul down so as not to be able, at once, to receive it properly. But have patience, and you will see what great graces God is preparing for you by means of suffering. Without it you would not, perhaps, have been worse than you are; but you would never have reached the degree of perfection intended for you. You have given yourself wholly to the service of God, but you have not yet resolved to sacrifice to Him this or that vanity. Does not an inclination to some trifling external pomp still linger in your heart? Have you entirely given up that longing after wealth and honor for your children? Or does not some purely human friendship still dispute with God the possession of your heart?" You have yet to take a step, in order to arrive at perfect freedom. It may be but a little thing that is required of you, but you have not yet offered this last sacrifice. Of how many graces do you not deprive yourself by this puerile trifling! There is question, we say, of but little things; and yet, nothing is harder, nothing costs us more than to break the last weak thread that unites the soul to itself and to the world. In this state of weakness, the soul partially feels in what it is wanting; but the mere thought of the sacrifice makes it draw back terrified. The evil lies so near to the heart that only by violent and painful means can it be eradicated. Therefore it was that this sudden shock was necessary for you. When you least expected it, a skilful hand plunged the knife deep through the sound flesh into the diseased part. How long without this painful operation would you have lingered? The illness that confined you to a bed of suffering; the bankruptcy that threw you into misery; the humiliation that covered you with shame; the death that you mourn so deeply,—all this accomplished in a moment what your own half-formed resolves could never have effected, what the guide of your soul so often fruitlessly attempted.

If these calamities accomplish God's designs over you, if they disgust you with creatures and force you to cast yourself unreservedly into the arms of the Creator, it is certain that you will offer more thanks to God for these marks of

Utility and Necessity of Sufferings. 71

His love than you formerly did prayers to avert them. In your afflictions you will recognize your Lord's greatest favors, in comparison with which all other considerations will appear trifling. The temporal blessings which God up to the present bestowed upon you and your family, were considered a special proof of His goodness; but now you see clearly, you feel deeply that God never evinced more love for you than when He apparently destroyed what He had formerly done for your earthly happiness. Was He not generous to you when He gave you riches, honor, health, and children? Now in depriving you of them, He is extravagant in His blessings.

We do not speak here of the merit of patience. It is certain that, in one day of tribulation, we often gain more for heaven than in years of prosperity, though spent ever so holily; for we must acknowledge that we do not trust the virtue that is practised in the midst of worldly success.

The great Apostle to the Gentiles gloried only in his chains, his stripes, his scourges, and shipwrecks. Of his prayers and apostolic works he makes no mention; for in continual combats against self, extraordinary graces and the greatest vigilance are necessary to prevent self-love from creeping in.

Prosperity makes us earthly and effeminate. It is a great deal if a prosperous man takes the trouble to think of God once or twice in the day. His pleasant surroundings occupy him so agreeably that he easily forgets all else. Misfortune, on the contrary, with its dark and desolate thoughts, raises our gaze heavenward· and by the hope of joys awaiting us, we strive to mitigate our sorrow. We may, assuredly, in every condition and under all circumstances glorify God. The pious life of a happy Christian honors the Lord exceedingly; but how much more does he honor Him who in suffering praises His holy Name? The first may be compared to a faithful and punctual courtier, who follows his prince everywhere, in the council and chamber, sharing all the pleasures and feasts of the court;

but the second, to a brave general who, in the midst of a thousand dangers and at the sacrifice of his own blood, wins battles and cities for his king. Would not such a prince owe more to the general than to the courtier?

If the rich, the happy, receive temporal blessings from God with gratitude, and use them rightly, they certainly honor Him; but when one whom Providence has robbed of all earthly possessions, one whom He visits with tribulations of diverse kinds, remains faithful and follows Him in the rough path of suffering, the power of divine grace is revealed in him in a manner much more perfect.

Judge for yourself what their reward will be who, in suffering, have glorified the Lord. What glory, at his entrance into heaven, awaits the Christian whose life here on earth was a series of sufferings, who appears before his God covered, so to say, with blood and wounds! He has followed his Lord in all things, he has been the faithful companion of the Divine Sufferer. Only in eternity shall we understand the infinite love with which God has loved us, in affording us the opportunities of acquiring a reward so rich. Then shall we reproach ourselves for having, whilst on earth, complained of what was to be for us the source of eternal felicity. Why should we not cultivate these sentiments now? Why should we not now praise God for the sufferings for which we shall eternally thank Him in heaven? Why should we envy the successful of this world, since they will one day envy us our sufferings?

St. Augustine cannot sufficiently wonder that God, in His unlimited power, infinite happiness, and perfect independence of all creatures should, by an explicit command, oblige them to love Him, and even make them participate in His greatest happiness. But I wonder yet more at His goodness in that He not only imposes so blessed a duty upon His enemies; but that, in a manner, He compels them to fulfil it.

Yes, through suffering, God forces even the most perverse to return to His friendship. By what other road could

Utility and Necessity of Sufferings.

they find their way back into His arms? The Word of God, the reception of the holy Sacraments, ordinary graces, keep Christian souls in the path of virtue. But a man overwhelmed with domestic and public affairs; a wife who has become the slave of vanity and pleasure; Christians, in fact, whose life is spent in sin and forgetfulness of God, must suffer or be eternally lost.

I know the efficacy of the Divine Word, I know that it is sharper than a two-edged sword; yet we daily see that it fails to pierce the hardened hearts of men, we daily behold the sinner resisting it. How much has not been preached against the ever-growing evils of pride and vain show, which consume the daily substance of rich and poor; against that passion for gaming, which robs one of the time and money with which heaven could have been purchased? But what impression do all these earnest admonitions make upon the mind of those to whom gambling has become a formal business, or who squander the most unreasonable sums in vain dress? The one forgets in a moment what he has heard; the other remembers but to ridicule it. Some even feel insulted, and think they have reason to complain of the preacher. Now, what can God do to lead such persons back to the path of duty? There is no means left except poverty. Through bitter want, they must be forced to sell their vain ornaments, and for the future support their family by their labor. Go and preach prayer and retirement to that woman so vain of her beauty and of the compliments paid her. Do you fancy that your admonitions will be well received, or that she will even listen to you? To save her soul, an illness must disfigure her, or some public confusion forever banish her from worldly society.

When will you speak to the rich, to the pleasure-loving voluptuary of conversion? He thinks not of going to hear the Word of God, still less of sending for you and entreating your earnest admonitions. And supposing he lent you a willing ear, how could a serious, a religious thought find place in a mind filled with pictures of earthly pleasures and worldly affairs? Grace so ready to insinuate itself into souls, can find no entrance into such hearts. But shall we despair of the eternal salvation of these men? Is there no means left to snatch them from the abyss of ruin? Yes, the Lord has still one means by which He calls to Himself the elect who, blinded by prosperity, have turned away from Him. This last saving means comes in the shape of tribulation, illness, the sudden death of a dear relative, the loss of property, etc. What fruit will this adversity bear? It will incline the soul estranged from God to sorrow. Wholesome suffering will turn it away from the most seductive pleasures, will bring it to the knowledge of its crimes and debaucheries, and will lead it, finally, into the arms of its truly religious friends. The soul in time of trial recognizes the evil she has done, she seeks its source, she looks for help. Now one can speak to her of sin, of conversion, and of confession. She will herself feel soon the happy necessity of an earnest change of life, since it has become impossible for her to continue longer in sin.

This sufficiently demonstrates that we should, under all circumstances, meet misfortunes cheerfully. They render the just more just; they, in a measure, force the sinner to penance. They only upon whose hardened hearts trials and tribulations have failed to make an impression; they that are not improved in the furnace of suffering; they that, perhaps, become therein worse, have cause for affliction. Such obstinacy is the surest and most evident sign of condemnation. A Christian who leads a godless life, and whom God does not chastise, should, if a spark of religion is yet alive within him, tremble; but a sinner who does not bend under the rod of God's chastisement, may be counted among the reprobate.

CHAPTER V.[1]

Of the Good Use of Sufferings.

THE goodness of God chastises those whom He loves. Why, asks some one, does God take pleasure in seeing us suffer? Could He not make us good and perfect without first plunging us into pain and misery? He certainly could, for to Him nothing is impossible. In His almighty hand, He holds the hearts of all men and moulds them as He pleases. But God, who could have saved us without suffering, has not so willed, just as He has subjected men to the weakness of childhood and gradual growth, instead of creating them in the full vigor of manhood. He is the Lord. We have only to be silent, and adore His infinite wisdom without desiring to fathom it. All that we know is that we can become perfect only when we are humble, disinterested, disengaged from ourselves, and when we refer all things to God.

Without a miracle it is not possible for grace to free us from ourselves, or to snatch self-love from us without causing us pain. If a soul filled with self could in an instant die to all vanity, it would be as great a wonder as to go to bed a child and to rise up a man of thirty. But God does not work miracles every day, either in the natural or supernatural order.

God conceals His work in almost imperceptible progress. What He does, is not only done by degrees but often also by simple and natural means, so that human wisdom sees in it little of the finger of God. Such results are frequently ascribed to means which appear wholly natural. Were we accustomed to see miracles in God's works, in what would

[1] This chapter is taken from Fénelon's Works. See also, "The Following of Christ," II. Bk., ch. 11 and 12; III. Bk., ch. 47 and 49.

the merit of faith consist? God wills that in this life we should believe without seeing.

That we should live by faith has a double object. The just man must be tried by it. He must, in the darkness of this life, renounce his own judgment; and the sinner, who in his presumption has not merited to see the light, shall be blinded by it. He sees the works of God and knows them not. True understanding, he alone deserves who distrusts his own wisdom. Man's proud knowledge is not worthy to enter into the councils of God.

God wills also that the workings of grace should be concealed in the darkness of faith. He allows them to act slowly and painfully. He makes use of the inconstancy and ingratitude of creatures, the disappointment and weariness found in all earthly enjoyments, to wean us from the false pleasures of this world. He frees us from ourselves by showing us our own weakness and perversity, and by allowing us to relapse repeatedly into the same faults. All this seems quite natural to us; and through a long course of apparently human means, He purifies us by degrees as in a slow fire. We would gladly be cleansed at once in the flame of God's pure love; but what would so sudden a destruction of self and its faults cost? It is our boundless self-love alone that makes us desire to become perfect in an instant and at small cost.

Why do we revolt against the length of our crucifixion? Only because we cling to self. It is this very clinging that God designs to uproot; for so long as we are occupied with self, His will cannot be accomplished in us. Besides, of what have we to complain? Our misfortune is that we cling to creatures and still more to self. For this reason, therefore, God arranges a series of preconcerted circumstances, which gradually detach us from creatures and eventually from ourselves. It is a painful operation; but our perversity renders it necessary, and its very necessity makes it painful. If a man's members were sound, there would be no need of surgical cutting or cauterizing. Such operations are required only when the wound is deep and the flesh corrupt. The more pain the surgeon causes, the more certain it is that the wound is dangerous. Would it be considered cruelty on the part of the surgeon to continue cutting and probing as long as he found it needful? Certainly not. He acts through a principle of love and duty; he would not act differently toward his only son.

Thus does God deal with us. He causes us pain only when forced to do so. His paternal Heart does not wish to afflict us; but He is compelled to cut into the sound flesh, in order to heal the wound hidden deep in our heart. He must take from us what we love too much, what we value more highly than we do even Himself. He deals with us as a mother with her little child. She does not regard his tears when she takes from him the knife with which he might inflict upon himself a mortal wound. We weep, we shrink, we cry *Ah!* and *Woe!* We struggle against God like children who, with hands and feet, strive against their mother. But God lets us cry and meanwhile heals us. He visits us only for our own good even when He appears to annihilate us. He acts thus for our own advantage and to spare us the suffering that we would bring upon ourselves. Had God left us that which we bewail, it would have cost us eternal tears. What we thought lost, was really so only when we fancied that we possessed it. God has taken it into his own safe-keeping intending to restore it in eternity. God deprives us of the object of our affection, in order to infuse into us a purer, a more constant, and better regulated love for it, that we may secure the eternal possession of it in His bosom.

In this world nothing happens without God's willing it. He does all, orders all, directs all. He gives to every creature all that it possesses. He numbers the hairs of our head, the leaves of the trees, the grains of sand on the seashore, and the drops of water in the ocean. At the creation of the world His wisdom weighed and measured even the least molecule that enters into the physical constitution of the sun. He it is who, at every moment, breathes into us new life. He has counted our days and holds in His mighty hand the keys of the gates of death which He alone can open or can close. What appears most striking to us is in His eyes of little importance. A few years of life, more or less, make no difference to Him. What matters it whether this mortal covering, this body of dust, be consigned to corruption a little sooner or a little later?

O how short-sighted and treacherous is our judgment! A youth dies in the bloom of life. We are shocked. "What a fearful loss!" we say. But whom does the loss concern? What has the deceased lost? Some years of life filled with vanity, deceit, and danger of eternal death. God took him away out of the midst of sinners. He snatched him suddenly from the corruption of the world and his own weakness. What do they lose to whom the departed was dear? They lose the poison of worldly happiness; they are roused from intoxicating pleasures, from long forgetfulness of God and their own destiny. They will gain through the cross the strength to resign their will to that of Divine Providence. By this stroke God saved the deceased and leads the relatives to resignation, to freedom of heart, so that they may go on courageously in the work of their eternal salvation.

O how true it is that God is infinitely good, infinitely loving; that His paternal Heart has compassion on our actual sufferings! Even at the moment in which the thunder of His wrath could annihilate us, and when the temptation is strong upon us to complain of His harshness, He loves us and has compassion on us.

What difference now between two persons who lived a hundred years ago, one of whom died twenty years before the other? Both have been dead a long time. The separation which then seemed so long and so hard, now appears to them as nothing; and it was in reality only a very short one. Soon shall the separated be reunited. The memory of their brief parting will scarcely remain. We act as if we were to live hundreds of years—yes, even forever. What foolishness! How quickly the dying follow the dead! He who sets out only two days after his friend upon the same journey, finds that the distance between them is not so great. Life flows on like a stream. The past is only a dream; the present is flying at the very moment in which we think to hold it, and is buried in the abyss of the past. The future will follow in its train; and it, too, will vanish rapidly. Days, months, and years press upon one another, drive on like the restless waves of the ocean, in endless pursuit, one of the other. There comes a moment, and all are engulfed. Hours of trial and nights of suffering which, in their actual endurance, seemed to us eternal, will, when all is over, appear to have been very short!

It is self-love alone that makes us so weak and sensitive. The invalid upon his bed of pain counts hour after hour. To him the night is unending; and yet it is in reality no longer than other nights. Cowardice makes us exaggerate our sufferings. They may, perhaps, be great, but our imagination magnifies them. The best way to shorten them, and to maintain patience to the end, is to abandon ourselves generously to God. Suffer we do, indeed, but God wills it so, in order to purify us and make us worthy of himself. The world smiles upon us, and the happiness we derive from it enfeebles our heart. Should we desire to live, till the terrible moment of death, in life's sensual merrymaking, its splendor, its vain joy, its proud triumphs, its love of itself, its enmity toward Christ, its horror of His cross, which alone can sanctify? The world will soon turn its back upon us. It will reject us with ingratitude, will number us among the things that are no more. Who, then, can wonder that the world will ever be the world; that is, always unjust, deceitful, and treacherous! And yet we are not ashamed to love it, and even wish to be still more entangled in its meshes. But God aims at disengaging us from it. He wishes to free us from its accursed slavery, in order to admit us to the blessed freedom of them that have renounced all things to follow Him. And how do we look upon his wise designs? Alas, we become disconsolate! If we allow ourselves to grieve over the disesteem of so miserable and abandoned a world, we are indeed our own enemies. We do not desire what is good for us, and we sigh for what brings us trouble. What an unworthy cause for so many tears, so many pangs!

If God tries us on the most sensitive point, so much the better! Adore the hand that strikes, let no word fall from the lips other than "I have deserved it! The chalice is bitter, but with my Saviour I must drain it to the dregs. Christ dying for His executioners has taught me to love, to bless, to pray for my persecutors."

Let us redouble our prayers in the time of combat, anxiety, and temptation. In the Heart of Our Saviour dying on the cross, we shall find strength to love those whom pride tempts us to hate. A cross loved is only half a cross, because love sweetens everything. Whoever is poor in love, is rich in suffering. Happy the soul that suffers much and suffers in the proper spirit! How unhappy would I be, if I were not to suffer with Christ, since I am here below only to be purified by the cross!

God tries us by sickness and exterior want, and from all we must derive profit! Every cross that God sends is necessary for us. We suffer much only because we cling too tenaciously to that of which God must divest us. We oppose, we delay the work of God in us. We thrust from us the healing hand and force our Heavenly Physician always to begin the cure anew. We should suffer far less if we abandoned ourselves entirely to God.

The cross accepted in a spirit of sacrifice, is never fruitless. Blessed is he who is ready for everything, who never says: It is too much! Blessed is he who builds not upon self, but upon the All-powerful, who wishes for no more consolation than God gives, and who feeds only upon the Divine Will!

The Good Use of Sufferings.

The cross is, for faithful souls, so assured a sign of mercy, and one so rich in the promise of an abundant harvest, that faith should make us rejoice in it despite the resistance of nature. We find peace when in resignation, and by it we offer to Him the sacrifice of our sweet pleasures. God urges the soul to the utmost to put off all that is not Himself. What else remains but courageously to embrace the proffered cross, and to allow ourselves to be crucified upon it? When He, our good Father, has tried us sufficiently, then He consoles. But His manner of doing so is not like that of creatures, whose sympathy only serves to nourish self-love. The consolation of God is true and lasting.

It is a great grace to establish one's peace in resignation to God's will and the privation of exterior comfort. We learn thereby to persevere courageously in trials. God has every right to dispose of His creatures, and their sinfulness deserves all kinds of humiliation and of crosses. These two thoughts should be our strength in trial. Let us permit God to be the Master, for men are impotent. Often when all seems lost, all is gained. God with His own hand casts down, and with His own hand raises up again.

Happy the man that suffers, if he but suffer rightly and satisfy divine justice! How much do we not owe this justice, and, strictly speaking, what sufferings have we not deserved! Instead of eternal pain, God sends us some hours of illness. Instead of the loss of the vision of God, instead of the rage and despair of the infernal spirits, the All-merciful sends us only a few short days of suffering in which to adore the hand that strikes through love. Such crosses call for gratitude, and not for complaints. Our heart must tell us that they are graces. Had God stricken us with leprosy, He would still smite us lightly; for how much more frightful is the leprosy of pride, of sin, and of self-idolatry, than that of the body!

A self-chosen cross is worth almost nothing.[1] God alone

[1] If the author here speaks of self-imposed crosses, which are almost worth

understands by what sort of self-denial to train the soul. The cross that God sends us shatters our pride, though not without our co-operation. We must do our part. When before God we calmly renounce our own will, then, and then only, has His grace the power to humble and to purify us. Abandon self and self-love! As long as we remain attached to them, we expose ourselves to men's antagonism, to their malice and injustice. Our humors do not harmonize with the whims of others, our passions resist theirs. Every desire of ours is a tender spot, to which the touch of our fellow-creatures causes pain. In self-denial alone is found peace; and peace will always be the more perfect in proportion as self-renunciation is more entire.

nothing for the benefit or the future reward of the soul, he certainly cannot mean self-imposed penances and mortifications. They are often necessary and restrain the passions. They are practised and recommended even by the saints, and, when sanctified by obedience, they will be gloriously rewarded in the life to come.

Self-imposed crosses, whose worth is to be suspected, are only those undertaken through self-love and against God's holy will.—*Translator.*

PART II.

TRUE PIETY THE INDISPENSABLE FOUNDATION OF INTERIOR PEACE—THE WAY IN WHICH GOD LEADS SOULS TO PEACE AND PERFECTION.

THERE are many souls of good-will, but their erroneous ideas of piety are prejudicial to interior peace and progress in perfection. The second part of our work, therefore, shall be to consider this matter.

I. To show the just idea of true and solid piety.

II. To enumerate briefly the way and means by which God usually leads souls to sanctity.

III. Important delusions and errors are pointed out which hinder us on our way

CHAPTER I.

The Foundation of True Piety—Points in which we Should Imitate the Example of the Saints.

WE here speak not to those who serve two masters and, under the outward appearance of piety, enjoy all the pleasures of this world. Our words are directed only to those that with an upright will cling to God alone. Few of them know, at least practically, in what the service of the Lord consists, and in what way they may safely and easily comply with their ob'igations. They either neglect the most important rules of the spiritual life and hold to the least, which their imagination suggests as duties; or they forget the sad state into which original sin has plunged us, and aim at an unattainable ideal of perfection, which prepares them only for discouragement, sadness, and dejection. Both hinder progress in virtue and, after years of effort, many souls realize the words of the Apostle: "We have labored all the night and taken nothing."[1] Yes, truly, they have worked in the dark, for no light from above has shone upon their endeavors; and, in their striving after perfection as in every other undertaking, good-will without true knowledge and right understanding does not suffice. We shall, then, give a short but clear idea of true piety, which leads the soul by union with God here below to peace, and above to eternal happiness. This idea is founded on the right knowledge of our relations to God and on the duties proceeding from them. God is our Creator and, therefore, our Lord and our Master. He can lawfully dispose of us and all belonging to us according to His pleasure: our thoughts, desires, actions, etc. But, in His goodness, He would not only be Lord, but also Father and Saviour to us; and from this should spring our fidelity toward Him. Our first obligation is entire submission to His sovereign law. The creature must always be ready to renounce himself, that is, his inclinations and desires, and bring them as an offering to God's will; for he has received his existence only in order to fulfil the will of his Creator. St. Francis de Sales says: "Piety is nothing else than the inclination and readiness to do all that we know to be pleasing to God."

Our second duty to God as our Father and Saviour, is love and confidence. From this duty anxious, timid souls only too often stray, seeing in God only a stern master. Such an opinion is injurious to the truth and honor of God, and is, for the souls entertaining it, a source of interior anguish and disquiet.

From what has been said, the nature of true piety may

[1] Luke v. 5.

The Foundation of True Piety.

be easily understood. Whoever serves God with unbounded resignation, offering his self-love in sacrifice, and this with full and loving confidence in the divine goodness, is truly pious; he will fulfil all his obligations. He will worship the Lord through love, adoration, and prayer in conformity to the Divine Will; in patience, in suffering he will honor Him; he will also observe all the rules of Christian justice and love, thus fulfilling his duties toward his neighbor; finally, he will not neglect his duties toward himself, but courageously fight against his disorderly passions. By subduing them he will again establish in his soul that beautiful order once reigning there, but which sin destroyed.

This is, in few words, the idea of true piety. What follows merely enlarges and explains particulars. But it is easily understood that one can attain to various degrees of this idea of perfection, for there is a very great difference between the lowest degree of self-denial, which freedom from every mortal sin secures, and that perfection which is attained by overcoming one's self in every imperfect emotion, even in the least things. Treading this path to the end, has been the work of a whole lifetime for the greatest saints. One advances but slowly along it; and it is not given to all to reach the term, though all should aim at it. When Our Saviour tells us, " Be ye perfect as your Heavenly Father is perfect," the meaning is, strive unceasingly after that perfection although it is so high that you can never say to yourself, " I have reached it."

On the way of perfection there are two snares to be met. The first is cowardice. Many Christians are satisfied with themselves because, strictly speaking, they do all that is necessary to salvation. They concern themselves little about paying God more perfectly the love and submission they owe Him, and they think little of the danger to which they expose themselves by neglecting their most important duties, thereby endangering the salvation of their soul. To such we do not speak here. They must, by earnest and impressive admonitions, be aroused from their slothful slumber; they need assuredly not be warned against excessive fervor.

The second, and far more dangerous snare, is the false idea devout souls but too often have of their duties. Such souls are frequently to be found in almost presumptuous ignorance of the real obligations which the service of God requires of them. In their misunderstanding they make demands upon themselves far beyond their strength and the designs of God. It is most necessary that they should be disabused of such delusions; for they lead to errors highly prejudicial, render all efforts at advancement in virtue fruitless, and rob souls of that interior peace which should be secured to them by their good-will. We shall, therefore, in the next four chapters disclose the errors of those who, instead of the Divine Law, frame an imaginary code for themselves as a guide to perfection, which self-made laws are equally unreasonable and impracticable.

When such false ideas, unfortunately too wide-spread, have been rectified, we shall explain in the last chapters of the second part upon what the conditions of our spiritual progress depend, and upon what paths God's providence generally leads souls to perfection. First of all, let us make some important observations on the false ideas often conceived of the lives of the saints, and the so much recommended imitation of their virtues; for these points are one of the richest sources of the above-mentioned errors. The imperfect and unintelligible manner in which the lives of the saints are not unfrequently written contributes not a little to impress the reader with false views. The facts related are mostly inimitable, whilst wonders of dazzling glare are told. Said wonders are confounded by many with sanctity, whilst, in truth, they are but its accidental consequences.

God, through certain saints, has wrought visible wonders to crown them with glory before men for the honor of His Church. He has also inundated their soul with extraordinary graces, upon which rest the remarkable facts of their life without, however, their constituting holiness. Many others have amassed not less merit before God by a hidden laborious life. Bellarmine, who was for a long time spiritual director of the Roman College of which St. Aloysius Gonzaga was at that time a member, often said there lay in the vault of that house several young brothers of the Society who, in the holiness to which they had attained, were not inferior to Aloysius in perfection. Sanctity does not depend upon extraordinary graces, which are not the result of merit, but simply the work of the Divine Will. To one the Lord imparts remarkable prerogatives, and from another He requires a hidden and ordinary life. When, then, we read the lives of the saints, we must not abandon the imagination, so easily excited by the extraordinary, to enthusiastic reveries. By so doing, we should expose ourselves either to the danger of presumption by eagerly aiming to realize in ourselves what we have read; or to that of yielding to discouragement and diffidence in our despair of arriving at similar results, as if nothing but the extraordinary was to be learned from the great heroes of Christianity.

On the contrary, what we should imitate in the saints is wholly independent of the wonders met in their lives. We should take as a model the virtues which they practised; the fidelity with which they corresponded to the graces they received, no matter what they required of them; the great courage with which they sacrificed self-love in order to follow divine inspiration; and, finally, the heroic combat against inordinate inclinations implanted in them by original sin as well as in us. We shall now speak of a very common error. One often represents to himself the saints during their earthly career as they now are in heaven, that is, in the full splendor of glory and purity. They consider them entirely different from their fellow-men, beings to whom the weakness and corruption of our nature were strangers; and who, consequently, had but to will and to do, not to practise and combat for the acquisition of heroic virtues. When we are exhorted to imitate them, we bring forward the excuse: "Ah, but they were saints!" as if the attribute of sanctity changed them into wholly different beings or made them angels. We see upon reflection that this could not be; but practically we hold to the false views which are often enough expressed in our words and actions. Our sacred legends generally strengthen such an opinion, since the trials, the weaknesses, and the faults of the saints are passed over in silence; or, at least, very lightly touched upon. From such stories one cannot gain an insight into the interior life of the saints. The misery and weakness of nature to which they, as well as ourselves, perhaps more than ourselves, were subject, are not portrayed, although they more courageously and steadfastly than we sustained the combat.

And yet, this is the very point that should be placed before us to console us in temptation, to increase our courage, and to prove to us by the example of the saints that we are not only able, but also bound to imitate them. We must, at one time, behold them advancing to the combat; at another, shrinking back and wavering. We must hear the great Apostle to the Gentiles complaining of the revolts of the flesh, when hard pressed by its rebellion he cries out: "Unhappy man that I am, who shall deliver me from the body of this death!"[1] We must call to mind the weakness of the Prince of the Apostles who denied his Master three times; then we shall see that all is not lost even were we to fall into grievous sin. But we must not forget Paul's trust in God's grace, nor Peter's humble contrition, generous confession, and unlimited confidence in God, not to speak of the lives of other holy persons in which so much can be learned.

What the Apostle St. James says of the God-favored prophet Elias holds good in regard to the other saints; they were men like us, subject to sufferings like us. They also felt within them that lamentable consequence of the sin of our first parents, the continual conflict between the

[1] Romans vii. 24.

flesh and the spirit. Many among them were for long years chained down by their passions; and even after their conversion, the hard struggle against them was the daily bread of their life. Nor was the victory always theirs, for "in many things we all offend,"[1] says the same Apostle. Trifling faults were the natural consequences of their weakness. But they knew how to repair quickly those into which they were surprised, and their hearts remained upright before God; they sought the Lord magnanimously, and, by His grace, they persevered in the firm resolution not to refuse Him anything, though even He should slay them. This is what we should do to imitate them, for we shall, undoubtedly, fall into greater faults than they. Such grace as theirs we indeed may not share; but for that very reason we shall have a less severe account to render. God only requires us to correspond with the graces He bestows upon us as earnestly and as faithfully as the saints did to their extraordinary favors. If we do this, then shall we be their true imitators, although in virtue and merit far below them; for we shall have traded with the talent intrusted to us, and that is all that the Master exacts.

All Christians are called to perfection and holiness, but God has not intended for all the same degree or species of holiness. The Church herself tells us that no two saints are alike, and it follows that the grace of each is as different as the call. Christ teaches us the same thing in the parable of the unequal division of the talents which the master of the household intrusted to all of his servants, desiring each to gain a sum corresponding to the amount received. He declared them worthy of an equal reward, although all could not show equally great gains. He may hope for like treatment in spiritual matters who, having received little, has faithfully traded with that little. Let him present himself before God with the same confidence as the more favored who have richer gifts to bring. Would not the intention of the father of the household be misunderstood

[1] 1 James iii. 2.

if the former believed himself obliged to gain as much with his one talent as the latter with two? Would it not be unreasonable in him to undertake the same successful enterprises as he to whom a considerable sum had been intrusted? Were such the case, he would display more love of self than love for the honor and interest of his master. Besides, secret jealousy with its whole retinue of crimes and consequent dangers, would here creep in. That others were more favored by the master would give rise to chagrin, a delusion in the spiritual life against which one can scarcely be sufficiently on his guard.

By virtue of the superabundant promises of God, all may confidently expect from Him the ordinary graces necessary for the fulfilment of the common Christian duties, as well as others peculiar to their state. In addition to this, every soul can, by prayer and faithful correspondence with graces already received from the infinite liberality of God, impetrate as many new ones as are compatible with the Lord's designs over it. Therefore, no soul should, by refusing to advance as far as God wishes to lead it, wilfully set limits to the goodness of God. But it would be unpardonable arrogance to lay claim to the extraordinary graces and special gifts granted to the saints who, in their humility, esteemed themselves unworthy of such favors.

Christian lowliness accords not with ambitious desires such as these, and still less with that jealousy excited in certain souls at sight of the great graces granted to others but denied to themselves. It is also a delusion of self-love to lay claim to the particular prerogatives of the saints, to those heavenly illuminations, those unspeakable consolations which made prayer for them a delight; whilst for us, owing to our dissipation, our spiritual languor, it very often proves a laborious and painful task.

Certain persons think not enough of this. They are not satisfied with what they can accomplish in a reasonable way with the graces received. They would, with St. Aloysius, be without distractions at prayer; with St. Teresa, a stranger to every revolt of the flesh; and with St. Catharine of Sienna at Holy Communion, inflamed with glowing love of God. In their inability to realize their vain desires, they fall into disgust and weariness; they no longer do what they can, because they cannot do what they wish. Then comes the reflection: "Why strive after perfection?" till, at last, they become so relaxed that even the most binding duties are no longer fulfilled. The foundation of their error lies in this, that in the spiritual life, the indispensaable maxim of moderation is neglected in spite of that impressive warning of the Apostle: "Be wise in measure!"[1] We would laugh at a child if we saw it abandoning undertakings suitable to its strength, in order to emulate those of a giant; and yet the souls of whom we speak act not more wisely. Ah, if we only rightly comprehended wherein the imitation of the saints consists!

[1] Romans xii. 13.

CHAPTER II.

We must Serve God according to His Will and not for the Gratification of our own Inclinations.

GOD means us to serve Him as He wills, and not in accordance with our own tastes and humors; He means us to follow the Commandments which He has given us, and not those that our unruly imagination would substitute for the divine; it means that, renouncing our rebellious thoughts, we make those of God our own. Rightly to understand this, is of the highest importance, because it is the surest foundation of spiritual progress and the basis of interior peace. But such insight is wanting to many souls who have more good-will than knowledge and experience, and it is the particular need of the scrupulous. The greater part of the mental anguish which this latter class creates for itself, arises not from actual duties, but from others which are self-imposed. They are not satisfied with the Commandments of God and His Church; they must have more. The worst of this is, that they are as stubborn as they are inexperienced. They do not wish to be enlightened upon their erroneous ideas of true piety. Devotion, according to them, consists in certain exterior practices, good and praiseworthy, to be sure, but which are only a means to an end. The souls of whom we treat frequently attach undue importance to such devotions, whilst overlooking wilful and considerable faults. Not unfrequently they impose upon themselves most rigorous obligations for the practice of certain acts, thus nourishing in the soul sentiments quite inconsistent with man's earthly existence. In spite of daily experience, they seem to forget to what weakness, as well as positive inability, the sin of our first parents has condemned us. For example, they think they could and should so school themselves as to banish every distraction in prayer, ward off every revolt of the flesh, control every indeliberate evil thought and emotion. They fancy that to serve God perfectly, they must no longer endure temptation; whilst, on the contrary, our temptations to evil are in proportion to our resistance. They seem not to know that they have within them two beings, the old Adam constantly fighting against us, intent upon naught but evil, and the new man born of grace. The latter is forced to live with the former, to feel the effects of his corruption, to endure his incessant attacks, and to advance in virtue only by continual struggles.

In consequence of their ignorance, or rather their mistaken notions, scrupulous souls form for themselves a religion simply impossible, and impracticable save in theory. Thus they even expose themselves to the danger of despair when, in spite of all their efforts, they do not succeed in carrying out their chimerical designs. Most wonderful is the contradiction of which they are guilty; for whilst aiming at the impossible, they deny to God what He most justly requires of them, namely, the sacrifice of their vain ideas, and submission to their spiritual guides. And so they languish for years in a most lamentable state. They make many efforts, and they suffer still more, but without achieving anything. They make no progress in virtue, they have no merit, because *self-will* is at the bottom of all their actions, which before God are worthless. They do not serve God according to His will; on the contrary, they make to themselves most false and most insulting representations of Him. Sometimes they see in Him a hard and menacing master, ever ready with scourges to chastise them in His wrath; sometimes they liken Him to the lords of this world, who take not into consideration the good-will of their subjects; who are satisfied only with perfect service: who have no patience with a poor servant who in spite of his desires, is unable to satisfy their demands. Represent to yourself a very active but awkward servant, who is always on duty, though only to do something precisely different from what he has been told, always following his own judgment instead of orders received. Could such service satisfy a master? This is but the true picture of those souls whose self-deceit we here aim at healing. The first steps such souls have to make, in order to extricate themselves from their unhappy thraldom, is earnestly to strive, in obedience to their director, to acquire a knowledge of their real obligations and a just idea of true piety.

They must comprehend the condition of man on earth since the commission of the first sin, that they may learn to distinguish what is possible to us and what is beyond our control. They must understand that we have lost by original sin almost all command not only over visible creation, but also over the powers of our own soul; that that which was once subject to us is now almost the master; and that with our numerous enemies both within and without the devil leagues to lead us astray. Our free-will alone remains, with which, aided by divine grace in our various combats and trials, we may gradually gain what we have lost. But in the first place, we should bear the evil effects of our misery with the thousand trials inseparable from this incessant interior war; and, in child-like trust in God's mercy and in humble mistrust of our own weakness, perseveringly continue our efforts to resist the adversary and satisfy the demands of God. I say in humble diffidence of our own strength; for were we to confide in ourselves, experiencing so often as we do our own weakness, discouragement alone would be our portion.

We cannot here enumerate all the deceits to which the souls referred to above are exposed in the path of virtue. Equally impossible would it be to particularize the imaginary duties with which they overburden themselves and distort the law of God. Most of these difficulties would be obviated, if they would reflect upon what we have said.

We must Serve God according to His Will.

We shall now treat of three matters more in detail, partly because they occur so frequently in the Christian life and partly because they are of the greatest importance, viz., the Sacrament of Penance, Holy Eucharist, and prayer. These three practices, prescribed us by the law of God, should prove the greatest consolation of our soul. But alas! too many make them a source of true torment by imposing upon themselves I know not what kind of imaginary obligations. This causes them to live in continual anxiety and excitement, and not unfrequently casts them into despair. We deem it necessary, therefore, to lay down some just principles by which such souls may correct their false ideas.

CHAPTER III.

Of the Sacrament of Penance, and of the Peace and Comfort found in its Reception.

ALMIGHTY God instituted the holy Sacrament of Penance in order to lead us to that purity of conscience without which neither salvation nor perfection is possible. By its means He would increase sanctifying grace, or restore it if lost, and to all souls impart peace and rest. Confession is a medicine to be taken when necessary or useful, and not an ordinary nourishment, to be partaken of several times daily.

But why, for certain souls, is this Sacrament the source of continual anxiety and agitation? Why do they busy themselves with it as if it were their only occupation of life? Simply because, owing to their false judgment, they misrepresent the divine precepts; because they convert a remedy into poison; because they impose upon themselves obligations utterly impossible to be fulfilled.

In order to cure souls affected by this obnoxious malady, and save others from similar errors, we shall here give the exact and simple rules to be observed in the reception of the holy Sacrament of Penance. We shall go through five points which, according to the Catechism, are requisite to a good confession.

I. THE ACCUSATION OR THE CONFESSION ITSELF.—In the first place, we must discriminate between the necessary and the merely advantageous and voluntary accusation.

1. *The Necessary Accusation.*—What must we confess? —All mortal sins of which there is no doubt, with their number as far as we can reasonably remember, and such circumstances as change or alter the nature of the sin; as when, for example, a theft is committed in a church. Cir-

cumstances which only aggravate the sin—for instance, the greatness of the amount purloined, and the like—the penitent is not, according to the unanimous opinion of learned theologians approved by the Church, obliged to confess. It suffices if he answers the probable questions of the confessor. If, uncertain whether he has committed a sin or not, he mentions his doubt, he has done more than he is strictly bound to do. He who suffers from scruples would in this case do better to keep silent. A sin forgotten is pardoned all the same; but if it be a mortal sin, it must, when remembered, be mentioned in the next confession; nor need one ever repeat a sin of which he has accused himself in a valid confession.

This is strictly all that God makes obligatory on the sinner in his avowal. We substitute our own judgment for the Law of God when we make it a duty to recite a whole litany of venial sins with their attendant circumstances and histories, to do which fully would be simply impossible. Hence arise a thousand anxieties and scruples for having omitted what was purely impossible to confess, and what we might without sin have freely passed over.

2. *Useful Accusations.*—Their object is venial sin. To confess venial sins is by no means essential either to the perfection of the accusation or the remission of sin. Our passing them over in silence should never give grounds for just or even reasonable anxiety; but in general such accusation is useful to all. Those who are so happy as not to commit mortal sin must if they will confess, accuse themselves of venial sin; otherwise they would have no matter of accusation. It is, therefore, a wholesome practice to confess venial sins. But does this mean that one must detail them with anxious exactitude and exaggerated minuteness, as so many pious souls do? Assuredly not. They who frequently receive the holy Sacraments will, on the contrary, draw far more advantage from their confessions if they select from their daily, unavoidable imperfections a small number of the most prominent and deliberate faults,

and those, especially, which proceed from a disorderly affection or strong inclination; for example, from some aversion, from envy, love of ease, ambition, etc. Of these faults let him accuse himself, not with meaningless anxiety, but with generosity which does not stoop to extenuate expressions or to palliate excuses, but treats self as an enemy who is neither to be calumniated nor spared. Thus performed, our confession assumes a frank and definite character: one declares his faults briefly and simply, omitting all excuses and histories. This method of confessing has, among other advantages, this also, that the particular attention of the soul is directed to the most important and dangerous faults, namely, those whose source is a sinful inclination of the heart, and which for this reason one would gladly leave unmolested. These faults are just those that prove a serious obstacle to our spiritual progress. They might even endanger our eternal salvation, as they imperceptibly lead to mortal sin. Faults of pure weakness or surprise injure the soul far less; consequently, the confession of them is much less beneficial.

But it must be remembered that either to confess or to omit venial sin is optional; and that no one need be disturbed on this head, he may leave out of his confession what he will.

3. How can one distinguish between mortal and venial sin?—You will tell me that in order to make use of the foregoing rules one must be able to discriminate mortal from venial sin. Undoubtedly under certain circumstances it is difficult to determine the line of separation. But I think that he who lives a truly Christian life will in most cases find the distinction not so very hard to make; and in cases of doubt, and for his greater peace, he may accuse himself of the sin in question, although strictly speaking he is not bound to do so. For anxious, scrupulous souls, it is in general better for them to be silent on their doubts; yet in this, as in all else, the direction of their spiritual guide must be their rule.

We shall give here a few general directions by which it will be easy to distinguish, in most cases, whether a sin be mortal or venial.

To a mortal sin belong three points : 1st. Weighty matter ;—a jesting lie, for example, or a vain, self-conceited thought, is not sufficient for a mortal sin. 2d. Full knowledge of the evil ; that is, the deliberate consciousness that what one does is a mortal sin. This excludes all cases in which the sin proceeds from surprise, or in which the soul is not full master of her powers ; as, for example, in half-slumber, and the like. 3d. Full consent of the will to that which the understanding knows to be mortal sin. As long as the consent remains imperfect, or we are conscious of a certain hesitancy, a deferring, or a reproach of conscience in consequence of our neglect in combating the temptation, the sin is only venial.

But if these three essential conditions to mortal sin are really found in a God-fearing soul, they produce disturbance so violent that she perceives it immediately, and she readily comprehends that some great change has taken place in her. It will not, therefore, be difficult for her to know the mortal sin she may have committed, and which is in such violent contradiction with her ordinary life.

For the rest, to judge correctly of what has passed in the soul during temptation, we must remember, says St. Francis de Sales, that we do not experience at the moment of temptation so lively a horror of it as before and after. Consequently we dare not at once conclude, particularly if leading a Christian life, that we have actually consented because in the decisive moment we felt in a certain way irresistibly drawn to the evil.

To venial sins belong almost all the faults that originate in character, that proceed from carelessness or vanity, and, in general, all that the majority of good and tolerably well-instructed Christians have not defined as mortal sin.[1]

---

[1] It is, of course, to be understood that in doubtful cases the decision is left to the confessor.—*Translator*

As to temptations to which no consent has been given, one is never obliged to mention them. If we speak of them, it is merely because in holy confession we seek not only the remission of our sins, but at the same time interior direction, counsel, and consolation. Silence on such points, however, can never render a confession invalid. He who suffers from extraordinarily severe and dangerous temptations of long standing does well to disclose them from time to time to his confessor, in order to learn from him how to act under them. A particular blessing rests upon humble obedience such as this. God often rewards it visibly by freeing the soul from the attacks of the Evil One; but we must not be ever and always returning with trifling, every-day temptations, such as distractions in prayer, and the like. When once told to despise them, to pass them over in silence, the repetition of them is, to say the least, a loss of time.

II. THE EXAMINATION OF CONSCIENCE.—In order to comply with the rules above mentioned concerning confession, a tranquil, reasonable examination of conscience suffices. A Christian who lives devoutly and goes often to confession need not examine himself on mortal sin at all. Should he have had the misfortune to commit it, it will without any effort on his part recur to him as something extraordinary. It is equally unnecessary to examine one's self upon a sin of thought, whose commission was immediately followed by a doubt.

Daily experience demonstrates how useless are all such after-thoughts in this case; for however long one may rack his brain, that will never appear clear which just after its commission was doubtful and mysterious. The more reflection is given to the matter, the more uncertain and doubtful it will appear, added to which, the soul becomes excited, and renews dangerous impressions and sentiments. Whoever wishes to include in his confession such doubtful matters, should simply mention them as doubts.

One who leads a pious life and confesses every week

ought to find a quarter of an hour more than sufficient to examine himself upon venial sins and acquire a knowledge of the state of his conscience. As has been said, strictly speaking, one is not bound to confess these faults; and the faults that are forgotten can be remitted by every good work performed out of confession. From this it may easily be seen how unfounded is anxiety on this point.

III. CONTRITION.—Contrition, says the Council of Trent, is an interior sorrow and horror for sin committed, united to the determination to sin no more. But the sinner can have true sorrow in his heart without experiencing a lively sense of it. Man loves and hates many things without knowing it till some occasion reveals his sentiments. A son loves his father without being conscious of it; but let the father be taken ill, then love, awakened in the heart of the child, fills it with sorrow. The same in a degree holds good with pious souls in regard to contrition. We cannot judge their want of contrition from their lack of feeling, especially as the motives of sorrow, as hatred of sin, etc., are of a supernatural nature; and the supernatural never makes so lively an impression on man as the purely human. "It is not necessary," says Gerson, "that contrition for sin should be so keenly felt as grief for some temporal misfortune. It is enough if our sins displease us to such a degree that we are resolved, should the occasion again present itself, not to commit them." Let us, then, never confound the essential conditions of contrition with the accidental. According to its nature, contrition is exclusively the business of the will. At times it works upon the feelings, and we are moved to tears and sighs. That is very consoling, and may often prove good and salutary, but necessary or essential it never is; should such feelings be wanting, we need have no disquietude.

True contrition consists in change of heart. The will that once clung to evil now casts it off, sincerely bewails the sin committed, and would be heartily glad thoroughly to undo it. This is the nature of every act of contrition.

With the help of divine grace, refused to none that asks, this will not be too difficult for pious souls. But if one has, as a general thing, only venial sins to confess, and wishes to be quite sure of his contrition, let him include in his confession the mortal sins of his past life; for to be sorry for them in this general sense is both sufficient and easy, and suffices for the validity of confession. By this means we may obviate all anxiety upon this point.

It is very praiseworthy to seek, as far as possible, for perfect contrition; but one must not confound the desirable with the essential, and become scrupulous when he thinks he cannot attain it. Contrition may be perfect in two ways. Either it is perfect in its motive, viz., sorrow for sin because by it God is offended; or it is perfect in its intensity, that is, in the extent and vehemence of its sorrow. Intense sorrow, in its highest degree, remits even the temporal punishment of sin. But this highest degree is very difficult to reach, and in truth is very seldom attained; but it is not necessary to the forgiveness of sins. Contrition which possesses only a very low degree of intensity, but which is perfect in its motive, suffices for the forgiveness of sins even without the Sacrament of Penance when it cannot be received. How much more abundantly, then, will it prepare the soul for the worthy reception of the Sacrament! The perfection of contrition is in the motive from which it springs. It is not so rare nor so difficult as many think. Before the coming of Christ this sort of contrition was held up to men as the only penance, the only means of salvation; and it must have been an easy one to fulfil. How much more, then, may a Christian who leads a God-fearing life and strives after perfection feel assured that he possesses such contrition when he prays God for it, reflects earnestly upon it, and then recites the act given in his prayer-book. Suppose, for instance, that perfect contrition were really wanting, then imperfect suffices for the remission of sin in the confessional. Imperfect contrition is such as is born of the consideration of the heinousness of sin, its evil consequences, or the fear of hell and purgatory. A few moments' reflection must easily produce such sorrow in a Christian soul. From what has been said it follows that the sorrow required for a valid and efficacious confession is by no means so hard to obtain as many suppose.

Yet a word upon the way and means by which one who frequently confesses should awaken sorrow. He should first employ a few moments in begging this grace of God; then cast a glance over the time that has elapsed since his last confession; recall the faults and sins committed in his past life; make a short reflection on the goodness of God, His greatness, and benefits; on sin and its evil consequences,—and the like suitable subjects, which produce abhorrence for past transgressions. If the penitent should not feel so much moved as he desires, let him humble himself deeply before God, and lament his sins with his whole heart, but without allowing his fears to discourage him. Then let him approach the holy tribunal with confidence. Let him not imitate certain souls who make exertions as fruitless as they are ridiculous, in their eagerness to acquire what is a free gift of God, and in no way necessary to the pardon of sin, viz., tears and sensible devotion.

IV. THE RESOLUTION.—This is inseparable from true and effective sorrow. It may be easily understood from the foregoing, that the resolution, at least in regard to mortal sin, is rarely wanting to a pious soul who has prepared for the Sacrament of Penance, according to the foregoing formula. With regard to venial sins, the resolution to avoid them all is simply an impossibility; but the will to avoid the most deliberate and to decrease the number of the others, as far as our frailty permits and our measure of grace renders possible, must not be wanting.

It should be especially borne in mind that the good resolution is a present disposition of the will; and that, consequently, with the fear, yes, even with the probable prospect of a relapse, particularly into small faults, it is very consistent to make it. There is no question of the dispositions of to-morrow. God alone knows what they will be, for our will is unstable and changeable. We are only asked how it is to-day, at the moment of our confession. If good, then so too was the confession, come what may in the future. In order to test your good resolutions, do not employ time in picturing yourself in extraordinary occasions, in which, perhaps, you will never be placed; neither must you draw up an agreement or treaty with yourself which would excite your imagination. This is often imprudent, and moreover unnecessary. Would you on another occasion commit the fault you are now on the point of confessing? No. Very well. Then be at peace: you have the requisite dispositions for the pardon of your sins; and you will see by this purpose of amendment, joined to the grace of the Sacrament, that the number of your weaknesses will by degrees diminish. It is often, also, useful at confession to make a particular resolution upon some special fault that has caused the most mischief in your soul since your last confession, and to which you can afterward direct your particular examen. In this way indifference cannot creep into the reception of the holy Sacrament of Penance.

V. SATISFACTION.—As regards satisfaction, or the penance imposed by the priest, we have to perform it quite simply, like any other pious practice. There are no special conditions to be fulfilled, if the confessor has not expressly specified them.

Now, what is to be gained or learned from all we have said in this chapter on the holy Sacrament of Penance? Nothing more nor less than that pious souls rarely make bad confessions, though they could draw far more profit from them if they went to work more quietly. Take, then, the following words as a rule of conduct: If you have reasonably done your utmost to comply with the conditions here given for a valid confession, approach the holy Sacrament with confidence, with a feeling of thanksgiving and faith in the blessed fruits thereof. When you have left the confessional, think no more of your sins, for God Himself

The Sacrament of Penance.

no longer thinks of them. Do not torture yourself as to whether you have forgotten anything, or how you may repair your supposed faults in the reception of the Sacrament, but be entirely at peace. Peace of soul makes us strong to aim at the true fruit of confession—the amendment of life; anxiety and excitement, on the contrary, weaken our strength, because they close the heart. For the rest, when we treat of scruples, we shall return to this point. May, then, all souls take to heart what we have said, and no longer disfigure the Divine Law by substituting for it their own false judgment and unreasonable demands!

CHAPTER IV.

Of Holy Communion—What is required to receive worthily, and tne Reason that It is for so many a Subject of Fear.

THE reception of the Holy Sacrament of the Altar is, like confession, the source of a thousand anxieties for certain pious souls. Here, again, the fault proceeds from erroneous principles, by which they confound the useful and the perfect with the necessary and the essential. Indeed, the greater part of scruples before Holy Communion is connected with the preceding confession. One doubts whether it was valid, and fears to commit a sacrilege by presenting himself at the Lord's Table. Whoever, by the study of the preceding chapter, has found peace with regard to his confession, will thereby be much less troubled at Communion. But there are others who, under other pretexts, hold aloof from the Bread of Life. "How many anxious and scrupulous souls," says Fénelon, "miserably perish from want of this Holy Food of the soul! They consume themselves in subtle speculations and fruitless exertions; they fear, they tremble, they doubt, and seek in vain for a security which is not to be found here below. The unction of the Lord is not in them. They desire to live for Christ without living in Him and through Him; comfortless and weary, they languish unto death. Near the fountain of Living Water, they perish of thirst. They wish to practise perfection in all its externals; and yet they dare not nourish themselves with the Bread of Life. They would carry the heavy yoke of the Commandments without seeking in frequent Communion and in prayer the spirit and consolation of those Commandments."

Our task is to lead those deluded souls back to sound

Christian truths. We shall first briefly and clearly show forth fundamental principles; and then, upon the authority of the most reliable theologians, descend to particulars. In order not to commit a sacrilege, and that the Holy Communion may be useful and salutary, there is only one condition necessary, namely, a reasonable belief that one is free from every mortal sin. When a person has sincerely revealed the state of his conscience to his confessor and received from him the command to communicate, he has in obedience the infallible assurance that he is free from mortal sin. Let him, then, despising all after fears, approach the Table of the Lord. God will never reproach him with having obeyed his lawful superior.

However, as the fruits of Holy Communion are proportioned to the more or less perfect preparation, it is to our interest to prepare for it as well as we possibly can. But when we possess the essential dispositions, why should we be troubled and absent ourselves from the Source of Life? It is true, also, that frequent Communion is not to be allowed to souls that retain an attachment to deliberate venial sin, that are very little concerned about their perfection, and that with voluntary tepidity draw near the Holy Table. It is the business of spiritual guides, however, to judge of the state of souls, and to direct them accordingly: the individual has nothing to do but to allow himself to be so guided, leaving casuistic decisions to authorized directors.

Upright and generous souls, conscious of their own imperfections, and who honestly wish to be better, should, in obedience to their spiritual director, communicate often. Your involuntary failings and passing weaknesses do not debar you from the Divine Banquet: they do but still more increase the necessity of nourishing your soul with the Bread of the Strong.

But some will not admit these principles. They allow themselves to be dazzled by a secret pride; without knowing it, they lean more upon themselves and their own merits than upon God's mercy. They would wish to draw near to the altar in such a state as to be able to say: "I am satisfied with myself!" We should seek to be freed from such egotism and self-love. He who has the sensible perception of interior grace and consolation approaches Holy Communion confidently, especially when he finds himself moved to tears, when he is free from every humiliating temptation; in short, when he beholds nothing in himself but what would inspire elevated thoughts of his own virtues. But when, in spite of all his efforts, he remains dry, cold, and dissipated; or has, particularly in the presence of another, committed a fault after confession,—ah, then he will hear nothing more of Holy Communion! Behold a soul filled with self. She fancied she was able to resist every humiliating temptation, and she has, since her last confession, experienced certain emotions contrary to holy purity; she thought sensible devotion her due, and now she misses it; she would appear at the Lord's Table spotless in her own eyes, and yet some unavoidable encounter drew from her almost involuntarily a word of impatience. Ah! she no longer desires to communicate, for the apparent glitter of virtue and innocence upon which she rested her whole confidence has deceived her. Now, an humble soul, on the contrary, one that expects all from the mercy of God, would at once go forward in obedience, with confusion it may be, but without fear, to the Feast of Love. She will, humbled and confounded, it is true, but still firmly determined to remain faithful to Him, open her poor heart to the Heavenly Guest. And certainly all the sensible devotion and faultlessness with which a vain soul might be able to adorn herself would not be so agreeable to the Lord as this humble obedience. This truth is of the utmost importance; but there are many who would rather not understand it. They are not satisfied to appear at the Heavenly Banquet in the nuptial garment; they wish, if we may so express it, not a single pin to be wanting to their spiritual ornamentation.

Other souls even desire to be able to give to themselves an account of the progress they make by means of Holy Communion. They forget that, as a rule, God hides from us our progress in virtue in order to save us from the delusions of self-love. In the beginning of a conversion one more easily perceives his advancement, for he has, for the most part, only external enemies to combat. He can consequently say: "I have gained that victory, curbed this passion, renounced that inclination, etc." But later on, the progress of the soul is generally hidden, sometimes even from the director himself. This may easily happen, since true progress in virtue is quite compatible with certain very palpable faults which God leaves us for our humiliation, and which with all our good-will we are not able to overcome. Should one, therefore, turn away from the Table of the Lord because he does not perceive in himself manifest progress? By no means. We must not only increase, but, above all, support our life; and to do this without nourishment would be impossible. It is a sufficient argument for frequent Communion if It preserves you in the state of sanctifying grace, and if through Its efficacy you continue, it may be weak and imperfect, yet sincere and upright. Such dispositions secure your eternal salvation; and perseverance in them may in general be taken as a genuine although imperceptible sign of progress. Finally, this question applies far more to the director than to the soul; for the latter has only to allow herself to be formed in child-like simplicity, assured that no other virtue can make her more pleasing to God.

Let us now hear what the most experienced masters of the interior life say on this subject:

"Whoever seeks an excuse to absent himself from frequent Communion," says St. Francis de Sales, "acts as did those that were invited to the banquet mentioned in the Gospel parable. Their excuses, though seemingly plausible, irritated the father of the household." Almost all the excuses with which souls arm themselves are merely so many accusations against themselves. Some say they are not perfect enough. But how are they to become perfect if they turn away from the Fountain of all perfection? Others, that they are too weak. But the Holy Communion is the Bread of the Strong, the Bread that gives strength. Some shelter themselves under the plea of sickness. But in Holy Communion they will find the Physician to whom they should say: "Have mercy on me, O Lord! for I am weak."[1] Many make their unworthiness their excuse. But does not the Church herself put into the mouth of the purest soul the words of the humble publican: "Lord, I am not worthy that thou shouldst enter under my roof"?[2] Others, again, assert that they are overburdened with business. But such Jesus calls to Him in this Divine Sacrament, saying: "Come to Me, all you that labor and are burdened, and I will refresh you."[3] Many fear to eat the Food of Angels to their condemnation. But do they not in this very act expose themselves to eternal damnation by absenting themselves from the Source of eternal life? Finally, many take refuge behind the screen of humility; but this is false humility, for how can we learn to receive the Body of the Lord rightly when we so seldom do it? Only in much practice can we learn any science perfectly.

"Christian soul," says the pious Gerson, "you have indeed sinned by your inordinate attachment to the perishable things of this world; but Jesus Christ, your Spouse, commands you by the mouth of the prophet to return to Him. He promises always to receive you lovingly. He will not despise a contrite and humble heart, had you contemned and abandoned Him a thousand times. If one of your fellow-men gave you this assurance, you would believe him, you would fly to his arms. It is God who now speaks to you. He tells you all this. He promises you forgiveness—nay, He even commands you to return to Him; and yet in your mistrust you dare not approach Him! You say

[1] Ps. vi. 2.   [2] Matt viii. 8.   [3] Matt. xi. 28.

you are not pure enough.—For that very reason you should flee to the inexhaustible Source of all purity, that you may be purified. You suffer hunger.—Take the Bread of the strong. It will nourish and quicken your soul. You are ill and languid.—Approach the most loving Physician, who alone is able to heal every malady. You are assaulted with constant temptations against holy purity, and no spiritual exercise is able to free you from them.—Go to Jesus Christ, touch with faith and confidence the hem of His garment, receive the Holy Host, His Sacred Body and Precious Blood, and you will find strength and freedom. Are you entangled in thousands of other temptations which, like the coils of serpents, surround you?—Raise your eyes to the God-Man who bled for you on the cross. His glance alone will heal all your wounds. You complain of your poverty and abandonment.—Fly to the holy Tabernacle. You will there find Jesus Christ your almighty, infinitely rich, and good King, ready to share all His treasures with you. You feel weak, faint, and blind.—But do you not know that this Heavenly King not only invited the lame and the blind to His Banquet, but even compelled their attendance? You bewail your inconstancy and many faults.—Eat this Heavenly Food of the soul. It will restore you. It will make your heart strong and generous. You are sad.—Drink, then, of the Wine that rejoices the hearts of men. Are you confused and distracted?—Seek refuge in Him who calmed the raging billows of the sea, and said to the stormy winds: 'Be still!' Fly to Him who alone is the Source of true peace; to Him who gives us the assurance that sufferings and tribulations are our portion here below, and that our heart will never find rest save in Him. We languish in banishment far from our eternal home.—Receive often the Bread of Angels. It will encourage you and strengthen your faltering steps up the holy mountain of the Lord. What do you fear? Why are you sad? Why disturbed? Hope in God! Put your whole confidence in Him, and He will save you from every trouble and tribulation. He Himself will nourish you, and you shall not be confounded. Sighing and lamenting, you ask yourself: 'Where is my God?'— Your God is in the Holy Feast in which Christ gives Himself to you as food, in which the remembrance of His Passion is renewed, in which the soul is filled with grace and receives the assured pledge of eternal blessedness!"[1]

"You are always in anguish drawing near to the Holy Table.—Subdue your fears by love. You consider yourself unworthy to communicate.—Were you to labor millions of years to make yourself worthy, you could not succeed. He who invites you to come to Him must make you worthy, and He will do it if only you carefully cleanse your heart of all that is displeasing to Him. Are you not yet prepared to receive Him?—Then put your hand to the work, and do what in you lies. Should you find yourself in the unhappy state of mortal sin, seek promptly the means of freeing yourself from it. Do not defer till to-morrow, for who knows whether you will then be in life? But if there is no just obstacle to prevent your communicating, why deprive yourself of so great a benefit? You feel so tepid, so distracted, so earthly-minded, so racked by interior anguish, pained by scruples, tormented by temptations against holy purity, so weak in faith, faltering in hope, cold in love. You cannot determine to draw near to Jesus, because you discover in yourself no worthy preparation for the reception of so honorable, so perfect a Guest.—Ah, say rather that you cannot allow yourself to be healed by the best and most loving of Physicians! You should follow the example of St. Peter, who, in his astonishment at the miraculous draught of fishes, cried out: 'Depart from me, O Lord! for I am a sinful man.'[2] O great Prince of the Apostles! what do these words mean? If you were really a sinful man, you would not dare beg Christ to depart from you; on the contrary, you would implore Him to remain always near you, to heal your wounds and to cleanse your soul from its sins. Zaccheus, a publican and sinner, did not act like

[1] Gerson. De Præparatione ad Missam. [2] Luke v. 8.

you. With what fervor and joy he made haste to receive the Lord into his house! And the salvation that came to him proves conclusively that he was right, and acted wisely. Christian soul, you say with the centurion in the Gospel: 'Lord, I am not worthy that Thou shouldst enter under my roof: speak but the word, and my soul shall be healed!'[1] But not through humility, but negligently and slothfully do you imitate his beautiful example. If it is humility that deters you from receiving Jesus, why does not the same humility impel you to obey Him, when, by His own words and those of the priest, He commands you to draw near to His Holy Table? And if the sense of your unworthiness keeps you at a distance from Him, why does not the thought of His infinite gentleness, goodness, and mercy draw you to Him? Approach, then, your Divine Lord, and say to Him: 'Thy mercy, O my Divine Lord! has always received me graciously.'[2] Would a sick man act reasonably in avoiding the presence of a skilful physician who could cure him?—You will, perhaps, reply that the physician will not permit the sick man to partake of nourishing food until all the bad humors are expelled; and that you too, before receiving the Body of Christ, should make yourself worthy, according to the words of the Apostle: 'Let a man prove himself: and so let him eat of that bread and drink of the chalice!'[3] I am not willing, Christian soul, to repress in you sentiments so noble and just, or prevent your making the very best preparation for Holy Communion. On the contrary, I strive to impress upon you the necessity of this preparation. I tell you only that in the beginning it need not be accompanied by perfect health of soul. We may have the spiritual life in us, although still subject to small faults. Under such circumstances Holy Communion does not make us weaker, but it weakens and expels our defects. It is, then, not enough for you to distrust yourself in your humility: you must also cast yourself confidently into the arms of your Saviour. How could

[1] Matt. viii 8.   [2] Ps. xxii. 6.   [3] I. Cor. xi. 28.

He refuse to receive you graciously, since He so mildly invites you? And in receiving you so tenderly will He not press you closely to His heart, to give you strength and health?"[1]

Bellarmine is of the same sentiment. In his "Art of Dying Well" he says with St. Ambrose, St. Bernard, and St. Bonaventure, that the Body of Jesus Christ is not only a nourishment for holy and perfect souls, but also a means of health for the weak and languid. The Church herself has condemned those who assert that all who have not a perfect, a pure, an undivided love of God should be kept from the Holy Table.[2] It is useless to add anything more to this, for such authority should suffice to quiet timorous souls. How unreasonable, then, to hold aloof from Holy Communion because of temptations and weaknesses, when even a mortal sin once confessed cannot deprive us of it!

[1] Gerson.   [2] Propos. 23d, damnata ab Alex. VIII.

CHAPTER V.

Of Prayer and the Manner of Fulfilling this Duty. Of the False Ideas often Formed of this Exercise.

INSTRUCTIONS on prayer are to be found in many parts of this book; therefore we shall, in spite of the importance of the subject, treat it very briefly in this chapter. So important is prayer, that St. Augustine does not hesitate to make the whole perfection of the Christian life depend upon it. He says: "Whoever knows how to pray well, knows how to live well." Again, let no one doubt of the truth of these words of the Psalmist when he exclaims: "Blessed be God, who hath not turned away my prayer, nor His mercy from me!"[1] Be firmly persuaded, then, that mercy will not be wanting to you so long as you do not neglect prayer.

But, alas! many souls entertain entirely false ideas of this pious exercise; so that what should conduce to their consolation becomes a species of torture. They burden themselves with a thousand imaginary duties, and, above all, they think their prayers must be without distractions, as if it depended upon them to curb a restless, unbridled imagination. Then they fancy that a vigorous contest is necessary; whereas distractions are best combated by contempt. Again, they consider it their bounden duty to aspire to the sweetest, the most beautiful sentiments, the tenderest effusions of sensible devotion; and not unfrequently they make laughable exertions to weep, to sigh, etc., as if the ebullition of the blood had anything to do with the good-will which alone has weight with God. And when such souls have,

Ps. lxv. 20.

through God knows what sort of means, brought themselves to those purely human sentiments and emotions of affected sensibility, they are apprehensive of its evaporating at every movement: they hardly venture to draw a breath, lest their whole stock of devotion should escape. In meditation they aspire to lofty thoughts, to sublime and exalted considerations, by which they draw so much the less near to God as they are the more satisfied with themselves. Some give themselves entirely to vocal prayer. They write for themselves interminable litanies, from whose prescribed form they dare not omit a word. Going to Holy Communion, they suppress the good sentiments and devout thoughts that God gives them, in order to read from their prayer-book the twenty pages they have imposed upon themselves. To pass over a single one would, according to their code, expose them to the danger of destroying the fruits of the Sacrament, or even committing a sacrilege. These long prayers constitute their devotion. If urgent circumstances or claims of charity force them to omit some part, terrible fear seizes upon them, and they do not venture to receive Holy Communion. If they imagine they have forgotten any of the formula, they go over it again and again, once, twice, thrice; yes, we have even seen persons for whom the whole day did not suffice to finish their morning prayers!

This is called using the means for the end. Vocal prayer is certainly a most excellent thing when practised with rule and measure, and according to the intention for which it has been instituted. This intention is to assist us when our mind no longer furnishes matter for pious considerations. It will then incline our will and fix our attention upon its expression. But when God Himself speaks to us and raises our heart to His, let us put away words, and be satisfied with the simple elevation of the mind to Him. This constitutes the nature and essence of prayer. There are pious souls who will not comprehend this. Their notion is, that all must follow the same beaten path. If anything should happen to disturb the order of their devotions, all is lost. The worst is, that they imagine they have fulfilled the whole Christian Law when on their knees they spend half the day reciting prayers, in which too often the heart has no share. Of the mortification of self-will and the retrenchment of faults there is no question. So self-deceit is, by these souls, added to the pain they inflict upon themselves for long hours, all for nothing and against nothing.

Thus they bring piety into disrepute with worldly people, who are inclined to confound true devotion with affected sanctity.

Whoever, in the fulfilment of his duties, mixes up his own overstrained ideas with the Divine Law renders the performance of duty an impossibility. He makes a frightful tyrant of God, who is the best of masters. He exhausts his strength in useless aims and efforts, and renders himself unfit for all good. The amendment of faults by such a one is out of the question. He falls into scrupulosity, loses sound understanding, and not unfrequently gives up his religion altogether, since he sees the impossibility of practising it after his own fashion. How could one possibly follow so many rules, a single one of which, viewed with the eyes of this class of persons, would be sufficient to keep him chained to the ground?—The examples of issues thus sad are not so rare as one thinks.

In contrast with these errors, let us portray the true principles of prayer as the greatest masters of the spiritual life have given them. Prayer, says Christ Himself,[1] consists not in many words. Prayer means simply the raising of the heart to God, to say to Him either how much we love Him, or how intensely we desire to honor Him, or how urgently we feel the need of His assistance. All this is wholly independent of the influence of the imagination, which one must never confound with the heart.

"Our prayer," says St. Francis de Sales, "is not less useful to us, nor less pleasing to God, when we have many distractions in it. On the contrary, it is then more bene-

[1] Matt. vi. 7.

ficial to us than at a time of greater consolation, since it costs us more effort. The only thing required of us in time of distraction is the will to conquer, and not wilfully to yield."—" He who wills never to be distracted," says Fénelon, "is never distracted." And one can with truth say, the prayer of such a soul is perfect. As soon as you remark a distraction let it pass unnoticed. Put it aside without taking the trouble to combat it. Turn your thoughts peaceably and gently to God. So long as you are unconscious of distraction, so long is it not a distraction of the will; as soon as you become aware of it, raise your heart to God! . . . "He who during prayer thinks that he is praying," says St. Francis de Sales, "does not pray with perfect devotion, for he turns his attention from God to think of the prayer he is making." Fear of distraction is itself the greatest distraction. Nothing in the spiritual life is so much to be recommended as child-like simplicity. Would you see God in prayer?—Look at Him, and with renewed ardor direct your whole attention to Him. When you turn to meditate upon self, you no longer see God, but only self. He who devoutly applies to prayer considers not at the moment whether he prays or not; he thinks not of his prayer, but of God, to whom he prays. We must make a difference between the presence of God and the feeling of His presence, between faith and the feeling of faith. A martyr who, in his moments of suffering, has not his thoughts always turned to God does not on that account lose this merit, nor does he give to God a less noble proof of his loyalty and love. It is precisely the same with the practice of the presence of God. We need only say quite simply, that He is our God, and that we are His weak, unworthy creatures. St. Francis acted thus. He spent the whole night long in fervent prayer, repeating the words: "O my God! who art Thou and who am I?" This humble sentiment of our own misery and the divine goodness supplies all effusions of sensible devotion, the absence of which is so painful to us; for true prayer is not the result of a strong imagination, nor of an effort of the senses, but of the spirit and the will.

"Would you pray with meritorious and desirable devotion?" says the celebrated Archbishop of Cambray. "Begin by considering yourself a poor man, dejected, miserable, naked, almost perishing of hunger. Then think that there is but one rich man from whom you can hope for an alms, and implore him to give it to you. Again, imagine before you an invalid covered with wounds and forsaken by all excepting the charitable physician who has pity on him, who nurses and heals him. This is a true picture of what we are before God. Your soul is poorer in heavenly goods than any poor creature in earthly treasures, and God alone can give you help. From Him only can you implore grace; from Him only can you expect assistance. Your soul is, without comparison, sicker than that of the poor invalid covered with wounds and dying. God alone can heal you. All depends upon whether or not you soften God's Heart by your prayers. He is almighty, but reflect that He helps only those that urgently pray for His assistance,—yes, I might almost say, those that torment Him for it.

"Consider, also, the difference between the prayer of the proud, self-conceited Pharisee and that of the humble publican. The former recounts his virtues, the latter bewails his sins; the former thanks God for his performance of good works, the latter complains of his commission of evil; the former was confounded in his self-righteousness, the latter went down to his house justified. The sinner that deeply humbles himself by a glance at his errors is worthy of the divine mercy; whilst many self-righteous souls who perform their good works to be seen by men have a severe judgment awaiting them. Their good works have all been disfigured by pride and self-complacency.

"As they do some good, they say within themselves: 'O Lord, I thank Thee that I am not as other Christians!' In vain self-satisfaction they form a very lofty idea of themselves; they imagine themselves to be highly privileged predestined souls, to whom alone are revealed the secrets of the kingdom of God.

"Woe to them that pray in this disposition! Woe to us if our prayers make us not more humble, more watchful of our faults, more resigned to God; if they do not infuse into us greater love of a more retired and humble life!"

From the examples quoted of the beggar in the presence of the rich man, the sick man and his physician, the sin-laden publican, we may clearly see what prayer is, and in what dispositions we ought to pray. "And as to distractions," says Fénelon, "you must have patience with yourself. You must not yield to discouragement when you suffer from the inconstancy of your mind, which inconstancy must be endured. Indeliberate distractions do not turn us from God: on the contrary, nothing is more pleasing to Him than the humble patience of a soul that never wearies of ever turning anew to Him. When at prayer, there is no question of extraordinary, elevated thoughts, rapturous visions, nor tender sensibility, which God suddenly gives, and can as suddenly withdraw. He who places the value of his prayer in these things, so flattering to self-love, will soon fall into discouragement; for such favors vanish as quickly as they come. Their loss will lead him to esteem all else as lost. Simple, confiding, and loving converse with God is true prayer. Accustom yourself to this. Pour out your heart unrestrainedly to the loving God; consult with Him about everything that interests you. Speak confidingly, openly, unreservedly to Him as to one for whom you entertain affection, and who, you feel assured, loves you also from His Heart. He who is satisfied with a prayer of whose constraint he is conscious, treats with God as with a mighty personage whom one honors and visits only ceremoniously, no affection on either side. Such intercourse is marked by studied phraseology. The visitor is constrained, and soon becomes weary. He can scarcely wait to be formally dismissed. Truly interior souls, on the contrary, commune with God as with the best of friends. They do not weigh their words in golden scales, because they know with whom they have to do. They speak to God out of the fulness and simplicity of their heart, conversing with Him of matters connected with His glory and their own salvation. They tell Him of what faults they sigh to be freed, what duties they have to fulfil, over what temptations they must gain the victory, what snares self-love lays for them, and what passions or inclinations are threatening to domineer over them. They tell him everything, hearken to all He says, and in all things follow His counsels and commands. Such prayer is not a ceremonious entertainment: it is a friendly, an unrestrained conversation. God is the Friend of the heart, the Father upon whose bosom the child lays its tired head, the Spouse to whom grace has united the soul. One humbles himself before God without discouragement, fully confides in Him, and wholly mistrusts himself; he never forgets himself when there is question of correcting his faults; but he does forget himself, that he may never hear the alluring flattery of self-love."

In regard to vocal prayer, we are far from dissuading souls from it, for it is useful and often very necessary; but it should be performed reasonably and properly. If you would draw profit from vocal prayer, pray quietly. and try to feel what you say. Let your mind comprehend the sense of the words you utter. Never hurry to get through quickly. Half a psalm said devoutly is better than a dozen recited hurriedly. If obliged to interrupt your prayers, be not disturbed. Pause gently, and if afterward you have time, resume where you left off.

These are true principles to be applied in prayer. We shall refer to them again, although what we have said seems to be sufficient. These truths are more soothing and consoling than are the false ideas of many pious souls exciting and discouraging.

CHAPTER VI.

The Knowledge of God and of One's Self the First Condition of Solid Virtue and True Peace.

THE soul that aspires to solid virtue must strive, first and foremost, to attain a true knowledge of God and of herself. As we have already said, nothing is more difficult, and at the same time more rare, than a just, practical idea of God and of our dependence upon Him. Like children of an accursed father, we are conscious of a secret dread at the bare thought of our offended Lord and Creator. Like Adam, we flee at the sound of His voice, and tremble in His presence as in that of an enemy. We draw near to Him with diffidence; we do not venture to confide in His mercy, though it is our only refuge. Faith, indeed, extols God's goodness to us; and in conformity with duty, we theoretically believe. But practically the sentiment of fear prevails more or less over us. There lives, as it were, a natural germ of mistrust and anxiety in our breasts; and the enemy of our salvation does what he can to develop the same. He knows well what he can produce from such weeds; and, according to the words of Holy Scripture, we can run in the way of the divine commandments only when our heart is enlarged by confidence. We must, above all, labor at stifling our mischievous, narrow-minded, and cowardly sentiments. We must be firmly persuaded that a God who for love of us shed His blood, can desire nothing so much as that His sufferings should promote our deliverance and eternal welfare. Never let us separate the consideration of our misery from the exhaustless mercy of the Lord. "His mercy is above all His works."[1] The thought of our misery would plunge us into discouragement and despair, instead of inspiring true humility. In another place we shall speak of the necessity of greater trust. Here we shall remark only in passing how indispensable it is that we judge God rightly, and relinquish sentiments that reflect so little honor upon His loving Heart. We have now come to a consideration which will require more elucidation, namely, the knowledge of self.

Self-knowledge is extremely necessary to us. Indeed, the old philosophers regarded it as the foundation of wisdom, and they inculcated upon their pupils the motto, "Know thyself!" In fact, this knowledge of our moral formation is indispensable in the work in which we are at once the material, the instrument, and the artificer. How can we draw a model without knowing ourselves perfectly? And, alas! is such actually less difficult than necessary? There runs through us all, more or less, a secret vein of self-esteem, a sentiment natural to fallen man, in so far as it is a reminder of his past greatness. A modern sophist held it as an axiom, that man is by nature good. Although it rightly applies only to the first man, who came forth from the hand of his Creator in the full splendor of original justice, yet we are very willing to admit it as true of all. Our self-love would not then be founded on so mean a basis. We now too easily forget to what sad desolation the sin of our first parents has doomed man and his whole posterity. An evidence of this is, alas! strongly presented to the world by a class of men who, like the Pharisees of the Gospel, allow themselves to be deceived by self-complacency. They make a vain display of their virtues, dreaming not that they owe everything to Divine Justice.

Our self-sufficiency is ever ready to sound our own excellence. It praises our just judgment, our acute penetration, our noble-mindedness, our disinterestedness, our kind heart, the equality of our temper, besides a thousand other

[1] Ps. cxliv. 9.

distinguished characteristics. It draws a portrait very flattering to self-love. Although a certain sense of propriety does not permit us to place ourselves upon a level with the greatest men and ascribe to ourselves all their good qualities and perfections, yet we raise ourselves at least above the multitude, and without much difficulty find many to whom we may readily prefer ourselves. We rarely acknowledge the charge brought against us; though, for the sake of politeness, we sometimes admit that we are not without faults. In short, self, considered at its best, must bow assent to the words of Bossuet, who so truly and emphatically says: "Though I may be penetrated with the sentiment of my own misery and weakness, yet as soon as I am contradicted in anything, I find a thousand reasons for the justification of my own ideas. The aversion and contempt that I had previously conceived of self are gone. Self-love grows strong again; or rather, it then becomes clear to me that not for one moment was I free from it!"

These lofty opinions of self make us presumptuous. We become pretentious, we nourish contempt for others; we grow sensitive, suspicious, jealous of others, impatient, conceited, and ambitious; in short, that innate pride which the Holy Ghost designates as the root of all evil[1] grows strong within us. These false notions, in which our self-love delights, are so deeply implanted in our heart, that we must, as it were, tear out the eyes of our nature if we would see the matter in its true light.

But faith uses quite another language. It unveils to us our disgraceful, sin-stained origin, and in it the source of that fearful corruption which runs like a noisome weed through our energies of soul and body. Faith tells us that from youth our senses are inclined to evil; that our passions are always leavened with revolt against reason; that they incessantly urge us to the evil which they condemn; and that they make the practice of the good, whose beauty they recognize, extremely difficult. It shows us clearly our

[1] Ecclus. x. 15.

ignorance in the most important things; it tells us that our restless imagination incessantly hinders and perplexes the understanding; and that, finally, we are of ourselves unable to promote the work of our salvation. This faith holds up to our view quite a different picture of ourselves; and its workings are, likewise, diametrically opposed to those of self-love. The true knowledge of self is the source of humility, modesty, patience, and diffidence in self; and these are the conditions of true confidence in God. He only who does not build upon his own strength directs his glance straight to God. As upright humility, or the knowledge of the truth that God is all and the creature nothing, serves as a foundation to every virtue; so this humble and correct idea of ourselves makes the blooming of all virtues in our soul possible, and brings us into just relations with God, with men, and with ourselves.

But if the knowledge of our depravity is to bear true fruits of salvation in us this general idea of faith does not suffice. Experience must be added thereto. Long, and in the midst of a thousand toils and dangers, must we endure this corruption of which the Gospel speaks; and this our own experience clearly proves. Occasions for doing so are never wanting to those that would serve God sincerely, and barter evil inclinations for Christian virtues. For this end we must fight incessantly against the evil that domineers over us, that is incorporated with our innermost being. When we have given ourselves to this troublesome task, viz., that of observing our interior emotions to control them, we discover the depths of the abyss we explore, and passions of which we never dreamed. Ah, how often will not wounded self-love recoil at the humiliating spectacle! We might close our eyes and conceal so bitter a truth from ourselves, but in so doing we should renounce virtue, which can only be acquired at this price. We must courageously, and in their full extent, examine the wounds of our soul. This humble glance is the most wholesome remedy for its most dangerous wound, viz., that of pride. We must pluck up courage to stare our misery in the face, in order to learn it better. But the sight of our miseries must never be separated from the thought of God's mercy, which is infinitely greater than our depravity. Discouragement would follow an opposite course.

Not less important is the knowledge of the difference between emotions that proceed from free-will and those that spring from concupiscence. The latter is much more the sin of Adam than ours. It has come to us from our first parents as an unhealthy inheritance, that can render us unhappy, but by itself never guilty. Concupiscence, it is true, incites us with a certain violence to sin; but the continual resistance that we oppose to it constitutes our merit. Justly, then, does the Holy Ghost call life here upon earth not a continual sin, but a continual warfare. For our evil inclinations, the result of original sin, we shall not have to answer, but only for sin committed with free-will. This most beautiful remnant of our past happiness, viz., free-will, by consent to sin, makes common cause with it; for from free-will alone springs the moral action, with its merit or its guilt.

But how many souls appear, at least practically, not to understand this difference!

They confound impressions, sensations, attractions, emotions, with resolutions of the free-will. They forget the essential truth, that the will always remains free in the midst of the storms that rage in the soul; and that, with the assistance of divine grace, it is always able to resist the disorderly emotions of nature and the attacks of hell. Dear reader, imprint these principles deeply on your mind, for they are a source of light in the direction of the soul. He who does not study them can know himself but half. Again, there is here no question of dealing with the speculative, but with practical knowledge. Experience will make this truth gradually become one with flesh and blood.

A man does not, however, attain to this self-knowledge and disengagement in a single day. The celebrated Archbishop of Cambray unfolds to us quite a different picture of such interior transformation.

"God," says he, "gives us the interior light as an intelligent mother places some work in the hands of her daughter. The first task over, then comes a second, and a third, etc. Have you done all that God has given you to do? Then He will soon give you something else. He does not leave the soul idle, or without a means of making progress in disengagement from herself and exterior things. But if, on the contrary, you have not yet perfectly accomplished the first task, He hides what the future has in store for you. It is with you as with a traveller who is wandering over a wide plain. At first, his view extends no farther than to the little strip of blue bordered by the distant horizon. He fancies that to be the end of his journey. But when he has reached it, he beholds a yet broader expanse of country stretching out before him. Even so one imagines in the way of disengagement and self-spoliation that he has surveyed all at the first glance. He resolves no more to turn back, no more to cling to self or anything else in the world. He would rather die than even for one moment defer his whole-burnt offering; but in the little daily occurrences of life God is constantly pointing out to us new and broader fields. We find in our heart a thousand things which we would have solemnly declared were not there. God points them out only by degrees, just as He wills to destroy and eradicate them. Every one of us carries within him a certain amount of corruption. He would die of shame were God to show it to him in all its abomination. Self-love would, upon beholding it, suffer unspeakable throes of agony. I speak not here of the vicious, of gross sinners, but of pious souls whose hearts are apparently pure and upright. What would they not discover in themselves if a ray of true light pierced their interior! There would be seen that silly vanity hiding in the secret folds of the heart, that self-complacency, that pride and self-seeking; there would be discovered a thousand secret aims and motives, as inexplicable as they are certain in their existence. We begin to remark them in ourselves only when God begins to drive them out of our heart." "Do you now see," says He to us, "what foulness lies concealed in the deep abysses of your heart? Can you still glorify yourself, boast of yourself?"

Let God do with us what He will. Let us be satisfied to follow faithfully the light that He will give us at each moment. It will bring with it everything necessary for the coming instant, and will prepare us for the sacrifices that are yet to meet us. At first, we have only superficially and in a general way the good-will to resign ourselves and to die to ourselves and to all we love; but soon shall the spirit of mortification penetrate the surface and strike into the depths of our will. It will spread until it reaches the centre of our heart, and leaves no room for creatures. It will never cease its growth until it drives out all that is not God.

CHAPTER VII.

Patience with Self, the Second Requisite of True Piety and Peace of Soul.

MERELY to know the corruption of the human heart is not sufficient. It must also be patiently endured without yielding to anger or irritation. This latter course is that taken by many souls who, consequently, become discouraged at the sad sight of their miseries. They do not recognize in their faults and weaknesses the means placed by Providence in their hands for their greater progress in virtue.

St. Francis de Sales says on this subject: "Be good, and have patience with every one—above all, with yourself. . . . The virtue of patience is the most unmistakable sign of perfection; and they that strive after the pure love of God have much more need of patience to bear with themselves than with others. It belongs to perfection to bear one's own imperfections patiently. I say bear them patiently, not love or pamper them. Humility is nourished by patience with self. Let us acknowledge the truth, that we are miserable creatures who can do scarcely anything good; but God, the All-good, is satisfied with our continual efforts and the little we are able to do. He looks rather at the disposition of our heart and our good-will. . . . Precious imperfections, by which we know our misery; which exercise us in humility, in self-contempt, and in patience; and which do not prevent God from seeing the perfect dispositions of our heart!"

Oh, how remote are even some most pious souls from the sentiments of this great saint! How they detest their imperfections, even the sight of which forces them down from their throne of self-esteem, and whose use for their spiritual advantage they do not see ! Their desires aim at what the same St. Francis de Sales terms "a certain Christian perfection, conceivable but not practicable, upon which many make long discourses, but which no one puts into practice." Such souls seek before all else, as the support and foundation of their confidence, the flattering testimony of a conscience perfectly satisfied with itself, with the perfection of its works, the devotion of its prayers, and which is quite conscious of the excellence of its own sentiments. For God's views they substitute their own, convinced that He could not fail to be pleased with them so long as they are satisfied with themselves. Hence all their efforts are directed toward this one satisfaction, viz., to please themselves, believing themselves to be God's favorites. They nourish their soul with vain self-complacency which they appear to regard as a fertile field from which only precious fruits are to be expected. They exhaust their vital force in their attempts at never losing sight of the presence of God ; they sigh for perfect mastery over their imagination, into which no troublesome or humiliating suggestion of the Evil One must enter ; but which, on the contrary, must be always filled with pious and holy pictures. But their heart especially must ever be inflamed with the most tender and perfect sentiments, ever aglow with sweet devotion and burning fervor. Pleasure, joy, and sensible fervor must enliven all their good works. They must never be annoyed. No repugnance, no impatience, no inordinate passion, must ever disturb their interior tranquillity. If they could preserve such peace, all would indeed be well. They might present themselves before God with perfect confidence in their own merits—like a princess who, proud of her beauty and rich attire, might meet her royal consort with the firm assurance that she is pleasing to him. Such souls act toward God as toward a selfish friend, on whom one can depend only so long as one's riches or amiable qualities may prove attractive. But if, instead of this angelic devotion, they feel the weight, corruption, and weakness of poor nature, all is over with them, everything goes wrong. They sink into the abyss of discouragement, that sad state of soul which some one has so justly styled "suffering self-love." They turn away from the Table of the Lord. They do not venture even to pray. No joy or alacrity of soul! No more confidence! God, with His exhaustless mercy and goodness, is still theirs; but this thought has never been their true support. They have sought their centre in their own hearts, in their own imaginary virtues. Let these desert them and all is lost, all is gone; they remain helpless and in doubt. Try to rouse their courage, and you must give them the flattering testimony of self-righteousness possessed before the hour of trial, and about which they so often tormented and wearied their spiritual director. As soon as they feel that they have again found their beloved "self," nothing is wanting to them—they have all. In a word, the edifice of their virtue is not established on the immovable foundation-stone—Jesus Christ. It is built on sand, that is, on themselves, on their own worth, on their own efforts; consequently, the first storm sweeps all away. The godless leave to the Lord alone the whole work of their salvation; they exclude men's co-operation, under the pretext that it is unnecessary to do violence to self, since God in His goodness could never punish with eternal torments. The souls of which we have spoken above, whilst condemning this erroneous assertion, plunge into the opposite extreme. Certainly not in so many words nor speculative belief, for in that case they would be heretics; but, alas! they do so in the practical direction of their whole life. Their false notions spring from this, that they depend wholly upon themselves. This error is so much the more dangerous as, with the help of self-love, it glides into the heart almost imperceptibly; and besides, it closely touches upon the incontestable truth, that man without good works cannot reach eternal blessedness.

But what else is this proud devotion than the piety of

the Gospel Pharisee? The Lord condemned him, whilst justifying the publican; since the latter, in his humility, ascribed nothing to himself but his own sinfulness, and thus gained a claim to the grace of God.

Again, let us hear the renowned Archbishop of Cambray: "Our soul," says he, "is so infected with self-love that the sight of even its virtues defiles it a little; for it always appropriates a part for self. It thanks God for His graces, though at the same time it feels that it has to thank itself that these graces should be given to it rather than to others. This manner of ascribing divine graces to one's self is to be found in souls otherwise very simple and upright, and who are not even aware of the theft their self-love is committing. Their fault is so much the worse, as they are dealing with the purest and highest good, upon which account precisely God is particularly jealous. These souls cease to attribute their virtues to themselves only when they can no longer see them, when in some measure all has vanished from them. Then they cry out with St. Peter sinking in the waves: 'Lord, save us, we perish!'[1] They can no longer grasp self; all their efforts are to no purpose. They seem to themselves worthy of only rejection, abomination, and hatred, This false and Pharisaical self-righteousness must disappear, that the soul may enter into the true justification of Jesus Christ, whom one is never tempted to consider as exclusively one's own."

These self-righteous Pharisees are more numerous than is generally thought. Their first fault consists in this: The Pharisee seeks his perfection in his own works, superstitiously and firmly adhering to the letter of the Commandments without inquiring into their spirit; and many Christians do precisely the same. They fast, give alms, receive the holy Sacraments, attend divine service, and pray. But they do all without the love of God or of their neighbor, disengagement from the world, humility, and self-denial. They are satisfied with themselves if only they can

[1] Matt. viii. 25.

Patience with Self.

see before them a faithful record of good works. Whoever thinks thus is a Pharisee.

The second fault of the Pharisaical self-righteous is that to which we have already called attention. The Pharisee rests upon his righteousness as upon his own strength. This false prerogative offers consolation so great only because it gives a firm hold to nature. One finds an extraordinary pleasure in beholding himself just, in feeling himself strong, in contemplating his virtues, as a vain woman does her beauty in a mirror. When we so cling to the sight of our own virtues we tarnish them, nourish self-love and hinder our progress in self-denial. Here lies the cause of so many souls, upright of heart and full of the best desires, always remaining in the narrow circle of self, without advancing one step toward God. Under the pretext of watchfulness, they are ever busied with self. They fear to lose sight of self as much as others fear turning away from God. They desire the ever-present consciousness of possessing all sorts of harmonious virtues, which promise them the satisfaction of feeling that God is well pleased with them. This satisfaction enervates them, and this appearance of virtue renders them more deeply in love with themselves. And yet one should try to free such souls from their self-consciousness, instead of allowing them to feed upon it; should fortify them against their tender sentimentality, which has in it nothing lasting. This sensibility is to them what children's food might be to a man thirty years old. It weakens the soul and prevents its growth, instead of supplying it new strength. Again, souls whose piety and peace of mind depend upon their feelings stand in danger of losing all at the first rude blast. Their only anchor is sensible grace. Withdraw this, and all falls to hopeless ruin. They lose courage as soon as God sends them trials. They make no distinction between God Himself and the feeling of His grace. When the latter is withheld, they conclude that God has abandoned them. They are, according to the words of St. Teresa, blind in giving up prayer when by trials it begins to purify them, when it is becoming more beneficial to them and more fruitful in results. A soul that nourishes herself upon the dry bread of desolation and suffering feels poor in all good. With her unworthiness and misery ever before her eyes, she will never weary seeking God, although He may seem to repel her. She will seek Him for Himself without seeking herself in Him. Such a soul soars far above one that is ever desirous of convincing herself of her own perfection, who becomes disturbed as soon as she loses sight of her advancement, and is always longing for God to prevent her with new proofs of tenderness.

Let us follow God upon the dim path of pure faith, seeking not to see what He conceals from us. We shall go forward like Abraham, not knowing whither our steps lead, resting upon nothing but our own misery and God's mercy. Let us in simplicity and fidelity follow the beaten path, ever resolved to offer all we have to God. Let us guard against confiding in self and in our own works, sentiments, and virtues. Onward to God! Pause not to cast a glance at self, its satisfaction, or its fears. Let us leave to God all that concerns us, intent only on honoring Him at every moment of our life.

If we would calmly and courageously look our spiritual weaknesses in the face, we should derive great benefit from them. In one sense our wretchedness is our treasure, since it more quickly attracts upon us the fulness of divine mercy. Let us prove this by a comparison. What are we before God? "We are His beggars," answers St. Augustine. The Holy Ghost Himself corroborates this decision of the great Father of the Church when He says by the mouth of the Psalmist: "But I am needy and poor: O God, help me,"[1] and "I am poor and sorrowful: Thy salvation, O God, hath set me up."[2] Yes, of ourselves we famish in the most stringent penury. But it is precisely this that attracts the divine mercy upon us, when in humble senti-

[1] Ps. lxix. 6. [2] Ps. lxviii. 30.

ments of our poverty we fly to God for assistance. But instead of this, alas! by presenting Him our supposed spiritual treasures and merits, we too often try to force Him to pour down His favor on us as if it were our due.

Does he who is about to ask an alms clothe himself with the externals of splendor? Does he borrow a costly garment in which to present himself at the doors of the rich, there to solicit a paltry alms? Does he display haughtiness? Does he treat as equals those whose compassion he implores? Does he extort alms as the just reward of pretended services, as something due his dignity, his merits? The rich, indeed, need not his services, and certainly such perverse dealing on the part of the poor man could have no happy results. One would certainly turn away from him as from a cunning thief whose appearance showed that he wanted for nothing, and who, besides, made himself insupportable by his airs and presumption. It is said in Ecclesiasticus: " My soul hateth a poor man that is proud."[1]

And we, too, see that they who implore the liberality of their brethren observe quite another course. They endeavor to appear humbly before those from whom they ask the alms for which they gently and modestly supplicate; they wait at the door patiently even in the worst weather, and come back perseveringly when there is hope of getting something. No refusal, no unkind answer, frightens them away or prevents their return. They show themselves thankful for the least that is given them; they consider it always far more than their due; and if, as so often happens, they miscalculate, and are disappointed in their hopes, they become neither angry nor discouraged. They gain for themselves the good-will of the rich, in whose presence they comport themselves as respectfully as we ought to do at our prayers. But not yet enough. Far from concealing his misery, the beggar displays his indigence,—nay, sometimes exaggerates it, in order the more effectually to arouse the compassion of his benefactor.

[1] Ecclus. xxv. 3, 4.

The poor wear their rags with a conscious satisfaction. They bare their sore limbs and disgusting wounds unasked, and sometimes resort to lies and hypocrisy in order to assume a more pitiful appearance and more efficaciously to move hearts to compassion. They act thus because they well know what our pride does not wish to understand; namely, that in their sad position is seen a true picture of one's own spiritual condition. Their misery is their only treasure, because it alone wins the sympathy which can help them. Oh, were we penetrated with these sentiments; did we but give up that pride which leads us to serve God as great lords; did we resolve, in spite of self-love, to reduce ourselves to a state of spiritual beggary,—then only would we be able to offer up to God truly humble and efficacious prayers; then only would we endure our evils as sweetly and patiently as is recommended by the saints.

CHAPTER VIII.

We should Courageously Labor at our Advancement, and thereby, without losing Interior Peace, draw Spiritual Benefit from our Faults and Miseries.

TRUE patience with one's spiritual frailties is neither cowardly compromise nor culpable laziness. It rather presupposes two very virtuous conditions. The first is the upright, though in the beginning weak, will to fulfil all obligatory Christian duties, and for this we always have sufficient grace. The second is the strenuous, persevering striving after amendment, so that we are always endeavoring, even in less important matters, to diminish our faults and to resist our evil inclinations. In a word, patience with self presupposes the sincere desire of perfection; for we speak here to souls of good-will, but who are not yet perfect. What way must such souls adopt, or what have they to do in order to work successfully at their advancement in perfection? This we shall consider briefly in the present chapter. Here self-love leads souls upon a most dangerous way, which has very appropriately been termed spiritual pride. Spiritual pride shows itself particularly under two forms. Either one wishes to attain to a higher degree of perfection than God has destined for him, and for which the graces allotted him are insufficient; or he would suddenly, so to say, spring with one bound to the heights of holiness. Let us now view these two forms of spiritual pride separately.

In speaking of the first, let us remember what we have said of the true imitation of the saints. May we never belong to the number of those whom St. Francis de Sales reproaches with busying themselves to become "good angels," whilst neglecting to become "good men"! Let us beware of such deceit. It is so much the more dangerous as it conceals itself under the mask of zeal for God's glory, whilst in reality it is only self-glory that is sought. It is not for us to determine our own way. Our whole perfection consists in this, that we submit to God's will over us; and our highest wisdom that, step by step, we follow the guidance of His providence. It is not our affair to determine in what manner we shall serve God; accordingly, we must not desire to enter upon another state than that to which He has called us. In the various vocations, there is for each individual soul a particular way that is to lead her to perfection. To enter upon it properly is not less important for her than the choice itself. To impose upon one's self, without being called thereto, severe mortifications and heroic acts of virtue, or to aim at the high perfection of the saints, signifies less the imitation of those great heroes of Christianity than the aping of them in a forced, ridiculous, and presumptuous manner. This would be to impose upon a child a burden that a strong man is hardly able to carry. It would be to expose one's self to the danger of being crushed under the weight of falling a victim to sadness and slothfulness, vexation and discouragement. The failure of so presumptuous an undertaking very naturally produces in us dejection. To all I say: "Not to be more wise than it behooveth to be wise, but to be wise unto sobriety; and according as God hath divided to every one the measure of faith,"[1] as the Apostle tells us. Let us search with humble, upright minds, without ambition, jealousy, and pride, to know God's will over us. Let us do with as much generosity as judgment all that devolves upon us in fulfilling the Divine Will, and let us faithfully co-operate with the graces imparted. It was by this way, and by no other, that the greatest saints became holy.

[1] Romans xii. 3.

The second form of spiritual pride is the impatience with which we would suddenly reach a predetermined degree of virtue. This impatience is not less natural than dangerous. There are sick persons who will submit with considerable ease to a painful operation provided it be done quickly, but who cannot subject themselves to the lesser grievance of protracted treatment, in order to regain their health. How many souls would, like this sick person, gladly offer a generous sacrifice if at once they might thus secure the possession of the desired virtue; but they cannot bring themselves down to the combat of long years, without which virtue is not acquired! Under the false appearance of courage lies hidden true cowardice. It shows that one neither knows the ways of salvation nor the wants of his own nature; for if nature felt itself freed at once from all its weaknesses, it would, like Lucifer, become puffed up in its pride, and attribute to itself the glory of a victory so lightly won.

But God understands the matter quite differently. His work in visible creation is a true picture of the effects of His grace in souls. This is particularly observable in nature. We see the gradual, sometimes slow, sometimes more rapid, growth of the smallest germ. It is often stunted by obstacles from within or others from without, against which it, as well as all creatures having the conscious perception of vital power, must struggle, till it has reached its development and perfection. Just so grace works. It is, so to say, engrafted upon nature to ennoble it. And if God sometimes exempts a soul from the rules of gradual progress, it shows us that He is all-powerful, and untrammelled by any laws; nevertheless, we have no right to claim for ourselves exemption from the general law.

In the guidance of the chosen people departing from Egypt till their entrance into the Promised Land, God has given us a true and perfect picture of the ways by which He designs to lead souls to perfection. Let us consider them more closely.

The Egyptian bondage may represent the slavery of a soul weakened in the chains of sin. The glorious land of Canaan flowing with milk and honey is a beautiful image of spiritual perfection. The journey from Egypt to Palestine is short; and the Israelites would very easily have found their destination if the Lord had limited their wanderings to a few days. We shall now consider a soul that, in the beginning of her conversion, renounces with her whole heart her natural inclinations to evil. She, too, would find it particularly agreeable if from her sad condition she could be raised to the highest, to the most exalted virtue. But the design of God is different. He leads his chosen people into the solitude of the desert, in order to give them His commandments, to make known to them His Divine Will. He leaves them there to wander forty long years. He permits them to be oppressed by powerful enemies. He allows them to be victorious on the one side and defeated on the other, according to their greater or less fidelity in prayer, their greater or less docility to the commands of Moses, His chosen leader. More than once, the Israelites deviated from the Commandments of Jehovah, for which they were severely punished but never deserted by Him. His providence always turned the fault and its punishment to their advantage. Finally they reached the borders of the Promised Land; and here new trials awaited them. At every city on their route they encountered a strong enemy to be baffled. Sometimes the Lord granted them victory, as before Jericho, whose walls at the blast of the trumpet fell to the ground; or again, they endured ignominious defeats in punishment of new prevarications. When, without recourse to God, they followed their own judgment, they fell into the snares laid for them by their enemies. In fine, the chosen people never fully conquered the Holy Land. In their immediate vicinity,—yes, in their very midst, dwelt heathens whose constant hostility kept them always on the alert, to punish their transgressions of the Divine Law, and to force them back to God.

This is a true picture of the paths upon which God guides the elect to sanctity. The soul must wander through the desert of aridity, repugnance, disgust, and desolation in its spiritual exercises. It is precisely by such trials that God impresses more deeply His Law upon the heart. In the solitude of the cloister, as well as in the bustle of the noisy world, the saints must bear arms against enemies whom they may weaken, but in this life never entirely banish. They must not only submit to the involuntary emotions arising as consequences from original sin, but more or less resign themselves to such experience. They shall often fall into real faults. They must be prepared for the combat, and support it with all its alternating vicissitudes to the end of life. In this way they must accustom themselves to prayer, to obedience to their spiritual guide, and to the humiliating sight of their own misery.

Let all souls take to heart the following words of Fénelon: "I hardly wonder," he says, "that God permits you to commit faults even when you most dread to do so, even in moments of sensible devotion and interior recollection. It is a true favor from Him when He permits you at such moments to fall into faults, for it convinces you of your inability by your own strength to do otherwise. What more could the greatest graces effect in you than deprive you of your high opinion of self, and urge you at every moment humbly to have recourse to God? To make a good use of the faults that humble you in your own eyes is more beneficial than the performance of good works, however consoling.

"Give up prolonged and unprofitable reflections upon your faults; for such meditations retard your progress. They serve only to discourage, and to disturb the head and heart. Humble yourself. Bewail your failings as soon as you remark them. This done, put them aside quietly, and proceed on your way. Again, do not note down every fault with pharisaical exactitude. Do not look upon God as an enemy that lays traps for you, or as a spy that watches you only to ensnare you in some fault. See in Him rather the best of fathers, who loves you and will make you happy. Repose in Him the fullest confidence. Call upon His mercy with the most perfect conviction that reliance on creatures and self is empty and deceitful.

"God sends you humiliations to make you humble and pliant. When you are not humbled by such trials, you force God, though against His will, to deal still harder blows, and to let you feel more sensibly your pitiful weakness. Be simple and pliant, and you will appease His Sacred Heart. Say to Him with confidence, 'An humble and a contrite heart, O God, Thou wilt not despise.'[1] You will see, then, that the Lord will be moved, for He cannot withstand the submissive confidence of His little ones."

Let us hear St. Francis de Sales on this subject: "Our daily faults and imperfections," says he, "should certainly abase and humble us before God. . . . But we must not be satisfied with this; for humility and self-contempt are virtues which serve as a means to rise to union with God. Self-imposed acts of humiliation will help us on to it; but this will count for little if not accompanied by entire resignation to God, as St. Paul recommends in the words: 'Put off the old man, and put on the new man.'[2] We must not remain naked: we must put on God. When we have fallen, we must cast a rapid and sorrowful glance upon ourselves only the better to mount up to God again by a vigorous act of love and confidence. Our confusion for our faults ought neither to sadden nor disturb us. Were it to do so, it would be a sign that self-love is writhing. You are displeased with yourself because you are not perfect; but such displeasure arises from the love of self rather than from the love of God. Try to elicit acts of confidence, even if your feelings tend the other way. Say to God: 'O Lord, although I feel no confidence in Thee, still I know that

[1] Ps. l. 19.   [2] Eph. iv. 22. 24.

Thou art my God, and that I am wholly Thine. I place all my hope in Thy goodness, and I remit myself wholly into Thy hands.'

"It is hard, certainly, to awaken such acts, though by no means impossible. It is on such occasions that we should show our loyalty to the Lord. You may find very little pleasure or satisfaction in such acts, but you must not be concerned on that account. Tell me not that your lips utter what your heart does not feel; for if your heart did not will it, your tongue could not frame a word. Have you succeeded in awakening an act of confidence? Then be at peace. Speak to God of other things without further attention to interior distractions and embarrassment. To conclude, I repeat once for all, it is very good to mortify yourself by a glance at your miseries and imperfections. But one must not stop there and lose courage. He must at once raise his heart to God, and confide in Him rather than in self."

These principles are so important, and yet so little understood, that we cannot dwell too long upon them. We quote what the Abbé Grou says on this subject in one of his learned books: "Souls that would really and truly belong to God, are often very much astonished at the faults they commit through human frailty. They allow themselves to be disturbed; they yield to anxiety, discouragement, and false shame. All this is the result of self-love, which does more harm than all other faults. If you wonder that you have fallen, you do very wrong, and you show how little you know yourself. On the contrary, your astonishment should be that you have not committed greater and more numerous faults. Thank God for those from which He has preserved you. You fall into disquietude as often as you perceive a fault, lose interior peace, suffer intense anxiety, are almost distracted, and busy yourself with it for hours and days. Is this right? Assuredly not. You should never allow yourself to be disquieted. When you feel that you have fallen, tranquilly rise again with a heart full of love for God. Return to Him, implore pardon, and think no more of it until you go to confession. Should you even forget the fault in the confessional you must not be troubled. Or, supposing that, through false shame, you can scarcely declare your faults to your father confessor. What will he think of me? you say; I have so often promised him to do better. When, with child-like openness and humility, you acknowledge your failings to him, he will esteem you only the more highly; but if you declare them with difficulty and repugnance, he is forced to think you proud: he will lose confidence in you, since he sees your want of candor. But I now come to the worst. You torment yourself, as St. Francis de Sales says, that you have become impatient. What misery! Do you not see that this is pure pride? You are full of shame and vexation, because in the hour of trial you displayed less strength and vigor of soul than you had previously ascribed to yourself. You would like to be free from faults and imperfections in order to contemplate your own spiritual beauty, and to be able to say: For a day, nay, for a whole week, I have had nothing wherewith to reproach myself! Finally, you lose courage; you give up your pious exercises one after another; you consider perfection as something impossible, and you despair of attaining it. You will at last say to yourself: What use is there in overcoming myself, always watching over myself, aiming at interior recollection and mortification of the senses, since I neither decrease the number of my faults nor become better? This is one of the most cunning devices of the enemy. Would you escape it? Never, then, yield to discouragement, no matter into what faults you may have fallen. Say to yourself: Should I fall twenty, nay, a hundred, times a day, I shall rise again each time and proceed on my way. What matters it that you have fallen, provided only that you reach the end? God will not reproach you on that score. It often happens that stumbling is the consequence of running too fast. Our zeal is so great that we do not give ourselves time to make

We should Labor at our Advancement.

use of certain precautions. Timid and reflecting souls always wish to see where they are about to step; they take roundabout ways at every moment in order to avoid dangerous places; they are always fearful of incurring even the slightest stain. In this way they do not advance so quickly as others, and death overtakes them half-way. The holiest soul is not the one that commits the fewest faults, but the one that has the most courage, the most generosity, and the most love. It is the soul that overcomes herself the most, that fears not to stumble or even to fall and soil herself a little on the way, provided only she advances.

St. Paul says: "To them that love God, all things work together unto good."[1] Yes, all things work to their good, even their faults, sometimes very great, which God permits in order to cure them of vain self-confidence, to point out to them what they are, and of what they are capable. David recognized that his sins had strengthened him in mistrust of himself. "It is good for me," said he to God, "that Thou hast humbled me; for thereby have I learned Thy justifications."[2] The fall of St. Peter was for him a most useful lesson. It humbled him, and prepared him to receive without danger the richest gifts of the Holy Ghost, and to become the head of the Church of Jesus Christ. In the midst of the glorious success of his apostolate, St. Paul remembered that he had once been a blasphemer and persecutor of the Church, and thus he was preserved from vain-glory. And for the same reason God would not free this great Apostle from a humiliating temptation, which served as a counterpoise to his sublime revelations.

If God knows how to draw such benefits from even the gravest crimes, who can doubt that He makes use of our daily faults for our sanctification? God permits, as all teachers of the spiritual life say, certain faults even in the holiest souls, of which, in spite of all their efforts, they cannot wholly correct themselves. He will by these weaknesses make them see and feel what, without His grace,

[1] Romans viii. 28. [2] Ps. xliii. 20.

they would be. He wills that they should not become proud on account of the graces He bestows upon them; that, on the contrary, they should ever receive them in humility, and preserve diffidence in self. They will thereby escape the snares of self-love, maintain fervor by prayer, practise watchfulness, confidence in God, and have continual recourse to Him in prayer. When the child, eager to walk alone, falls, it comes back to its mother with greater alacrity to receive comfort from her. It is taught by that fall to remain by its mother's side.

Our faults often become for us occasions for great acts of virtue, which otherwise we could not practise. God not unfrequently leaves us those faults for this intention. You give way to your humors, you are testy with your neighbor, you yield to impatience. God permits it thus, thereby to give you the opportunity to practise an act of humility by which you repair your fault and make good the scandal you have given. The fault was committed in the first heat of excitement; the satisfaction with deliberate self-victory. The reparation is, therefore, more agreeable to God than the fault was displeasing to Him.

God makes use also of our faults and exterior imperfections to conceal our sanctity from others and to procure us humiliations from them.

He is a skilful Master. Let Him act; His work will not be a failure. Firmly resolve carefully to avoid all that could in the least displease Him. And if in spite of your resolution you commit a fault, regret it for His sake and not your own. Love the humiliation which arises from it, and pray the Lord earnestly and perseveringly that every one of your false steps may redound to His greater glory and your own good. He will hear your prayer, and you will by this means advance more rapidly in virtue than if you led a life apparently regular and holy; for the latter would be less conducive to the uprooting of self-love.

If God desires anything good from us, we should not refuse it under the pretext that by so doing we might commit faults. A pious work imperfectly performed is better than one not done at all. You refrain so frequently from giving a necessary rebuke, because you fear becoming excited or violent; you avoid intercourse with certain persons, lest their faults put your patience to the test. But how will you acquire virtue if you avoid the occasions of practising it? Do you not, by such reserve, commit a greater fault than that of which you were afraid? Endeavor to act through a good intention; fly whither duty calls you; and be persuaded that God is sufficiently indulgent to pardon a fault committed in His holy service, and to which the desire of pleasing Him exposed you.

CHAPTER IX.

Of the Transition from a State of Sensible Devotion to that of Pure Faith and Spoliation.

WHEN a soul that has lived in a state of innocence, or for a time has borne the yoke of sin, turns with upright will to the service of God, a state of sensible devotion and spiritual consolation is usually hers in the beginning. This is necessary, to lighten the first difficulties met in the path of virtue. In this state such souls feel powerful impulses of grace which strengthen and support them.

They gain victories without effort; they are conscious of their progress, and from this consciousness springs either great facility in the exercise of virtue, or in case of difficulties a more active, more courageous zeal in surmounting them. The state of sensible devotion shows itself more or less in a soul, according to the degree of perfection to which God has called her. It is good,—yes, in the beginning, even necessary. Still it is a state free neither from danger nor imperfection. The struggles, the victories, the virtues, the pious sentiments, of which the soul cannot fail to be conscious, produce in her by degrees such self-sufficiency and complacency that all further advancement in the path of perfection will become an impossibility. If she remain in the peaceful enjoyment of such a state she will fall a victim to the subtle whisperings of pride. But now comes a time in which God withdraws that sensible consolation, for which withdrawal, however, He has gradually prepared her. The soul is not thereby shorn of grace. The solid, the essential part of His grace, as well as her previously acquired virtues, are still hers. The intention of Almighty

God in so doing is to unite the soul more closely to Himself, though she in some manner loses the consciousness of this union, or at least ceases for a time clearly to understand and taste its sweetness.

What pen can describe the desolation of a soul thus passing from light to darkness, from sensible consolation to spiritual disgust and impotence, the very thought of which is sufficient to deject? She shudders. Desolation seizes upon her. She looks upon all as lost, and at every moment is ready to proclaim herself vanquished. Spiritual exercises are performed with repugnance, because she sees in them naught but defeats. Her weakness is such that she doubts whether or not she has complied with even her essential obligations. The most trifling difficulties frighten her, the remembrance of past fervor consumes her, and with Job she cries out, "Who will grant me, that I might be according to the months past, according to the days in which God kept me?"[1]

Oh how fatal might not such trials prove to interior peace! And yet they establish in the soul the secure foundation of true peace, since they besiege its cruel enemy, pride, in its most hidden lurking-place. In confirmation of what we have said, let us again hear the great Archbishop of Cambray: "Nearly all who would render service to the Lord," says he, "think in so doing of their own interest. They desire to gain, and not to lose; they seek to be consoled, and not to suffer; to possess, and not to want; to increase, and not to diminish. And yet the whole interior life consists in losing, in sacrificing, in diminishing, in being despoiled, in becoming little, in renouncing those gifts of God to us so sweet, so as to hold firmly to God alone. We are like the sick, who desire vehemently to be restored to health. How many times in the day do they feel their pulse! The physician is called in to calm them. He must prescribe all kinds of remedies, he must assure them of their improvement. We do nearly the same thing

[1] Job xxix. 2.

in regard to our spiritual physician. We go round and round in the narrow circle of every-day virtues, and never take one bold step beyond. The spiritual director acts like the physician. He quiets, consoles, encourages, speaks kind words, fosters our tender delicacy for our dear self, and orders only mild, trifling remedies to which nature soon becomes accustomed. As soon as God takes from us the milk of little children, namely, sensible devotion, we think all is lost. We prove thereby that the means make us forget the end, and that we seek self in all things. Privation is the bread of the strong. It strengthens the soul, uproots self-seeking, and offers it a holocaust to God. But, alas! no sooner have we tasted this bread than we grow sad and dejected. All has gone to ruin, in our estimation; whilst in reality all is being purified, is striking firmer root. We are prepared to let God make out of us what He will, provided only it is something very grand and perfect. But so long as we will not give ourselves up entirely to this annihilation, we cannot become whole-burnt offerings, consumed by the flames of divine love. We would enter upon the life of pure faith, and yet retain our own judgment; we would become little children, and still be great in our own eyes. . . . What a picture of false piety!

"If we are willing to belong to God only whilst we find joy and consolation in His holy service, we resemble the multitude that followed the Lord, not for the sake of His teaching, but for the multiplication of the loaves. We say with Peter: 'Lord, it is good for us to be here; and let us make three tabernacles.'[1] But, like the Prince of the Apostles, we know not what we ask. Intoxicated with the sweets of Thabor, we disown the suffering Son of God, we will not follow him to Calvary's Mount. We snatch at spiritual illumination, sweetness, and sublime elevations; the mind would see and understand; the heart, feel and taste. Does that mean death to self? Is that the just

[1] Mark ix. 4.

man who, as St. Paul says, lives by faith, and is nourished by it? . . .

"Some souls never get beyond the state of spiritual consolation. Others, on the contrary, God leads further by depriving them of that with which He had once nourished them. Such souls easily fall into a state of dryness, disgust, and weakness. Then everything becomes burdensome to them. No friendship, no conversation, no intercourse, can ever again console them. They feel that God has withdrawn from them, with all His gifts and graces. The pangs of death are theirs; a sort of despair takes possession of them. They are insupportable to themselves, and life becomes tedious. In God's love even, and in His holy Law, they feel no more joy. They are like the sick fainting from want of nourishment, and yet experiencing naught but disgust at the sight of the daintiest food. Speak to them of friendship—the mere sound of the word causes pain and brings tears to their eyes; a trifle overpowers them. They themselves know not what they want. Their friendships and their sufferings are like those of little children. They can give no reasonable cause for them. What they have felt or what thought, vanishes like a dream at the moment in which they utter it. Every word on the state of their soul seems to them a lie; for what they say ceases to be true as soon as they begin to speak about it. Consistency exists no longer for them. They cannot answer for anything, promise anything; they have not even the power to describe what takes place within them. Their humors are as little under their control as are the cell and its furniture subject to that of a religious. Changing and mutable, nothing belongs to them as their own, and their heart least of all. It is incredible how this childish instability, these puerile whims, humble a soul formerly so wise, so strong and virtuously proud in her own eyes. Now, God does not permit souls to suffer thus for His own pleasure. He tries them only to purify; He merely deprives them of the graces which they appropriate to themselves, in order to give them back to them a hundred fold as soon as He sees they may be possessed without danger.

"Our virtues need purging, for their sight nourishes in us the natural life. Our disorderly nature finds even in the graces that cost her most the constant nourishment of her own free choice. Self-love feeds not only on macerations and humiliations, on prayer and self-denial, but also on great sacrifices and unlimited spoliation. It is on this account that God permits that we should lose sight of even the consciousness of our giving up all to Him; for only painful trial ends our purgation. . . .

"Do you now see how necessary it is that God should gradually deprive you of His gifts of grace? They, even the purest and choicest, are useful only in the beginning to advance in virtue. They would soon become to you obstacles to higher perfection. Your grace is sullied when you ascribe it to yourself. Therefore God takes from you what He once gave. He will not deprive you of it forever. He will return it purer and better when there is nothing more to be feared from your faults.

"We cling to the sensible; hence our delusions. Many souls are so blind and so sensual that they grasp at feeling, in order to reach security; and yet these feelings deceive us, because they are a bait for self-love. So long as we enjoy sweetness and consolation, we know no fear of sin. In our superabundance we exclaim: 'Never shall I waver!' But let the intoxicating draught be withdrawn, and, alas, alas! we think all is over. By acting thus we substitute our own happiness, our own lively imagination, for God's good pleasure. Naked faith is the only safeguard against such deception. Trust not to your imagination, your sentiments, your own taste. Aim not at the brilliant, the extraordinary. Cling to God alone in pure, naked faith in the simplicity of the Gospel. Take from the hand of the Lord the graces that He gives you, but do not attach your heart to them. Refrain from judging of your state. Obey, in the ready belief in your own capability to err, and in the ability of others to direct you; finally, let your every movement be stamped by simplicity and a good intention according to the light of faith. Do this, and be assured that you are on the right road.

"Such a practice will be to you the best sign that your way is much securer than would be that of sweetness and particular lights. Make the experiment, and you will soon see that it is so. If you courageously follow it, it will lead to perfect spiritual death. Beautiful sentiments and interior consciousness of virtue indemnify self-love for exterior sacrifices, and nourish subtle self-seeking. But are you interiorly and exteriorly divested of self? exteriorly by Providence, and interiorly by self-spoliation? Then is your martyrdom perfect. You are, in consequence, secure from every species of deceit. Read the 'Following of Christ' (bk. iii., ch. vi.), and you will understand that when God takes away interior sweetness from you, it should be your consolation to be deprived of all consolation. O how agreeable to God is a crucified soul when she descends not from the cross, but dies thereon with her Saviour!"

These words of Fénelon point to the end to be attained, if by cowardice the soul does not set limits to her perfection. This end means "death to self." The soul reaches it when she exercises herself long and perseveringly in self-denial and an unlimited surrender to God. It means again when, as the 'Following of Christ' says, "She gives all for all." Some particulars upon this species of spoliation will be given in the coming chapter.

CHAPTER X.

Of Self-renunciation and the Total Surrender of Self to God, the Last Condition for Obtaining Constant Interior Peace.

THE soul that strives after perfection can belong to God as entirely as is necessary to her peace, only when she denies herself; that is, when in the sight of her Creator she accounts herself nothing. "Whoever does not renounce all," says Christ, "cannot be My disciple."[1] We shall now clearly unfold in what this renunciation consists.

All can readily perceive that forbidden gratifications, unjust possessions, vulgar vanity, must be renounced; for the Law of God commands us this. But it will not be so readily comprehended that one should also renounce lawful possessions which, because of his position, he is even obliged to preserve. Such possessions are a good name, the independence accruing from a respectable income and happy domestic relations, the consolations of friendship, and a thousand similar things.

In all such instances renunciation consists in detachment of heart. Conscientiously and without anxiety they must be preserved and used with moderation; but one's happiness must not be founded upon them. The use of such goods is reasonable when accompanied by moderation, though at the same time real necessities must always be distinguished from imaginary ones. Nature would gladly procure the latter; it would indulge the one and refuse the other all nourishment. What does it mean, for instance, after the example of Christ, to renounce those persons who

[1] Luke xiv. 33.

Total Surrender of Self to God. 155

are the dearest to us, and whom we are even bound to love? It means to love them only for God; to enjoy their friendship with rule and measure, and according to necessity; to banish from our heart all passion and jealousy; to be prepared to lose or be separated from them, if God so wills, and to seek our true peace of heart not in our friends, but in a more worthy object. By such a mode of procedure we, according to the advice of the Apostle, use creatures and the world as if we used them not; we do not desire to enjoy, but only to take what God gives. It preserves peace of soul amidst the thousand vicissitudes of life; because in loving resignation to the Lord we abandon all that we prize or possess.

But granting that we have in this manner given up all our surroundings, then comes the last great sacrifice—that of self; for the main cause of all our anxiety and suffering is our blind love of self, which borders on idolatry. Only when we shall have sacrificed our idol shall we find healing and peace. God lays His hand upon us first exteriorly, taking from us the creatures to whom we cling inordinately. By so doing He lays the indispensable foundation-stone. Then He goes further, and attacks us interiorly, in order to free us from self. We loved all these things only because of self; and this self God now pursues without rest or mercy, if only He can lead us to a higher degree of perfection. Sensual, worldly men find the privation of sensible satisfaction fearfully hard; for they, if not in theory, at least in practice, consider the body the most important part of self, and pamper it accordingly. But when this weakness is overcome there still remains hard work till we have renounced our understanding. Our judgment, our wisdom, and virtues are to us what beauty is to a frivolous worldling. We delight in them, we esteem them very meritorious. We congratulate ourselves upon being wise, enlightened, and free from the errors of our neighbors. What refined self-complacency lies in this! How much we should displease God if we deliberately allowed self-love to hold such sway in our heart! We must, on the contrary, renounce also the natural satisfaction that our interior advantages may produce in us.

"Remember well," says Fénelon, "that the purer and more exalted God's gifts are, the more jealous He is of them. He had mercy on the first man, but the rebel angel He cast without mercy into the depths of the abyss. The angel and the man had sinned by pride. But the angel had received more perfect gifts from the Lord; therefore his revolt was more severely punished than was man's disobedience.

"But you ask me how you can practise this self-denial. To this I answer that, as soon as the necessity of self-denial is acknowledged by the will, God takes the soul by the hand, and by every event of daily life leads it onward in the path of renunciation.

"Not by painful reflections and continual effort of the mind does one renounce himself. Only he who preserves himself from every species of self-seeking, who does not wish to dispose of himself according to his own ideas, is ever truly lost in God.

"You feel an emotion of pride, of self-satisfaction, of self-confidence, of impatience with the weaknesses of others, or with the weariness incidental to your vocation; you feel tempted to seek your own satisfaction, follow your own attraction instead of the voice of your guide. All such emotions must be relinquished as entirely as a stone dropped into the depths of the water. Recollect yourself before God, and do not act until your soul has regained its calm. But if distracting occupations or your vivid and excitable imagination prevent this instantaneous interior recollection, you must by the uprightness of your will and your sincere desire aim at self-possession. The will to recollect one's self is a sort of recollection. It suffices to despoil the soul of her own will, and to make her a pliant tool in the hand of God.

"But if in an unguarded moment some purely natural and sinful emotion escape you, be not discouraged. Proceed peacefully, bearing in God's sight the humiliation entailed by your fault, but going to Him full of confidence. Your interior confusion humbles you before God, and makes you die to self. You best repair your fault when, yielding at once to the influence of grace from which your infidelity had for the moment withdrawn you, you overcome the chagrin and vexation of self-love.

"The main thing for you is, by perfect simplicity in your dealings, to renounce your own wisdom and be prepared to relinquish the favor, esteem, and approbation of men just as often as God wills it. It would indeed be impossible to enumerate the peculiar and special sacrifices that God may require of a soul. They are as varied as are men themselves. Every soul has its own, in accordance with its necessities and the designs of God. How can we know of what God wills to divest us, since we know not to what we cling? Each is held by innumerable ties whose existence he himself could never guess. We realize how closely we clung to them only when God takes them from us.

"The renunciation that God requires of us is not generally what we ourselves, perhaps, thought. God surprises us in the most unexpected manner; in trifles it may be, but trifles that wound self-love most sensibly, and inflict upon it a true martyrdom. Great, heroic acts of virtue would flatter pride. But to rejoice at insignificant and repeated sacrifices calls for more self-abnegation, more mortification, than would do many great ones; and this cheerful pliancy in little things is precisely what God exacts of us. He allows the soul no rest. He twists and turns her on all sides, until He has made her perfectly pliant and flexible.

You must bear from others and from yourself all possible annoyances. You have spoken too freely, or you have forgotten to say what was most necessary; you are praised, censured, forgotten, elevated to the first rank, then deposed; you are judged falsely, and you cannot justify yourself; you have spoken to your own advantage; a trifle perplexes you, renders you irresolute, throws you off your guard; you grow angry like a little child, and give open expression to your vexation; your dryness gives your friends subject of offence; you are, without foundation, jealous and mistrustful, and you own your childish jealousy to the object of it; you speak freely to certain people, and you are not understood; you appear inconstant, artful, and not to be depended upon; you feel dry, indolent, inert, distracted, with nothing to counteract these miseries, for even God has become wearisome. These are some examples of what may afford matter for interior renunciation. I have placed them here just as they occurred to my mind. The list, however, is by no means exhausted. There are hosts of others, which God in His wisdom will mete to each one as seems good to Him. . .

"One word with regard to a temptation to which the soul is often exposed when endeavoring to practise self-denial. Certain selfish intentions pursue her in speech and action. Reflecting afterward upon self, she thinks she has yielded to self-complacency, sought after human applause, relished the consolations of virtue too much; in fine, she sees self everywhere. This greatly afflicts a conscientious soul, and she laments over it. To calm her, one must remind her that good and bad depend entirely upon the will. As long as such emotions of self-seeking are involuntary, they do not derogate from the perfection of self-renunciation, do not make us displeasing to God. They are but seldom voluntarily indulged by a soul truly divested of self and wholly given to God. They, on the contrary, who in spite of their sincere piety are not quite dead to the pleasant things of life, to a good name, to the sweetness of friendship, still seek self a little in all these things; not blindly and impetuously, to be sure, but occasionally, and so to say, in a passing way. This is proved by their chagrin, their deep affliction when threatened with the loss of these things. We cling to self without knowing it. Only a blow aimed at it discovers to us the depth of our heart and

Total Surrender of Self to God. 159

forces us to make a sacrifice. The moderate use of temporal blessings secures to us as direct a step toward self-renunciation as a loss borne peacefully...

"There comes a time in the spiritual life when one cannot clearly understand one's own secret self-seeking. God permits the interior light to shine only brightly enough to give power to sacrifice it. Jesus Christ addresses the soul: 'I have yet many things to say to you, but you cannot bear them now.'[1] We see our good intentions and our good-will; but we should be shocked if God allowed us to see the numberless cords that still bind us down. We do not, indeed, cling to them with full deliberation, with a determined will; we do not say to ourselves: 'I cling to this, and I will cling to it.' But still we hold on to it. We fear to dive into our heart lest we should too plainly see how tenaciously we are clinging to that idol. We feel our own weakness; and yet we venture not to pursue the knowledge of it too far, lest we might grow to know it too well. We are sometimes suddenly inflamed with an impatient zeal for our own perfection, we desire to discover every obstacle thereto in order to sacrifice it; but this zeal is as rash and indiscreet as that of St. Peter when he cried out, 'I am ready to die for Thee!' though a few moments after found him trembling in the presence of a weak servant-maid. We desire to behold all our weaknesses at one view; but God spares us the sight by dimming for the present moment our interior light. He will not permit us to see what we cannot then and there uproot. Ah, the admirable indulgence of Divine Goodness! He never urges us to a sacrifice without giving us the necessary light; and He never grants us that light unaccompanied by the strength necessary for the sacrifice. Until that hour strikes for us we are with regard to such a sacrifice like the Apostles who, when our Lord spake to them of His approaching sufferings, understood Him not. Upright and vigilant souls may still be in ignorance of the secret spoliation God

[1] John xvi. 12

has in reserve for them, and which he keeps concealed until they are advanced a step farther in pure faith and disengagement from self. We must not aim at outstripping God. Let us be true to Him in all that we know, for then only shall we be in peace. He will enlighten us upon whatever it may be good for us to know. . .

"Happy he who in the work of self-denial never hesitates to follow grace! Happy he who only fears not following quickly enough! Happy he who always performs in the cause of self-conquest rather too much than too little! Happy he who, when asked for a sample, courageously presents the whole fabric to God, and allows Him to shape it to His own liking! Happy he who esteems himself nothing, and who never implores God to be forbearing with him! And lastly, blessed is the soul whom the prospect of such despoilment does not intimidate!

"Some may imagine such a condition unendurable; but oh, what a mistake! It is then that the heart is free, then that it is enlarged, then unshackled by rule or bounds. Then does it, in accordance with God's promise, become one with Himself! . . .

"O my God! Thou alone canst give true peace! The more unsparingly self is sacrificed, the greater is the soul's freedom. When, without delay or hesitancy, she is ready to lose all, then does she possess all. Her condition is a picture of the blessedness tasted by the heavenly spirits. They are forever lost in God, and their blissful rapture will endure eternally!

"O Spouse of souls! Thou dost give to Thy servants here below a foretaste of that felicity. Created things can but circumscribe the heart; but when it renounces attachment to creatures and self, it enters, in a manner, into Thy infinity. Nothing holds it back; it becomes more and more perfectly lost in Thee; it expands as Thou dost fill it, and without nausea it is ever satiated! Such service, O my God! is true, pure adoration, in spirit and in truth. Thou

Total Surrender of Self to God.

seekest such adorers; but alas, how rarely dost Thou find them!

"When a soul has once given herself up entirely to the Lord, she aims not at multiplicity in her works, but all that she does is well done. With perfect confidence she remits the future to God. She accepts unconditionally all that God wills in the present or for the future, and she closes her eyes to useless anticipations. She endeavors to execute God's will at every passing moment. Sufficient for the day is the evil thereof; sufficient also the good. The daily fulfilment of the Divine Will is the coming of God's kingdom in us, and at the same time it is our daily bread. It would be an infidelity to anticipate the future which God holds concealed from us. It lies in His hand, He will make it sweet or bitter, long or short. Let it fall out as it may, the soul always prepares for it in the most perfect manner by renouncing self-will, to conform to the will of God. As the manna in the desert was possessed of all kinds of flavor, so this union with the Divine Will combines in itself all graces and sentiments suitable to every condition to which God may subject you.

"When the soul is prepared for this, she begins to gain ground, to plant her feet firmly on the edge of the abyss. She is as peaceful with regard to the past as she is in view of the future. Though esteeming self the worst of God's creatures, yet she knows that God is ready to pardon. She casts herself blindly into His arms. She forgets self, and perfect self-forgetfulness is perfect penance; for it is the martyrdom of self-love. It deals the death-blow to every attachment. How lightly the soul springs along when released from the oppressive load of self under which she once well-nigh sank. With astonishment she beholds how straight and simple is the way that lies before her. Once she labored under continual restlessness and spiritual constraint; an ever-new activity was deemed requisite. Now, however, she sees that but little is to be done; that, with no thought of the past or of the future, it is enough for her to look with perfect confidence to God as to a Father who leads her at every moment by the hand. If a passing distraction hides Him from view, let her turn again to Him without alarm, and again she will learn what He expects from her. A fault is committed—let her turn again to Him whom she has abandoned, let her atone for it by an act of sorrow, for sorrow is the proof of pure love. The transgression arises before her and fills her soul with horror; but such humiliation is both good and useful. The humbled soul turns back to God in recollection, peace, and confidence; the proud, on the other hand, bitterly and subtly discusses the fault and all that led to its commission.

"Experience is the best teacher. A simple, peaceful return to God will bring with it more light, will advance the soul far more, than useless and weary lamentations. As soon as you perceive that you have committed a fault, turn simply to God. Do not torture yourself fruitlessly; do not reflect so much upon it, nor weigh the matter so nicely. When in your spiritual desolation you make reflections, it is with yourself that you take counsel. Ah, wretched consultation in which God holds no part!

"Who will extend a helping hand to lift you from the mire? Yourself? Ah, it is you who have plunged into that out of which you are powerless to extricate yourself! And yet more—you yourself are the marsh, the cause of your misery. How can you hope to rise, since you are ever busy with self, ever nourishing self with the sentimental consideration of your own misery? This constant return upon self, this ceaseless reflecting upon self, is nothing more than a lamenting over self. A single Godward glance would bring far more peace to the troubled heart than this unending occupation with self. Renounce self, and you will find peace . . . . But how can this, this rising above self, be brought about? I answer, in this way: Turn quietly to God, and accustom yourself, little by little, to the habitual remembrance of Him. . . ."

Yet one more important observation. This and the pre-

Total Surrender of Self to God. 163

ceding chapter treat of the purification of the soul by renunciation and interior disengagement. Though intended for all, according to the degree of virtue to which God calls them, yet they find their full realization only in those souls whom God has separated from the multitude, in order to lead them to higher perfection. For these in particular we have inserted the foregoing instructions. In spite of this, however, all may draw profit from them if, in submission to a spiritual guide, they apply them to themselves. It would indeed be to err directly against this doctrine if one should make it a pretext to absolute self-guidance ; if, without a spiritual director, he should strive after this or that degree of perfection. As to this latter point, it is only for him who directs us to determine. He who assumes his own guidance exposes himself to dangerous illusions, and grants free play to self-love. God does not work in all souls alike. There are some to whom He leaves a certain return upon self, because it will support them in the exercise of the virtues, and in a certain degree help to purify them. It would be imprudent and dangerous to deprive them of such support. It would be to take milk from a child that cannot yet eat solid food. Never should a director take from a soul what serves as her nourishment, what God has left to support her weakness. To anticipate grace is to destroy its work. Fénelon says: "It is better to wait and open the door with a key, than to break the lock through impatience." These beautiful words should often be taken to heart by the spiritual guides themselves.

PART III.

OF THE MEANS FOR PRESERVING PEACE AMID SPIRITUAL WEAKNESSES.

CHAPTER I.

Various Instructions on these Means.

FIRST POINT.[1]

Fundamental Maxims on Liberty of Spirit.

A SOUL that seeks naught but persecution and contempt, desires or loves no earthly good, fears no temporal misfortune, flies from joy as from poison, and finds her happiness in suffering, is capable of receiving great consolation from God. But her confidence in Him must be firmly established; as soon as she rests upon her own strength, her support is gone. Great was the courage of St. Peter when he protested that he would die with Christ. His resolve was certainly most praiseworthy; but his zeal was defective in this, that it proceeded from his own will,—hence his fall. Thus it is that, without the assistance of grace, we can neither determine nor accomplish any good thing.

Our soul must be free from all desires foreign to her perfection. She must be wholly attentive upon what she thinks or does, never divided between the duties of the present and those that may come upon her in the future.

[1] This point, as well as the following, is taken from the " Treatise on the Peace of the Soul."

A man is not forbidden to arrange his temporal affairs wisely and carefully. Rightly understood, these things are in accordance with God's will, and they in nowise hinder either interior peace or spiritual progress. To utilize properly the present moment, no method is better than to present our soul before God empty of all desires, by which we appear before the Divine Majesty as poor beggars with nothing to do and no means of earning anything.

Perfection consists in that detachment of spirit which, free from all ties either within or without, wholly and entirely depends upon God alone.

SECOND POINT.

Of the Snares by which the Fiend seeks to Rob us of Peace, and of the Means by which to Defend Ourselves against him.

The Evil One tries to rob us, above all things, of Christian humility and simplicity; therefore he would instil into us confidence in ourselves, in our own efforts, when troubles and anxieties come upon us. He wills that we prefer ourselves to others, and thus, little by little, despise our neighbor. By vanity and self-esteem the devil loves best to gain admittance into a soul. The most skilful way of defending ourselves against him is to intrench ourselves behind humility. As soon as shame and self-contempt vanish from the heart, we lose the power to oppose the demon of pride. Let him once take possession of the will, and he rules as a tyrant, and with him reign all vices.

Watchfulness is not enough; prayer must be added to it, for it is written: "Watch and pray!" Peace is a treasure to be secured by these two means only.

Let us never permit our mind to be disturbed or distracted by anything. To an humble, peaceful soul everything is easy. Difficulties disappear before her, and she perseveres in good. But a restless soul effects little, and that little in the most imperfect manner. She soon wearies of virtue, and she suffers continually, though without merit.

Suppose that a thought of confidence or one of mistrust in God's mercy presents itself,—which should you entertain? which should you banish? Ah! nourish the thought of loving confidence in God. Look upon it as a messenger from heaven, and rejoice in its presence. But banish as a suggestion of the Evil One every thought that arouses in you a want of confidence in the infinite mercy of God.

When the tempter assails pious souls, he represents to them that their daily faults are far greater than they really are. He whispers that their duties are never rightly fulfilled; that their confessions are imperfect, their Communions tepid, their prayers worthless. By such scruples he aims at rendering them anxious, disquieted, and impatient. In the same way he tries to withdraw them from their devotional exercises, by suggesting the thought that all is of no avail, that God no longer regards them, that He has entirely forgotten them. Nothing can be more untrue than such insinuations. The distractions, the interior dryness, and the defects of our spiritual exercises may become extremely useful to us, if we only understand that, under certain circumstances, God expects nothing from us but patience and perseverance in the good begun. St. Gregory says: "From the prayers and good works of a soul deprived of spiritual consolation God receives the truest pleasure that He can possibly have in His creatures. The soul must, however, persevere courageously in her spiritual exercises in spite of coldness, disgust, and indifference. Her patience prays at such moments, making her as agreeable to God as if she actually prayed as she desires." The same saint adds: "The interior darkness of such a soul is resplendent with brilliancy in the eyes of God. Her patience under interior suffering constrains Him, in a manner, to bow down to her and fill her to overflowing with His grace."

Never, therefore, omit doing a good work, however great

may be the repugnance experienced in it. To act otherwise, would be to obey the Evil One.

THIRD POINT.

The Soul when Disturbed should strive to Regain her Calm as soon as possible.

Whenever you commit a fault, great or small, were it even voluntary or a thousand times in the day, observe the following rules:

As soon as you perceive the fault, cast a glance upon your weakness. Turn humbly to God, and say to Him in peaceful, loving confidence: "Thou seest O my God! what I have done. Thou knowest of what I am capable. What can sin produce other than sin? But Thou hast granted me the grace of repentance. Pardon me also my fault, and grant me Thy assistance never more to offend Thee!"

Having prayed thus, lose no time in thinking whether or not God has forgiven you. Turn in humility and peace with your former confidence and tranquillity of mind to your occupations, and do not reflect upon what has occurred. Should you fall frequently, you must at the last fall do precisely what you did after the first. This will bring to you a twofold benefit: first, you will at every fall turn back to God, who, like a good Father, is always ready to receive you; and secondly, you lose no time in disquiet and vexation, which might so disturb the soul as to retard her return to peace and quiet. If they who, on account of their faults and failings, are so often disturbed and discouraged could comprehend rightly these secrets of the spiritual life, they would see how much time they waste, how much injury their agitation does them, and how different is their sad condition from that of a discreet, humble, and peace-loving heart.

FOURTH POINT.[1]

Of Watchfulness over Self.

That we may learn to watch over ourselves, and yet not be too much occupied with self, the following remarks will be of use:

The wise and prudent traveller is attentive to his steps. He carefully examines the road before him, though without turning to consider the progress he has made; for that would be a loss of time.

A soul that God really leads by the hand (for we are not speaking here of those that have not yet learned to walk—those that are still seeking the way) should, in peaceful and child-like simplicity, carefully watch over her steps. This watchfulness must be limited to the present; and it must consist solely in attention to the will of God, and not in returns upon self. We need not try to obtain certain knowledge of the state in which we are, since God does not will such certainty to be ours.

Would we walk unremittingly in the presence of God? Then we should never cease watching over ourselves. Such vigilance is, however, full of simplicity, love, peace, and disinterestedness; whilst that which seeks only satisfaction with self leads to nothing but pain and disquiet. We must walk in the light of the Lord, and not according to our own illumination. We cannot consider the sanctity of God without experiencing a holy horror for the slightest fault. Walking in the presence of God and with interior recollection, we must also attend to examination of conscience. This prevents carelessness, and makes confession easier. But this examination of conscience must be made simply, gently, and without disquieting returns upon self.

[1] This point is from Fénelon.

FIFTH POINT.[1]

Of Mistrust of Self.

Mistrust in one's own strength is so necessary in the spiritual life, that without it one cannot overcome the least perverse inclination. We must be thoroughly impressed with this truth, for we are only too prone, though without good reason, to esteem ourselves something. Self-confidence is a consequence of our nature's corruption; but the more natural it is to us, the more difficult it is to understand it. God, who sees all, abhors it. He would have us convinced of the truth that we possess no grace or virtue that does not proceed from Him, the source of all good, and that without Him we are not able even to think anything pleasing to Him. Mistrust of one's own strength is a gift of Heaven, which God grants to souls whom He loves—sometimes by holy inspirations, or again by hard interior sufferings; sometimes by almost unconquerable temptations, or finally by means known to Himself alone. Notwithstanding the gratuitousness of the favor, it is His divine wish that we do on our part what we can to acquire this virtue. It will infallibly be granted to us if we make use of the four following means:

The first is often to place before our eyes our lowliness and nothingness, acknowledging that of our own natural strength we are incapable of accomplishing anything good and meritorious for heaven.

The second means is that we humbly and earnestly pray to God for this essential virtue; for He only can give it to us. We must acknowledge that it is not only wanting to us, but also that of ourselves we are quite incapable of acquiring it. We must kneel down at Our Lord's feet, and implore it of Him with a firm confidence of being heard. Lastly, we must patiently await the granting of our peti-

[1] This and the two following points are taken from the "Spiritual Combat" of Scupoli.

tion, and persevere in prayer as long as His divine providence pleases.

The third means is to accustom ourselves gradually to diffidence in self, to the unreliableness of our own judgment, to fear the violence of our evil inclinations and the innumerable multitude of our enemies. The latter are without comparison more artful, stronger, and more skilful in the combat than we; yes, they even change themselves into angels of light, to lay snares for us in the way of salvation.

The fourth means is, after every fault to turn our gaze inward and consider carefully the extent of our weakness. God permits our faults only that, being enlightened by a new light, we may more sincerely acknowledge that we are miserable creatures, that we may learn to despise ourselves and arrive at the sincere desire of being despised by others. Without this last means we cannot attain to mistrust of self, a virtue that rests on humility and the experimental knowledge of one's own misery.

He who would draw near to the Fountain of Light, the Uncreated Truth, must know himself thoroughly. He must not be like the proud, who open their eyes upon themselves only when they have unexpectedly fallen into some shameful sin. When milder means did not effect what His mercy intended, God permits them such experience in order to cure their presumption.

God ordinarily allows every man to fall more or less, according as he is more or less proud; yes, I even dare to assert, were one as free from pride as was the Blessed Virgin he would never fall. Turn your faults into a means of gaining self-knowledge. Ardently implore the Lord to enlighten you, that, seeing yourself as you are in His eyes, you may no longer entertain so high an opinion of your own virtue. Otherwise you will relapse into the same fault,—yes, into still greater ones, perhaps, that might endanger even the salvation of your soul.

SIXTH POINT.

Of Confidence in God.

We have shown that mistrust of self is extremely necessary in the spiritual combat. But if this virtue stood alone and unsupported, one would be disarmed and vanquished by the enemy, and would soon take to flight. It must stand side by side with confidence in God; for the Lord is the source of all good, and from Him alone must we expect victory. If it be true that of ourselves we are nothing, then only prospect of dangerous defeat is before us, and we have every reason to distrust our own strength. But if, convinced of our weakness, we generously confide in God, we shall with His assistance gain great advantages over our enemy, since confidence calls down the grace of Heaven upon us. Four means are at our command for the acquiring of this most necessary virtue of confidence:

The first is, that we humbly ask it of God. The second, that with eyes of faith we attentively consider the infinite power and wisdom of the Creator, to whom nothing is impossible, whose goodness knows no bounds, and who, from the overflowing measure of His love for His servants, is at every moment ready to send them all possible graces, whereby they may lead a pious Christian life and gain the victory over self.

The only thing that He expects from them is, that they have recourse to Him in perfect confidence. And what is more just? For long years the Good Shepherd has unweariedly pursued the lost sheep. He follows after it on hard, thorny paths, with exertion so great as to cost Him His blood and His life. If at last He sees the sheep returning with the design of following His guidance, will He turn away the eyes of His mercy, because its sincere and upright will is still weak? Will He not rather carry it back on His shoulders to the sheepfold? O let us not doubt of this! The Lord with joy inexpressible takes up the strayed sheep, and invites the angels of heaven to rejoice with Him.

And if He so assiduously sought the drachma of the Gospel as to search the whole house to find it, will He repel the soul that, like the sheep strayed from the fold, makes ready to return to Him? Christ is the Spouse of our soul. He continually knocks at the door of our heart, and desires nothing more ardently than to find an entrance. His greatest happiness is to give Himself to us, and to heap His favors upon us. Now, how can we believe that He will refuse us entrance if we rightfully long for such a grace? Let us open wide the door of our heart and implore Him to make us worthy of His visit.

The third means to attain confidence is to recall frequently such passages of the Holy Scripture as excite to this virtue. Passages of this nature are not difficult to find. The Word of God repeats to us a thousand times the consoling assurance that he who confides in the Almighty shall not be confounded.

The fourth means by which we acquire confidence in God as well as mistrust in ourselves is, that in every good work, every temptation, and upon all occasions in general, we fix our eyes on the one hand upon our own weakness, and on the other upon the goodness, the omnipotence, the wisdom of God. We shall then meet courageously the most laborious works and the severest combats, for the fear of our own weakness vanishes before confidence in the assured help of the Lord. These two weapons united to prayer place us in a position to undertake the greatest enterprises and gain the grandest victories.

SEVENTH POINT.

A Mark of True Confidence in God and Mistrust of Self.

A soul filled with self easily believes that she is in possession of both the virtues mentioned above. But she not unfrequently errs, and the error is most clearly evident when she has committed a fault. If she is then disturbed and troubled, if she loses all hope of progress in virtue, it is a sure sign that she had placed her confidence in herself, and not in God. And the greater the discouragement, the less of these virtues does she possess.

If, on the contrary, the soul that mistrusts herself and places her confidence in God commits a fault, she is by no means astonished, disquieted, and vexed; for she immediately recognizes it as a consequence of her weakness and her want of confidence in God. Her fall, on the contrary, increases her mistrust in her own strength and her reliance upon the assistance of the Almighty. The soul abhors her sin above all things, she condemns the passions or bad habits that gave rise to it, she is keenly pained at having offended her God; but her sorrow is peaceful. It does not prevent her from returning to her accustomed exercises and pursuing her enemies till death.

Disquietude after the commission of a fault is sometimes looked upon as a virtue. This is an error. Although such disquietude may be accompanied by some regret for sin, it nevertheless originates in secret self-conceit, springing from vain self-confidence. When a soul that thought herself strong in virtue, one that despised temptation, is taught by experience that she, like all others, is frail and sinful, she is astounded at her fault as at something quite extraordinary; she yields to anger and discouragement. And why? Because she sees her support, that is her self-confidence, destroyed.

This never happens to humble souls. They have no high opinion of themselves, they lean upon God alone. If they fall they are neither surprised nor disquieted; because they clearly see, by the true light that beams upon them, that their faults are a natural consequence of their own weakness and inconstancy.

EIGHTH POINT.[1]

How greatly Diffidence and Mistrust Offend the Lord and Injure the Soul.

We cannot too often impress upon pious souls the importance of guarding against discouragement, distrust, and sadness, as well as the necessity of preserving at all times and upon all occasions holy peace and joy. In a thousand places of the Sacred Scriptures the Holy Spirit repeats this admonition to us, as if very specially to direct our attention to it. By disquietude, fear, and dejection we in no way honor God. Such dispositions offend Him. They express doubt of His goodness, remove us from Him, and deprive us of His assistance. Our vain apprehensions may lead to God's really permitting the evil we dreaded to come upon us. Confidence in Him produces effects precisely opposite.

Peter walked with feet secure upon the stormy billows, so long as he remembered the goodness and omnipotence of Him whom he was going to meet. But he began to sink as soon as, terrified by the roaring of the storm, he trembled and wavered in confidence: "O thou of little faith! why didst thou doubt?"[2] "Woe to them that are faint-hearted, who believe not God: and therefore they shall not be protected by Him."[3] Our first duty is, therefore, to banish faint-heartedness, which deprives us of the divine protection, and is in consequence the cause of so many faults and sufferings. On the contrary, we must strengthen ourselves more and more in hope, the source of all good, of peace and joy: "Ye that fear the Lord, hope in Him: and mercy shall come to you for your delight."[4] "He that adoreth God with joy shall be accepted, and his prayer shall approach even to the clouds."[5] "Delight in the Lord, and He will give thee the requests of thy heart."[6]

---

[1] This point is taken from the "Treatise on Christian Hope," by Father Gaud, S. J.
[2] Matt. xiv. 31. [3] Ecclus. ii. 15. [4] Ecclus. ii. 9.
[5] Ecclus. xxxv. 20. [6] Ps. xxxvi. 4.

Various Instructions on Preserving Peace. 175

"The joyfulness of the heart is the life of a man, and a never-failing treasure of holiness."[1] "The sadness of the heart is every plague."[2] Sadness infuses grief and bitterness into every act, by filling the mind with dark pictures and gloomy thoughts; weakening confidence in God, diminishing love for Him; destroying benevolence, compassion, and patience toward the neighbor; creating anger, impatience, hatred, and jealousy: and it goes so far as even to undermine the health of the body. In a word, it inflicts deadly wounds. Ah, then, suffer not thy soul to be sad, and put away gloomy thoughts! "Have pity on thy own soul, pleasing God: gather up thy heart in His holiness, and drive away sadness far from thee; for sadness hath killed many, and there is no profit in it."[3]

Attend to the fact that the last care of Jesus Christ was to impress His disciples with this consoling truth. In their person He exhorts all believers to take it to heart. In His most admirable discourse after the Last Supper, He left us His peace and His joy as an heirloom. He explicitly commanded His disciples to banish every fear and disquiet from their heart, repeating to them: "Let not your heart be troubled. You believe in God, believe also in Me."[4] In him who does believe every apprehension should cease. God is our Father, and His only-begotten Son our Mediator! "Peace I leave with you, My peace I give unto you: not as the world giveth, do I give unto you. Let not your heart be troubled, nor let it be afraid."[5] "These things I have spoken to you that My joy may be in you, and your joy may be filled."[6] "Ask and you shall receive, that your joy may be full."[7] "These things I have spoken to you, that in Me you may have peace. In the world you shall have distress: but have confidence, I have overcome the world,"[8] for Myself and for you. And when the Lord gave Himself to prayer for Himself and for those whom

[1] Ecclus. xxx. 23.   [2] Ecclus. xxv. 17.   [3] Ecclus. xxx. 24-25.
[4] John xiv. 1.   [5] John xiv. 27.   [6] John xv. 11.
[7] John xvi. 24.   [8] John xvi. 33.

the Father has given Him, turning to His own heavenly Father, He said: "And now I come to Thee: and these things I speak in the world, that they may have My joy filled in themselves."[1] The Apostles, impressed by these teachings of their Lord, never wearied repeating them to the faithful both in their words and in their epistles.

[1] John xvii. 13.

CHAPTER II.

Of Faults Springing from Weakness.

FIRST POINT.[1]

One should without Disquiet or without Mistrust Return to God when he has Fallen into Venial Sin.

WHEN the fiend cannot induce a soul to become careless in the commission of venial sin, when he sees that she hates and despises it, he tries to mingle a purely natural sorrow, a purely human sadness, in her contrition, by which he harms her almost as much as if he had succeeded in his first design. True sorrow, such as the Holy Ghost imparts to the soul, is rich in consolation; for it holds in itself the hope of pardon, and gives us even new strength to labor more assiduously at rooting out our faults. Purely natural pain, merely human sorrow which the devil stirs up, fills the soul, on the contrary, with perplexity and anguish, robs her of the hope of improving or beginning anew, and often exposes her to still greater faults.

There are many Christians who lead an otherwise pious, upright life, but who do not wish to understand this truth. Seeing themselves constantly subject to venial sin, they grow discouraged and vexed with self. Sometimes they complain of their evil nature; sometimes of the fickleness of their good resolutions; again of the defects or utter uselessness of their confessions, prayers, and Communions. They fill their mind with the thought that they will never be better; they sadden their heart with these and similar

[1] This and the two following points are from "Treatise on Christian Hope," by Father Gaud, S.J.

conceits, till works of piety and spiritual exercises become painful,—nay, even loathsome to them. They lose their time in trifling and anxious speculations upon what took place in their soul during the temptation; they put to themselves a score of questions as to how many minutes they resisted, whether their consent was immediate, whether with full knowledge, etc. They recommence this examination of conscience over and over again, becoming less satisfied with themselves the longer they proceed, and thereby increasing their interior disquiet.

Such persons, notwithstanding, go frequently to confession; but their heart is so full of doubt, anxiety, and sadness, that they are after it as much disturbed as before. They are in constant dread of not having rightly and minutely accused themselves, or of not being understood. Their whole life becomes an unbroken chain of suffering, disquiet, and apprehension, from which they derive neither profit nor advantage. They are, on the contrary, disheartened by these trials, which hinder their progress in Christian perfection, the essence of which consists in the love of God and confidence in His goodness.

True sorrow infused by the Holy Ghost into the soul generates no evil consequences. Such sorrow is a great grace from God. It is impossible for it to create discouragement in the soul, or hold her back from recurring with entire confidence to the Divine Goodness. It is impossible that it should infuse into her nothing but anxiety, distress, and impatience. True repentant sorrow casts the soul into the arms of God, where she finds strength and comfort. If for a moment perplexed, yet her embarrassment soon changes to confidence, which in turn attracts the divine mercy. The evil effects of the sorrow of which we have just spoken must not be ascribed to the Holy Ghost. They spring, undoubtedly, from the enemy of souls, and are strengthened by pride and self-love. We must heartily detest our sins, since they are opposed to the justice and holiness of God, to which they offer infinite injury; but we

Faults Springing from Weakness.

must consider, also, what thanks we owe the Divine Goodness, whose clemency has guarded us from greater falls, from eternal woe. After every misstep we must resolve anew to wage war against our evil inclinations, and, with ever-increasing courage, pursue them to death. Finally, we must with unshaken confidence seek refuge in God, and never abandon the hope that He will grant us the victory when His greater glory and our salvation call for it. He will either free us from our faults or by means of them render us humble. Let us confide in Him, and He will grant us the grace to live and die in His love, and in hatred of sin. "Fight like a true warrior; and if sometimes through human frailty you are defeated, renew your courage, and hope for greater graces from Me!"[1]

God commands us to hate our evil inclinations, and the multiplied sins springing from them; but He desires us to do so through love of Him, and not from pride. He wills that we repent of them, but only in such a way as will lead to our improvement and sincere return to Himself. He forbids us to yield to the sorrow that makes us sink only the deeper. An upright, humble soul hates her sins, because they are contrary to the justice and holiness of God; but she loves the humiliations that come to her from them, for justice requires that she should make use of this deserved humiliation, bear it patiently, and profit by her own shame to repair her fault. But a proud soul thinks little of all this. That her sin opposes the Divine Justice, matters not to her. She sees only the shame and abjection that her faults bring upon her; hence her impatience, her grief, her anxiety, her discouragement. But this is not that true hatred for sin which God demands. Instead of atoning for the fault, it increases it. Let us not be astonished, let us not be dejected, if we also, after long years in God's service, perceive in ourselves so much slothfulness, misery, and weakness. Astonishment or discouragement would evince our little progress in self-knowledge and self-hatred. It

[1] Following of Christ, Bk. III. c. 6.

would prove that we do not yet know how to rise after a fault, and that we are far from giving due honor to the goodness of God and the grace of Jesus Christ, as we are in duty bound.

After having committed a fault, think of God and not of yourself. Honor the Divine Truth and Justice. Remain humbly before God, acknowledging that He has nothing to expect from your perversity. Thank Him that you have not sunk still deeper. Be cautious in guarding yourself from the snares of your cunning enemy, who, making use of your chagrin and false shame, would drag you still deeper into hell. Rise quietly from your fall, and be assured that, by giving vent to anger against yourself, you commit a greater fault than that which you bewail. A child that has offended his mother by word or deed would outrage her maternal heart if he despaired of pardon or feared that she would disinherit him. Such a suspicion would certainly cause the mother more suffering than the fault itself. Be persuaded, then, that discouragement, lack of confidence, and mistrust of God's goodness and help injure and dishonor Him more than the sins which arouse such sentiments.

Do you feel restless, ashamed, and discouraged after a fault? Then let your first care be to regain peace and tranquillity of heart. Turn your thoughts from what has happened, and consider the infinite mercy of God, as well as the proofs which He has ever given you of it in preference to so many others. Having by such consoling considerations restored the peace of your soul, think seriously upon your offence, in order to repair it in the manner suggested above. So long as disquiet lasts, you are not in a condition to reason upon your fault, as is useful and salutary for you to do; and instead of repairing it, you would commit some new and perhaps more grievous one.

As soon as you feel disturbed, recall the fact that it is God's will that you resist such emotions as you would any other temptation. Such disturbance would hinder your clearly understanding the truth and acting with the Spirit of the Lord, whilst at the same time you open the door to the suggestions of the Evil One. The devil knows this; therefore he is always on the alert to cast you into disquiet and keep you there. Be not deceived by him, nor yet by the appearance of false humility, or the fear of God. Disquiet is always dangerous, and it is our first and most important duty to avoid it. Yes, even when imposing a heavy penance upon ourselves in expiation of a serious transgression, it must be with that interior peace which alone can enable us to see what is truly good for us.

"We preach to worldlings the fear of the Lord," says Father Huby, a very skilful guide of souls, "but I preach to religious and to pious souls confidence in God. I exhort them to take refuge in the Lord, particularly if they have fallen into some fault. I would that their confidence were as great at such moments as it is after Holy Communion. After the commission of sin courage is even more necessary to us than before; for then, being weaker, we need more grace and strength. Confidence in God gives both.

"We could not vex the Evil One more than by clothing ourselves with confidence after a fall. His aim is to hold us captive in constraint of mind which amounts almost to despair. This is not one fault only, but a whole series of faults. To frustrate this design of the devil, we must arouse as strong a confidence in our heart as possible.

"Why should one be discouraged if sometimes overcome? Our adversary the devil never ceases his attacks, although a thousand times repulsed in the same temptations. As far as his own state is concerned, he is sunk in despair; but he never loses hope of casting us into perdition. He expects to conquer by his own malice and our weakness. Why, then, should we not hope all from the goodness of God, from the assistance of His grace, which is infinitely more powerful than the snares of the evil spirit?

"We practise confidence in God more perfectly when

the dangers and sufferings to which we are exposed are greatest.

"The more fully a soul gives herself up to the Lord, the better will she be guarded by Him!"

SECOND POINT.

Frequent Relapses into Venial Sins are not always a Sign of Insufficient Sorrow for them.

We now come to a point which is usually a source of disquiet, distrust, and discouragement to anxious souls. What follows applies only to those who sincerely love God, and honestly aim at avoiding venial sin. These, in spite of their relapses, should not imagine that their sorrow for sin and their good resolutions against it were only specious and unmeaning protestations. There is a great difference between contrition for mortal sin and that excited by venial sin; between hatred of the first and horror for the second, between the determination to avoid the one and the resolution not to commit the other.

We cannot truly atone for one of our mortal sins without doing penance for them all. One cannot be sincerely converted to God if he hates only some of his mortal sins, and does not detest them all. One cannot worthily confess if he resolves to refrain only from some mortal sins, and does not extend this resolution to all. In the same way, one mortal sin cannot be remitted without all being pardoned. Mortal sin is incompatible with a life of grace, a child of God, and an heir of heaven. Every mortal sin separates the soul from God, kills her, makes her deserving of condemnation to hell. He that would be converted to God, let him do penance, and redeem his soul from death and hell. He must necessarily hate and detest sin; he must be firmly resolved to avoid all sins without exception. The determination not to commit mortal sin, can and should be carried into effect, since every Christian can and should keep himself free from it. "Therefore," says St. Augustine, "a

Christian who is pure in faith and firm in hope commits no such sins."[1] In the same sense is to be understood what St. John says: "Every one that abideth in Christ sins not,"[2] and "Whosoever is born of Christ sins not."[3]

It is quite different with the state of true servants of God who commit venial sin only. The resolution to avoid such sins cannot be kept perfectly; for it is of faith that the just with the help of ordinary grace are not in a condition always to avoid venial sin. The ever Blessed Virgin alone enjoyed this privilege. In regard to venial sins, our resolution to strive to avoid them consists more in an upright will and hearty desire to commit them no more, than in the hope of never falling into any; for we must believe that, in spite of all our watchfulness, devotion, and efforts we cannot preserve ourselves entirely from them. Pious souls, therefore, should neither be discouraged nor waver in confidence, although constantly falling into those venial sins of which they have so often accused themselves. "The just man," says the Holy Scripture, "falls seven times, and rises again."[4]

It is enough if we hate sin and bewail it, if we humble ourselves for it, and always endeavor to avoid it as much as possible. We may experience the heartiest, the most sincere sorrow, and yet relapse often enough; for whilst hating the weakness, one may at the same time remain weak. Even those that are so weak as to retain a deliberate attachment to some venial sin should not lose courage. Without much time and labor one will not succeed in overcoming every attachment to evil.

They that live in the greatest retirement from creatures and worldly affairs are even by this more exposed to relapse into the same sins. Since their exercises and occupations are always the same, their faults likewise are always the same. In general, our sins change their nature with the change of occasion. Similar occasions give rise to the

---

[1] August. de verbis Apost. serm. 181, n. 8.   [2] I. John iii. 6.
[3] Conc. Trid. sess. 6, can. 23.   [4] Prov. xxiv. 16.

same temptations and the same sins. This usually happens to souls that most sincerely detest venial sin, and are most earnestly striving after perfection.

But on this account we dare not believe that all our good purposes in regard to venial sins, all our watchfulness, labor, and prayer by which we implore to be freed from them, are lost and useless. To harbor such a thought would be to yield to one of the most dangerous insinuations of the Evil One. Our exertions all tend to procure for us the greatest blessings. God preserves us by them not only from many venial sins, but perhaps even from grievous ones. In consideration of our prayers and efforts to be free from daily faults, God will at the hour of our death really free us from them; and, in reward for our hunger and thirst after justice during this life, He will fill us with good things in the next.

THIRD POINT.

How God permits the Venial Sins of the Just and all their other Imperfections to Redound to their Greatest Good.

"The spirit of those that fear God is sought after, and by His regard shall be blessed. . . . For their hope is on Him that saveth them, and the eyes of God are upon them that love Him. . . . A preservation from stumbling, and a help from falling, He raiseth up the soul and enlighteneth the eyes, and giveth health and life and blessing,"[1] even making use of their weakness in daily faults to increase their strength. Thus He fulfils the words of the prophet: "When the righteous fall, he shall not be bruised: for the Lord putteth His hand under him." The Lord holds His hand under him that his fall may be less dangerous, and that he may rise more vigorous than before.

Deep and firmly rooted humility is the first and principal advantage to be derived from our faults. The gravest and

[1] Ecclus. xxxiv. 14, 15, 20.

Faults Springing from Weakness. 185

most dangerous of all evils is pride, and the vain complacency we secretly take in our virtues. To protect us from this deadly malady of the soul, God permits in us so many faults and imperfections. They serve to keep down the temptation to esteem ourselves above others. If, in spite of our great misery and many sins, it still costs us unspeakable efforts to humble ourselves, what a snare would not a superfluity of spiritual gifts be to us ? God dispenses to His servants His graces with weight and measure. He instils into them through the Holy Spirit a great longing for perfection, whilst permitting them to be tempted, to experience in themselves naught but obstacles to the fulfilment of their pious design, and to fall short in the rapid progress they desire to make. By this means they are, however, preserved from pride and vain self-complacency.

But how is this ardent longing after perfection which God Himself instils into His servants, those sighs and incessant prayers by which the Holy Spirit in them pleads for exemption from their sins and imperfections, compatible with the promise contained in these words of Our Lord: "Ask, and you shall receive ?"[1] Is it not written: "The Lord hath heard the desire of the poor: Thy ear hath heard the preparation of their heart."[2] Is it not also written, says St. Augustine: "Before they call I will hear; as they are yet speaking, I will hear."[3] "It is true," answers this holy Father of the Church; "but by deferring assistance God really helps, and precisely by means of this delay. He fears that He may not grant perfect health by a too ready compliance with our petitions." If He gave us at once all that we desire and long for, we should experience neither struggle nor opposition to good, we should ascribe the facility with which we receive God's gifts to our own strength or power. Such pride would be an obstacle to perfect victory. God the Master acts like a skilful physician. The latter, though forbidding his convalescing patient certain food, though refusing his petition for it, is really

[1] John xvi. 24. [2] Ps. Heb x. 17. [3] Is. lxv. 24.

granting it; not indeed according to his patient's desire, but agreeably to reason and the true interest of the sick man. One may even say that he grants the invalid's dearest wish, since a reasonable patient desires above all else his restoration to health. A skilful surgeon will sometimes keep a wound open in order to draw off poisonous humors and secure the recovery of the sufferer. In like manner God deals with His servants. He permits them to retain certain weaknesses and infirmities. He does not heal their wounds at once, because He knows well that a sudden restoration to perfect health would rouse in them a temptation to pride, and vain self-complacency would endanger the loss of merit previously acquired. Hence He allows them to advance in perfection only by degrees in order thereby to ground them in humility. He gives them His grace sparingly to secure to them the possession of the more essential virtues.

God permits the light of His countenance to shine upon us; and we are enlightened, we are filled with consolation and joy. He hides Himself; and dryness, hunger, and loathing are our portion. He turns to us again, and with Him return peace and enjoyment. "Thou visitest him early in the morning, and Thou provest him suddenly."[1] He leaves us impetuosity of passion, inconstancy of humor, mutability of desires, thoughts, and sentiments; and by all these variable emotions He leads us to unalterable calm and equanimity of soul, and that to such a degree that nothing can any longer take us by surprise, nothing can henceforth move us. We judge of all things equally, we despise and humble ourselves in everything; we depend no longer upon ourselves, nor upon our own disposition of soul; and at all times and under all circumstances we cling unalterably to God as to our only support.

Whoever is rightly penetrated with these sentiments is not hurt by falls. His faults render him humble and grateful; consequently, purer and more just. There are

[1] Job vii. 18.

certain lotions which are apparently calculated only to soil whatever they touch, and yet they really cleanse from stains. Precisely thus do pious souls make use of the faults and sins that so often creep into their best actions. They purify their souls with them from pride, their greatest fault. It is ordained that during this life the sight of our virtues should soil us, and that of our sins purify. "Not unfrequently is it the case," says St. Gregory, "that they who see themselves before God stained with many sins, are richly adorned with the costly garment of deep humility." And St. Bernard says: "Thus falleth the just on the hand of the Lord, and thus is seen the astonishing wonder, that even his sin contributes to make him more just." "For we know," writes St. Paul, "that to those who love God all works together unto good." Do not our own faults tend to our greatest advantage when they make us more humble and watchful? And if humility sustain him who falls, is he not upheld by God's own hand? "I was moved and dejected," says the prophet, "and already I fell; but he that cast me down has gained nothing, for the Lord upheld me."[1] Who would not here admire the goodness of God, who, so to say, at His own cost, that is, by the offences which we offer Him, heals us and leads us onward?

Humility is the most excellent advantage that we can derive from our venial sins. But it is not the only one; for God knows how, in consideration of our weakness, to impart to us several others. By our frequent failings He awakens, maintains, and increases in us the spirit of prayer. In this land of probation prayer should be our only consolation, our greatest happiness; yet, alas, of what coldness and negligence are we not guilty during this holy exercise! For this reason God makes use of our sins and temptations to preserve us from tepidity. When the sense of our miseries casts us down, then do we cry to God with all the power of our soul. As soon as suffering and danger cease

[1] Bern. in Ps. xc.

to oppress us, we likewise cease to pray with fervor. Either our misery must continue, or new afflictions must come upon us, to force us, as it were, to take refuge in God, to flee to Him for help. God desires that constant intercourse should be maintained between His goodness and our weakness. Hence in this life He does not endue our souls with perfect strength : He dispenses His graces to us but by degrees.

The fervor of penance shone with special brilliancy in the saints directly after the persecutions of the early Christians. The happiness of sacrificing self to the Lord by martyrdom, of washing away sin in their own blood, was denied to Christians after that date ; wherefore they sought to indemnify themselves by another kind of martyrdom, which, if it did not approach the first in barbarity, far outstripped it in duration. They offered themselves, by a long life of austerity and expiation, as holocausts to the Lord. But what induced them to wage so cruel a war against themselves, and thus become their own persecutors ? Nothing else than the venial sins which they discovered in their lives. They bewailed their least faults as others regret not even the greatest transgressions. Zeal for God's glory and justice consumed them, armed them against self, and led them gladly to devote themselves to a slow death, an uninterrupted martyrdom. Had they been free from sin, had they remarked no failings in their life, no stains upon their soul, the Church would have lacked her fervent penitents, and heaven their gleaming crowns. When a sinner grieves over his offences and atones for them all heaven rejoices with great joy, and by his penitential fervor he merits a place in the kingdom of God. "What joy," says St. Gregory, "shall there not be above over a just man who so honestly bewails his least sins and so severely atones for them ! To what glory does he not merit to be raised !" This is certainly not one of the least advantages which God permits to spring from the venial sins of the righteous. But there are several others yet to be enumerated.

Among all the Divine Commandments not one weighs more heavily upon our nature than that which directs us to love our enemies, to forgive unreservedly those who have offended or injured us in any way. Now, God, who Himself has mercy upon our weakness, makes use of our venial sins to render the fulfilment of this commandment sweet and easy. For who would not joyfully pardon his neighbor every contradiction and mortification when he thinks that by this means he himself will be absolved by God from the penalty due his own sins? What one man has to pardon another is well-nigh nothing; but the debt man owes to his Creator is infinite. Is it not, therefore, to be one's own enemy to refuse so advantageous an exchange? Let us not neglect to purchase the infinite mercy of God by our sweet and gentle mercy toward our brethren.

We are constrained to bear patiently all our own defects and sins, the inconstancy of our mind, the revolts of our passions, the changeableness of our humors, our constant interior rebellion. Should not this sad necessity make us indulgent toward the weaknesses of others? Should we not bear in others what we must endure in ourselves? You command yourself something, and you will not obey; you so often impose silence upon your thoughts, desires, and passions, and yet they resist you, so that "you do not that which you would."[1] How unjust, therefore, to think it strange that others should oppose your wishes! The Almighty, the Creator, suffers a creature to oppose His will and transgress His Commandments; and you, poor wretched worm, will you not endure that another worm like yourself should oppose you and resist your will?

We have now pointed out the chief advantages that the just may draw from their faults and venial sins. All these benefits are not the consequences of sin itself, but the effects of the infinite mercy of God and the grace of Jesus Christ, who in His goodness knows how to turn evil itself to our sanctification. Manure is nothing but foulness and cor-

[1] Galatians v. 17.

ruption, as St. Bernard very aptly remarks. And yet it enables the farmer and gardener to produce most beautiful flowers and the richest harvests of fruits. Even so does God make use of the sins and imperfections of His elect to bring forth the rarest and richest fruits of virtue in their souls. It will be given them to share in these graces if they hate their sins, humble themselves for them, take pains to uproot them, meanwhile losing neither courage nor confidence in God's goodness and Christ's grace. In this precisely, and in nothing else, according to St. Augustine, does the perfection of the just consist during this life. This holy Father of the Church has, in one of his works shown that perfection is not reached by aiming at a faultless righteousness altogether unattainable in this life; but rather in the constant remission of venial sins, and in the care to make use of them for advancement in virtue. All that has been said in this chapter will lead to the understanding of what is found in the writings of various teachers of the interior life; namely, that he who commits the fewest venial sins is not the most perfect. It may very easily happen that some one, owing to more frequent occasions, to his ardent temperament, his employment, or surroundings, may commit trivial faults more frequently than others; and yet, before God, be purer and more perfect than they that commit fewer faults. The most perfect souls are they who acknowledge and lament their faults most sincerely; who seriously endeavor to cut off their source, which are pride and self-love; and who make use of their sins to advance in humility and gratitude to the All-merciful God.

FOURTH POINT.[1]

Of Bearing with Self and our Daily Faults and Weaknesses.

It may easily be seen that there are many faults that are in various degrees deliberate, although not committed with the express design of offending God.

A friend will often upbraid another with a fault not intentionally committed to injure, although, perhaps, it may have been calculated to harm. In like manner God is displeased with faults against Himself. They are, in fact, deliberate; for although reflection is wanting, the will is active. It is in opposition to a certain interior light that should suffice to make us avoid the fault.

Such faults pious souls often commit. Deliberate venial sins, however, are rare when the soul has once given herself truly to God.

In proportion as the clear light of grace increases in us, our slightest transgressions appear to us graver; just as objects are dimly seen at night, but gradually become distinct as the sun rises above the horizon. Be convinced, then, that by the increase of interior light the imperfections you now observe in yourself will appear much greater and more malicious. You will also discover a thousand others in your heart that you would not otherwise have known. Yes, you will there find the very weaknesses that are most calculated to rob you of confidence in your own strength. But these painful experiences should not discourage. They should serve merely to divest of self-confidence. Nothing proves the true progress of a soul more than the power to bear the sight of her misery without disquiet or discouragement.

This is an important rule: Never commit a fault of which you are aware beforehand; and courageously bear the penalty of humiliation, as soon as you perceive that you have been so unfaithful.

[1] This point is from Fénelon.

If you see a fault before committing it, beware of resisting the Spirit of God. He warns you interiorly, and opposition would stifle His call of grace. Faults of inadvertence and weakness are nothing in comparison with those that arise from disregarding the voice of the Holy Spirit, who makes Himself heard in the secret depths of the heart.

But the faults of which you become conscious after commission will never be repaired by disquiet and vexation. On the contrary, such vexation is the clamoring of pride over what has confused you. After such faults, simply and quietly humble yourself. I say quietly, for to accept humiliation unwillingly and ungraciously is not to humble one's self. Disapprove and bewail your faults imposing some penance suited to the state of your soul, and do not seek consolation in vain excuses and palliations. Look at yourself before God in all your misery, without bitterness and without discouragement. Taste and enjoy in peace your own abjection. Thus will you draw from the serpent the remedy for its poison. Confusion borne patiently after little faults is to the soul a preservative from mortal sin. He who struggles against humiliations shows that the virtue of humility is wanting.

Do you wish to know whether your former confessions were good? Then, do not ask yourself whether you have forgotten any faults in them, but whether you have sincerely accused yourself of all that you knew. Light was not given you then as now; therefore you could not know all your evil inclinations. The more pure light streams into your soul, the more convinced you become that your depravity is greater than you believed. Be not astonished nor discouraged. It is not that you are worse now than formerly: on the contrary, you are advancing, for to your consolation be it said, we become aware of our evils only when they begin to heal. So long as your wound is not doing so, you do not feel its grievousness. Whilst you float with the stream, you do not notice the movement of the water. It is only when you begin to go against the current that you experience the force of the waves.

FIFTH POINT.

The Faults of our Neighbor should Disturb our Peace as Little as the Imperfections Found in every Human Virtue.

He has not yet sufficiently fathomed his own misery, and that of mankind in general, who is scandalized at the weakness and corruption of his fellow-men. Expect nothing good of them; then the evil in them will not surprise you. Do not indulge the delusion that humanity is of much account; but be persuaded that it is nothing, and less than nothing. Why wonder that a bad tree bears bad fruit? Rather wonder much more that Jesus Christ, upon whom as wild shoots we are engrafted, should permit us to bring forth, instead of our own bitter fruits, the sweet fruits of virtue.

Be not deceived! Every human virtue is tainted with self-esteem and self-confidence; but notwithstanding it still remains virtue. When you see in the same person little faults mingled with high and interior devotion, do not think his piety is not genuine, do not mistrust the sentiments or undertakings of such a person. Your own piety remains, indeed, both good and praiseworthy, in spite of the commingling with it of much self-love and impetuosity. And if that person of whom we speak were to express his sentiments to you regarding his faults, you would see that they spring much more from bad direction than from evil intention.

Zeal against the faults of others is in itself a great fault. To despise another on account of his weaknesses evinces a weakness that does not sufficiently know itself—a species of pride which soars aloft in order to observe human misery; whereas to measure it correctly it should be viewed from a level stand-point.

You fear that the knowledge and experience of human frailty might lead to contempt for the whole human race. This, in a certain sense, is much to be desired; but you must also acknowledge the good that God mixes with it. Alas! there are but few who without prejudice can view this combination of good and evil. Be convinced of this truth, that it was the enemy who sowed the bad seed among the good. The servant wanted to go and gather it up, but the good man of the house said: "No, suffer both to grow until the harvest."[1]

The important point is not to let such an aspect discourage and render us too distrustful. Many by nature open and confiding, become more close and distrustful than any others after the frequent and bitter experience of having their candor and openness betrayed. But that is going too far. God has always some true and upright servants. If these do not do all they should, compared with others they still do much, according to their strength and ability. They discern their imperfections, humble themselves for them, and struggle against them; and though slowly, they amend them. They give God the glory of what they do, and they call themselves to severe account for what they leave undone. God is satisfied with this, and you ought to be so too.

When you perceive in any quarter that God should be more perfectly served, then, without rule or measure, do you strive perfectly to honor Him in spirit and in truth. Such honor leaves to the creature nothing for self, and condemns as an infidelity every return upon self. O if once you found yourself in this holy, blessed state, you would be a stranger to every feeling of impatience at the faults of others! Your heart would be so enlarged that it would feel naught but indulgence and compassion for the narrow-mindedness of the selfish. Indeed, the more perfect one is himself, the milder he is toward his less perfect neighbor. It is only the imperfect who are impatient with the imper-

Faults Springing from Weakness. 195

fect. The Pharisee could not endure Mary Magdalen and the publican—those sinners whom Jesus Christ treated with divine gentleness and goodness. He who entirely renounces self, enters into the infinity of God, which is never wearied, never overcome. When will you acquire this freedom of the children of God, this broad, great-heartedness? Sensibility, or that tenderness of feeling which is so quickly wounded, and which is often falsely ascribed to a refined sentiment of virtue, originates in narrow-mindedness and love of self. He who no longer lives for self, lives wholly for his neighbor and for God. He, on the contrary, who lives for self gives himself to God and to his neighbor only in small and limited measure. The more he clings to self, the less he has to give to God. O may peace, truth, simplicity, freedom, pure faith, and unselfish love soon make of you a holocaust to the Lord!

A few of Fénelon's thoughts upon intercourse with the neighbor will aptly close this chapter: "You must despise the world," says he, "and still know how to hold necessary intercourse with it. You may renounce it from piety, but you must not withdraw from it through caprice or matter of convenience. Maintain, in conformity with duty, a reasonable intercourse with it. Neglect it not through sloth, but do not serve it through vanity. Preserve converse with men agreeably to the dispensations of Providence; but never build upon them, however good they may be. Never forget that God alone is the true friend of the heart. He alone is able to console. He alone understands all. The first low tone of your heart's cry to Him, He hears. None other than He can enter so fully into your needs and sufferings, and you are never burdensome to Him; therefore, choose Him for your friend, make Him your second self.[1] But as concerns your intercourse with men, be not too nice in your choice. If you find people peaceable and a little reasonable, be satisfied. Forget not, however, that we must be content with little and endure

[1] Following of Christ. Bk. I. c. 16.

much, if we would get along well with even the best people. Only under these conditions is harmony possible.

"In disagreements between you and your neighbor, you must always remember that to be in the right is the consideration that influences a Christian the least. The philosopher may indulge such a satisfaction. But to be in the right and to act as if one were not, to allow one's opponent to triumph on the side of injustice,—this means to overcome evil by good, and to secure peace for one's soul. No more convincing argument for your own vindication is required than the silent exterior acknowledgment that you are in the wrong. He who edifies does more for the truth than he who is zealous for the combat. Instead of trying to refute those that are in the wrong, it is better to pray for them. A stream flows much more rapidly when nothing is done to hold it back. Pray for those who are prejudiced against you, never become embittered against them, pity them, await their return to better feelings, and help to free them from their prejudices. One would not be human if he does not feel how easy it is to stray, and how much it costs to acknowledge this. The spirit of meekness, of indulgence, of patience and humility in examining the behavior of others toward us, secures us that peace of mind which is not compatible with the jealous, suspicious sensibilities of self-love."

CHAPTER III.

Of Discouragement.

FIRST POINT.

Evil Consequences of Discouragement.[1]

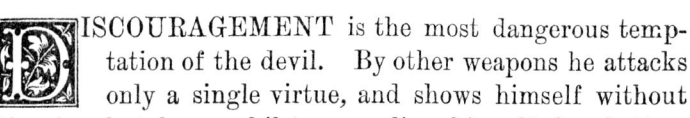

DISCOURAGEMENT is the most dangerous temptation of the devil. By other weapons he attacks only a single virtue, and shows himself without disguise; but here, whilst concealing himself, he shatters all the virtues to their very foundation. In other temptations one can easily discover his snares. In religion, often even in reason or in a Christian education, principles upon which to condemn the evil may be found. A glance at the sin that cannot be palliated; conscience raising its voice aloud; the spirit of religion awakened with increased strength—all these may serve to parry the insidious attack. But in discouragement nothing affords us assistance. We feel that our strength is not sufficient to accomplish what God demands of us; and yet confidence in help from above, which is so indispensable, is wanting. We feel so miserable that we desire to give up everything; and to this precisely the devil loves to lead us.

In other temptations one sees clearly the sinfulness of deliberate consent to their suggestions; but in discouragement the temptation takes a thousand different forms. One thinks he is acting upon a pure motive in harboring an emotion in which he sees no evil. And yet this feeling presents to the soul the persevering practice of virtue as something impossible, and thus exposes her to the danger of being carried away by her passions. Hence the importance of avoiding such a snare.

[1] This chapter is from a Treatise on Discouragement by Father Michel, S.J.

We must first be persuaded that discouragement is really a temptation, and nothing else. Every thought which is opposed to the Law of God, whether in itself or in its effects, is a manifest insinuation of the devil. We must weigh every suggestion according to this rule: Is the thought that troubles us against faith, hope, love, or any other virtue? If so, we must consider it a temptation, turn away from it, and awaken acts of the opposite virtue. Now the Divine Law obliges us equally to the practice of hope and confidence, as well as to that of faith and the other virtues. Contrary feelings and sentiments are, accordingly, not less prohibited than those that oppose the other virtues. A certain commandment requires us to make frequent acts of faith, hope, and love, thereby interdicting us every wilful, deliberate thought or reflection contrary to these three divine virtues. Discouragement is, consequently, of itself a temptation, in so far as it is opposed to Christian hope. But because of its evil consequences it is a particularly dangerous temptation, since it leads to the giving up of all pious exercises.

Would you prove this? Cast a glance at the ordinary doings of men. To what does not the hope of success, of happiness, of gain, of the gratification of desire or passion, not stimulate? It urges men to action, it animates them to exertion, it buoys them up in the combat. Take hope from man, and he will soon cease to aim at even what appears to him a desirable good. In the spiritual life discouragement works similar effects. It unfits men to reach their highest end.

A Christian soul that does not hope to succeed in the spiritual warfare, and acquire virtue, will undertake little or nothing, will never arm herself for the struggle. The most trifling exertion made in such a state only increases her weakness. By her discouragement she is, in anticipation, already half overcome. She allows herself to be conquered by the domineering sway of her passions. A glance at her weakness throws her into disquiet and irresolution.

Discouragement.

Wholly possessed by the thought of the exertion and weariness that the struggle entails, losing sight of the principles which should guide her, she miserably succumbs. Blinded by fear of defeat, she sees not the weapons that God presents her, with which she might so easily gain the victory; and thus she rushes unarmed into the snares of the enemy. She acts like a child that trembles in the presence of a giant, knowing not that a stone cast in the name of the Lord could bring him dead to the ground.

The despondent soul forgets that the goodness of her Heavenly Father is her protection and defence. To come out of the combat victorious she has only to flee to Him. . . .

Discouragement not only deprives the soul of discernment and reflection, but also robs her of the spirit of prayer. She then plunges headlong into the abyss. We can work out our salvation only with the assistance of divine grace, and it is but by uninterrupted and persevering prayer that we can obtain this grace. There is no means of good more recommended to us in the Holy Scripture than prayer. But the first effect of discouragement is to withdraw the soul from this holy exercise, under the pretext that she performs it so badly that it becomes, if not sinful, at least useless. Thus beset, the discouraged soul is defenceless in the hands of her enemy. Hence we may easily perceive the danger of this temptation.

The discouraged soul should never, never neglect prayer. There are among the various forms of prayer many, indeed, which presuppose interior peace. Such prayers are impossible so long as the storm of discouragement and despair agitate the soul. They are not at all to be recommended to a dejected soul. All that can be expected from her is the suppliant cry for help from a heart that feels its misery, that exclaims with the humble publican of the Gospel: "O Lord, have mercy on me, for I am a sinner!" or, still better, with our loving Saviour in His death agony: "Father, if it be possible, let this chalice pass from me;

but not My will, but Thine be done!"[1] Assuredly, an angel of the Lord will come down to strengthen the praying soul and, supported by grace, she will be able to resist the assaults of hell. But the most excellent of prayers in this temptation is always the awakening of hope, which is in direct opposition to it. Excite in the hour of combat repeated acts of confidence. If you tell me that your heart is so full of contrary sentiments that these acts appear to you false and hypocritical, I answer: "Your speech is vain, for there is question not of your sentiments but of your will." When the will is resolved into an act of hope, it makes use of the freedom given it. Such an act is highly meritorious before God, and at the same time the most effective means against the above-mentioned temptation. Daily experience proves this. Such a practice has often, in one day, freed a soul from the temptation to despair from which she had suffered for long years. Therefore, we cannot too urgently insist upon discouraged souls exercising frequent acts of hope.

SECOND POINT.

Why Discouragement occasions so much Harm.

Why does discouragement produce in the soul effects so sad? Listen to my answer to this question: "A disheartened soul is perfectly convinced of her oft-tried weakness; she feels keenly how hard it is to overcome herself, and how seldom she really does so. Wholly occupied with her own sad thoughts, she loses courage; she does nothing for God; she considers it labor lost to seek her refuge in the Lord; for she imagines that, in her present state, He would not even hear her. Strange effects of human pride, as if the good that we do and the happiness to which we aspire could be attributed to no one but ourselves. How greatly is such a state in opposition with the words of the Holy Ghost: "What hast thou that thou hast not received?"[2]

---

[1] Matt. xxvi. 39.   [2] I Cor. iv. 7.

Discouragement.

The despondent soul dwells only on her own efforts, her own strength : on these alone she counts; so that her discouragement decreases, ceases, returns, and increases accordingly as she acts well or ill. She forgets that the mercy of God, and not her own merit, is her support and help; that the good she does is an effect of the undeserved grace of God; and that the treasury of eternal mercy stands open to her in every circumstance, so that in the exercise of good works she can always receive the necessary grace.

If you try to convince such a soul that she ought, in imitation of the saints, to place all her confidence in the Lord, she at once replies : " They were saints, and faithful servants of the Lord. It is no wonder that they had confidence in God ; but as for *me*, I have no such reason to hope in Him." Moreover, she does not see that such a manner of speaking is opposed to the maxims of our holy religion.

Hope is a divine virtue, and, consequently, can be founded only on God. But the souls of which we are speaking make it a purely human virtue, since they found it wholly on man and his actions. No, never have the saints hoped in God, because they were faithful to Him ; but they were faithful to Him, because they hoped in Him.

Were the alleged objection correct, then no sinner could evoke an act of hope ; and yet it is precisely such an act that prepares the way for his return to God.

Remark that St. Paul does not say : "I have received mercy, because I was faithful," but "I give counsel, as having obtained mercy of the Lord to be faithful."[1] Mercy always goes before our good works, and obtains for us the grace to accomplish them. Never did the saints reflect upon their own merits, in order to strengthen their confidence in God ; on the contrary, they were deeply penetrated with this teaching of the Divine Master : "When you shall have done all these things that are commanded you, say : We are unprofitable servants : we have done that which we ought to do."[2] The more holy they were, the

[1] I Cor. vii. 25. [2] Luke xvii. 10.

more humble they became. In their humility they saw but the perfection to which they had not yet attained. Far removed from the presumptuous sentiments of the proud Pharisee, they discovered nothing in themselves that could rouse confidence; but they sought and found it in God, the immovable foundation of their hope. This plank upheld them. Let it likewise encourage you, and give your wearied soul new life.

THIRD POINT.

The True Foundation of Christian Hope the same for all Men.

According to the teaching of our holy religion, the foundation of Christian hope, namely, confidence in God, is the same for all men—for the saint and for the sinner.

Hope is, like faith and love, as we have already said, a divine virtue. It must, then, be founded upon God and His infinite perfections alone. This precludes any idea of personal merit from the motives of this virtue. We do not hope in God because we have served Him faithfully; but we hope in Him, that we may thereby receive the grace to serve Him with fidelity.

What, then, according to our holy faith, is the foundation of Christian hope? Pope St. Benedict XIV. tells us in the act of hope composed and published by himself: "O my God! I hope in Thee because Thou art true to Thy promises, and because Thou art almighty and infinitely merciful." In this act we see nothing human. All is founded upon God. Could there be, I ask, stronger motives of hope and confidence than these?

Our hope rests in all things upon God's mercy—upon that mercy which is more willing to heap graces upon us than we are to receive them; upon that love which more sincerely desires what is for our good than we ourselves, and which prevents us with its help without our deserving it; finally, upon that fidelity which in all our trials will give sufficient grace and strength in as far as we implore it.

Discouragement.

This mercy, which is infinite, and consequently far greater than all the malice of men, has made itself known in the most conspicuous and wonderful manner, viz., by God's resignation of His only-begotten Son to death, in order to save us. How could he afterward deny us that grace and assistance which, by such a sacrifice, He has so dearly purchased?

Secondly, the promise of the Lord secures to us the gracious effects of His mercy. God has promised to grant us assistance toward our eternal salvation when we pray to Him for it. He, the Infinite Truth, cannot deceive us. He is faithful to His promises. Holy Scripture calls upon us in a hundred places to take refuge in God, who solemnly assures us that He will Himself be our help and strength. Dare we, then, deliberately harbor the least fear that God will cast us away from Him or forsake us when we have confident recourse to Him?

Certainly, God deserves that we should call upon Him trustingly if we would be favorably heard. But do we not render ourselves unworthy of His benefits when we pray to Him, mistrusting that goodness of which He gives manifold proofs at every moment? St. James says: "For he that wavereth is like a wave of the sea, which is moved and carried about by the wind. Therefore, let not that man think that he shall receive anything of the Lord."[1] And we see how Jesus Christ in His earthly life worked miracles only where He found confidence.[2]

The infinite omnipotence of God is the third motive of Christian hope. Men often promise what it is not in their power to perform; but to God, the Almighty, nothing is impossible. No insurmountable obstacle can be placed in the way of His will when He wills to give us graces. In the inexhaustible treasury of His gifts He possesses means sufficient to lead us to sanctity. Never, then, let us fear to ask Him for too many or too great favors.

God, who is infinitely rich, possesses all goods, natural

[1] James i. 6, 7.   [2] Matt. ix. 22.

and supernatural. God, the Almighty, can communicate all these goods to us. God, the All-Good, is ready at all times, according to His promise, to give us everything necessary for our sanctification. These perfections of God are for all men the foundation of Christian hope. They alone can give to our confidence the unwavering assurance that it should possess.

FOURTH POINT.

The Passion and Merits of Christ a new Foundation for Confidence.

Our Divine Saviour, who died for all men, prayed for all, offered His sufferings and death for all, merited for them the strength needed in the combat of salvation, whose victory leads to eternal blessedness. Jesus Christ needs not His own merits. He has, therefore, made them over to us, and this in such a way, says St. Bernard, that they become our own property. If we offer these merits to the Heavenly Father, we obtain His powerful assistance against the enemies of salvation. Upon this truth Holy Church rests when she adds at the close of all her prayers: "Through Jesus Christ Our Lord."

To these considerations the Christian, racked with the memory of his sin-stained life, replies: "How can Jesus Christ look upon me favorably after the many offences I have offered Him? How can He still intercede for an enemy who has so long and so shamefully betrayed and despised Him?" I reply: How can a well-instructed Christian put such a question? How dare he doubt the mercy of his Mediator? Yes, Christ assures us that He is come to suffer and to die for sinners, to seek that which was lost. How, then, can the sinner think that he will be turned away when he cries for pardon? No, heaven and earth shall pass away, but the words of Christ shall not pass away. His promises concern sinners. Would He have suffered, would He have so cruelly died upon the

Discouragement.

cross, if there had been no sinners? The more sinful a soul is, the more resplendently are revealed in her the mercy of God and the power of the Saviour's merits. Could there be a greater crime than that of Judas? "Yes," answers St. Jerome, "there is one still more monstrous; viz., that of despair. Judas sinned more deeply in killing himself than in betraying his Divine Master."

Let us never fear to take refuge in the merits of our Redeemer. We honor these merits when we use them to obtain the necessary assistance from God; for it was with this design that Christ gained them and made them over to us. By our prayers and good works we appropriate them to ourselves, and direct them to their true end. It would be a singular manner of honoring Christ's merits if we did not venture to make use of them. That would be to run counter to the intention of the Divine Saviour. He who leaves unused the precious graces of Jesus Christ, testifies thereby not that he esteems them, but that he is indifferent to them. We acknowledge that we are poor, weak, and miserable; therefore we must strive after riches, health, and strength. To this end Christ donated His infinite merits: "Come to Me all," said He, in His boundless goodness, "and I will refresh you."[1] Do we not walk in direct opposition to the maxims, meaning, and intention of Our Lord when we fear to take refuge in Him?

The enemy makes use of everything he possibly can to discourage souls. For this purpose he not unfrequently takes advantage of false humility. Christian humility, in perfect harmony with reason, requires that we deem ourselves unworthy of God's favors; but it in no wise follows that we should reject the graces offered us, or abandon our petitions for those He has promised to prayer. Still more, the gratitude which we owe Jesus demands that, in conformity with His holy will, we make use of His sufferings and merits in order to receive the graces which He thereby purchased for us. We cannot give the Lord greater proof

[1] Matt. xi. 28.

of honor than when we correspond with the loving designs of His mercy.

How can we impetrate God's offended justice, how implore His compassion, if we do not support ourselves upon our Redeemer's merits? We appease God only when we offer these merits to Him. All in us calls for the just punishment of our offences; but all in His Son calls for mercy. As soon as we kneel contrite at the foot of the cross, as soon as we wash ourselves in the most adorable Blood of the Son of God, the Lord turns to us in mercy, and His justice is appeased. In the atoning death of the Mediator, "mercy and truth have met each other: justice and peace have kissed."[1]

FIFTH POINT.

To be Wanting in Confidence, is to be Wanting in Faith.

God, the most tender Father of His creatures, has done everything to preserve them from that fear which could keep them away from Him. He knew well that man, in the sentiment of his ingratitude and oft-repeated infidelity, would easily relinquish hope, and lose courage to return to His Creator in order to seek help from Him in his misery. Therefore the All-Merciful gave us not only the assurance that all who hope in Him should not be confounded,[2] but He still more clearly declared to us, on this important point, His paternal will, His formal command to hope in Him.

Unquestionably, only by the help of His grace can we fulfil this command. But would God have given it to us if He had not wished to help us? And since He has given it, how can He remain unmoved when, with an honest and upright intention, we cry to Him? How could He forsake us when, to obtain His assistance, we do what He Himself has prescribed? No, the Lord never breaks His word. If we are defeated in the combat, it will be only because we are wanting in faith.

[1] Ps. lxxxiv. 11.   [2] Ps. xxi. 6.

Discouragement.

The Holy Scriptures furnish us an example of this: Peter, at the word of Jesus Christ, hurried over the waves with a firm step to meet his Divine Master. The wind arose, the confidence of the Apostle wavered; he began to sink; the threatening danger, though it filled him with terror, also animated his courage and confidence anew. Peter sought refuge in the Lord, and He extended to him His helping hand. For our instruction, Jesus wished not to leave His Apostle in doubt as to the cause of his danger. He upbraids him with his want of faith: "O thou of little faith! why didst thou doubt?"[1]

How true a picture of what only too often goes on in the Christian soul! So long as the heart is all peace, souls go full of confidence to Jesus wherever He calls them. But let the storm of temptation arise, let the difficulty of virtue be felt, the soul becomes confused, and forgets that she is acting upon the word of the Lord. Fear arises, confidence wavers. Her first unfaithfulness diminishes her strength, and she begins to sink; she is lost if returning confidence does not quickly secure help from on high.

Peter would have been lost had he not called Jesus to his assistance. But the good Master would not let him sink to rise no more. Would you also, Christian soul, who have imitated the Apostle in his weakness, cry with him to the Lord instead of losing precious time in anxiety and complaints, you would certainly feel the protection of Jesus, you would experience His assistance; you would be spared the many faults, the many weary hours, that your want of confidence draws upon you. You have yourself alone to blame if you do not, in the moment of need, grasp the hand extended to you by the Divine Master. It is always stretched forth to you. You know the danger; you know the means of escaping it; therefore it is your own fault if you do not follow the interior light.

[1] Matt. xiv. 31.

SIXTH POINT.

No Victory without Combat; No Combat without Labor.

We can readily admit that the motives of Christian hope are firm and secure; but the devil knows how, under a thousand pretexts, to deceive the discouraged soul, and turn her away from her true end. Man by nature is slothful; he fears every exertion. As soon as he gives himself up to God's service, he desires to taste the sweets of his offering without its costing him the least trouble. Only too gladly does he forget Christ's assurance: "The kingdom of heaven suffereth violence, and the violent bear it away."[1] He does not reflect that it was by suffering Christ would enter into His glory, and that He has led His saints thereto only by the cross, by combats, sacrifices, and renouncement. Heaven is a reward; but it must be merited, by placing God and His holy will before all else, even that which is dearest to us. As soon as He demands it, we must be prepared to offer all to Him as a sacrifice, a whole burnt-offering. This is an incontrovertible principle. St. Paul declares that no one will be crowned who has not fought valiantly.[2] He who would claim the crown of justice without combating, contradicts the maxims of faith; and he who would fight without labor and exertion, contradicts sound reason.

We know well what God requires of us; and this knowledge is precisely what the devil employs to discourage us. He tempts us to yield to our innate sluggishness, and to omit the efforts necessary for salvation. It costs us nothing to follow our natural inclinations, but it is painful to us to fight against them. It is, consequently, an easy matter for the enemy to persuade us to choose the former mode of action.

In order to confirm us still more in our evil choice, he places before us the various sufferings we must expect in

[1] Matt. xi. 12.   [2] II. Tim. ii. 5.

Discouragement.

the service of God, the continual violence we shall have to undergo in fighting and overcoming self. At the same time the tempter conceals the interior peace he enjoys who gives himself up wholly to God, and the great consolation the hope of eternal reward imparts even amidst the most painful sufferings. He shows us our own weakness in its fullest extent; reminds us of the faults committed in spite of the best resolutions; and extinguishes, so to say, every thought of the mercy and power of that God by whose assistance we have so often obtained the victory.

The following picture will portray the progress of this fatal condition of the soul: Quite overwhelmed by the thought of our weakness and the difficulty of our work, we yield to dejection instead of exclaiming with the Royal Prophet: "If armies in camp should stand together against me, my heart shall not fear, because Thou, my God, art with me!"[1] In her sadness and dejection the soul hardly sees the assistance of Heaven. She depends little upon it, she scarcely ventures to pray for it; perhaps, too, she fears to receive it, since she must then renounce her cherished inclinations to evil. She imagines that she cannot continually do violence to herself, since she experiences in her soul so great opposition; therefore, in this condition of interior dejection she does nothing, or almost nothing, to overcome herself. The first fault she commits strengthens her in the fear that she will never succeed in the struggle, and confirms her opinion that she must await the time when her passions will be less violent.

To such a soul everything is hard. Her duties are disagreeable, because disgust and a secret longing for independence have taken possession of her heart. She either neglects her pious exercises or performs them so negligently that they fail to draw down God's grace upon her. Dissipation of mind and heart banishes the recollection that once accompanied her actions. She gives up her good works, resists grace and the twitchings of conscience, turns from

[1] Ps. xxvi. 3; xxii. 4.

holy thoughts, and allows her humors, fancies, and inclinations to guide her in all things, because in so doing she has no need to overcome self. In spite of the uneasiness by which she is, through the mercy of God, pursued, she would rather remain in this tepid and slothful condition than do violence to self for the love of God. This is exactly the point to which the Evil One desires to bring her. He wants to divert her from the care of her salvation, and through her discouragement he has obtained his end.

I have perhaps entered too fully into particulars; but by this means only can we learn to know the attacks of the enemy, and more easily frustrate his efforts.

I can understand the intimidation of a soul that contemplates as present the difficulties to be encountered in the service of God during a whole lifetime. But do the sufferings of the Christian life come upon us all at once? Has one to bear them in the whole? Certainly not. He bears them singly, sometimes this, sometimes that, as occasions offer. If there are some that often fall heavily upon us, there are others again that come but seldom. Against the first you must particularly arm yourself; the latter you will best ward off by the frequent exercise of the love of God. Our cowardice would indeed be great if we had not courage to oppose a single enemy, whose only weapon is often our own weakness. If you fear him, you are already conquered. If you call upon God, and with His help offer valiant resistance, the enemy will not long hold out. He will flee, and perhaps will not soon return.

Never consider as a whole those events that come singly. The soul has to account only for the actions of the moment. If, instead of acting thus, you fill your mind with thoughts of possible sufferings, it will be to trouble yourself about uncertainties, to set out to meet all sorts of temptations. By such a line of conduct one does not wait to be tempted, one becomes his own tempter. You act very unreasonably when you draw on your imagination for what may, perhaps, never happen to you. "Sufficient for the day is the evil thereof." [1] To put ourselves in the way of temptation is contrary to the teachings of religion and Christian prudence. [2]

The soul that does violence to herself to please God and in the hope of a reward, thinking in every suffering how she can make a holy use of it, will not only find her burdens lighter, but she will carry them with greater merit.

A religious, for example, feels strong repugnance to the continual restraint imposed upon her by obedience and the rules of her Order. If she looks upon this contradiction of her natural feelings, views this subjection as the yoke of a whole lifetime, she becomes perplexed and discouraged. But if she considers the restraint as but for one day, for some hours, or merely for the time that it will take for her present occupation, she will not find it so hard. Generally speaking, difficulties are but the matters of a moment; trouble vanishes as soon as a courageous resolution is made.

You deceive yourself, also, when you think that the effort which self-conquest now costs you will always remain as great and as painful. Experience drawn from the nature of things teaches us, that by the frequent performance of any action with purity of intention it soon becomes a custom, and thereby easier in its fulfilment. Do violence to yourself for some time in the faithful and punctual performance of a single action, and you will find that it will soon cost you no effort; the difficulty has vanished, and the pious intention has come, as it were, of itself. This experience is so lively, that it actually becomes a cause of alarm to many souls. They imagine that they have no merit for the performance of what no longer costs them a sacrifice. They do not consider that the true value of an action consists in the supernatural motive that animates it, and not in the labor it entails.

Again, our holy religion tells us that God rewards with special graces the fidelity with which, through love of Him,

---

[1] Matt. vi. 34.

[2] Farther on we shall see what is said on the difference between great, courageous souls and weak, desponding ones. At present we address the latter.

we have conquered ourselves; so that suffering becomes not only easy, but even sweet. Though God may leave us long the sentiment of suffering, yet He never permits us to be tried beyond our strength. Confide in His Divine Word, for It cannot deceive.

Never reflect upon the uncertainty of perseverance without remembering the promised helps and reward : the latter thought will always console and animate you anew.

SEVENTH POINT.

He who Anticipates Future Combats and Sufferings Tempts both God and Himself.

Against the foregoing assertion some one may perhaps make the following objections: "One must be prepared to fulfil his duties. Now, when I see mine before me, and, conscious of my own weakness to meet the gigantic struggle a whole life long, I say to myself: 'How is it possible not to tremble and be discouraged?'"

It has already been remarked that the effort does not always continue so violent and sensible as it is in the beginning; neither are you to measure future by present trouble. Correspond with the present grace vouchsafed you by Almighty God, and hope that in the future He will not withhold what is necessary.

Furthermore, God forbids presumptuous seeking after temptation. He has not promised His assistance to those who, by foolish and senseless anticipation, go to meet imaginary trials, and in fancy conjure up temptations that may perhaps never come upon them. You have not now the strength even to look these temptations in the face; and this for the simple reason, that the time for combat not being at hand, you have not yet the graces which God holds in reserve for the hour of trial. It is, then, no wonder that their sight appalls you. Why, contrary to the will of the Lord, do you thus tempt yourself?

Why should you desire to know how the heavy crosses, the

violent temptations, the obstinate combats that others have to endure, would affect you in case anything of the kind should befall you? God has promised to strengthen your will when He demands of you great sacrifices, but He has not promised to do so if you wilfully allow your imagination to place you in situations that are now and may perhaps ever be foreign to you. A truly Christian soul is humble : far from seeking the danger, she fears and avoids it. But you, through temerity, through secret presumption, hidden self-love, court the temptation. Then, do you wonder that your will is weak and irresolute? God gives us His grace not in accordance with our humor, but in proportion to our needs. Its measure is determined by His providence. This is precisely the temptation that often deludes the imprudent or badly instructed. They live in an imaginary future, filled with sacrifices which the Spirit of God has not yet revealed to them ; and they turn away from those of the present moment, which He really demands of them. Such souls, whilst pursuing shadows, lose sight of the reality.

To please God, pious souls must not in imagination extract the juice from every bitter herb, under the pretext that thereby real suffering is endured with greater magnanimity. Their intention may be good in itself, but God, far from willing, rather forbids such a practice. It is in reality nothing more nor less than tempting God. Hence, however good your intention may be, do not trust it; rather divert your mind from such thoughts. God expects you to be prepared only in a general way to avoid mortal sin and its occasions, and resignedly to carry the cross that His providence daily lays upon you. He is not desirous that you prepare in imagination for all kinds of crosses, and thus carry them before the time.

If without your concurrence such trials present themselves to your mind, full of love and confidence raise your heart to God, and say: "My God ! if thou dost permit this trial to come upon me, I hope in Thy promises and through the merits of Jesus Christ that Thou wilt help me to bear it aright." After this short prayer, put all such fancies aside. Give yourself to your present duty; show yourself on every occasion strong and courageous; and by such fidelity you will better and more safely prove your love for God.

EIGHTH POINT.

Aversion, Disgust, and Weariness in God's Service are not Unfrequently the Sources of Unreasonable Discouragement.

A soul that, in spite of persevering prayer, is constantly assailed by her predominant fault or some obstinate temptation, or that experiences in the service of God only disgust, weariness, and aversion, often falls into the grossest errors. The devil whispers that God does not hear her, and that her prayers are useless, thus plunging her into the abyss of discouragement. In this pitiable state she beholds in God only a hard-hearted, inflexible, exasperated Master, to please whom no one may dare to hope.

Such a soul, whom the Lord proves without abandoning, errs especially when she thinks that, because of her repugnance and weariness, what she does is not agreeable to God and meritorious to herself. This thought saddens her at first, then tortures her, and finally quite discourages her, if God does not hear her petition to restore her lost consolation, her sensible fervor. Let me now lead the soul back to the way of truth, and she will soon recover her peace: she will perceive that the state in which she is has been esteemed by her a bad one only because she has not judged it by sound religious principles.

Disgust, weariness, aversion, and their attendant temptations are not sins in themselves,—no, not even imperfections; consequently, there can be no possible reason why the fulfilment of duty under such trial should be less agreeable to God or less meritorious to the performer. Men, who do not see the heart, judge the value of an action by its exterior merit. Thence it is that the way in which an

Discouragement.

action is accomplished very greatly enhances or diminishes the value of said action in their eyes. But this is not the case with God. He penetrates hearts and their secret folds, He judges the uprightness of the intention by the sentiment itself, and not by its expression. To fulfil His holy will is all that He demands.

The indisputable evidence of this truth is found in the word and example of Jesus Christ. He tells us: "He that doth the will of My Father who is in heaven, he shall enter into the kingdom of heaven."[1] He does not desire us to fulfil His divine will with sensible joy, or that we find in it sensible satisfaction; but He requires that we accomplish it at any cost, and for this He promises us eternal happiness. When, then, the feeling of disgust and repugnance does not hinder a Christian soul from doing what God demands of her; or, in other words, when it does not prevent her from performing the duties of her state of life, it cannot be evil. It can neither retard her perfection nor deprive her of eternal life.

Our Divine Lord confirms this by His own teaching and example. He who was incapable not only of sin, but even of the least imperfection, deigned for our instruction and consolation to endure all our trials. It was for this reason that He allowed the devil to tempt Him to pride, vanity, vainglory, and presumption; and by a glance at His sufferings in the Garden of Olives He deigned to feel for man's ingratitude the deepest sadness and trouble along with violent abhorrence for the cross. But He was on this occasion not less an object of admiration to heaven and of complacency to His Heavenly Father; for His temptations, His dejection, and His natural aversion could not shake His faithful submission to the Divine Will.

Christ has plainly shown by this that such states of interior trial, even when reaching the highest degree in a soul, far from being evils, are not even imperfections; and

[1] Matt. vii. 21.

that, in spite of them, her works are meritorious and agreeable to God.

I cannot press home this truth emphatically enough; for I know that many souls, notwithstanding the teaching and example of Christ on this head, are still disturbed. They have read that one should serve God joyfully: hence, as soon as this feeling of joyfulness is wanting—a feeling that is in no wise demanded by Christ—they think they are far from God, even reprobate. They do not consider that such a disposition of soul does not depend upon them, but on God, as we shall more fully explain.

Let us judge matters according to true religious principles. So long as you do not assent to these temptations of disgust, weariness, and aversion, they are involuntary, they depend not upon you. Were it in your power to have it otherwise, you certainly would not experience what causes you so much affliction. The feeling, therefore, which does not depend upon you, to which you have not yielded, and which you have ever combated, cannot render you guilty before God. In His eyes you are accountable only for what you actually do or leave undone, for what depends on your own free-will.

This is a truth of which, according to the unanimous decision of the Church, you cannot doubt, and of which reason itself convinces. What idea should we necessarily form of God's goodness and justice if He punished men for what they could not avoid?

Hence it is certain that aversions and temptations do not in themselves make us displeasing to God. For the consolation of troubled and dejected souls, we may add that if, in spite of their trials, they still remain faithful to the fulfilment of their duties, they give God a greater, a more ardent, proof of love, receive more marks of His grace, and through their good works acquire more merit than if they were inundated with sensible fervor and experienced no difficulties at all. It cannot be doubted that our love for God is proved to be stronger the more enemies we conquer and the more obstacles we overcome in the accomplishment of His will. If this love were weak within us we could never succeed in opposing assaults so violent; but the less sensible our love, the more powerful it is, and the more meritorious.

Assuredly, the soul may often commit faults in these wearisome and obstinate combats, for such is the fate of man here below. But this is no cause for disturbance; such faults are soon repaired by the numerous sacrifices the soul perpetually offers to the Lord. If you carry your cross with resignation, if you follow the interior light of faith, if you overcome and deny yourself at every moment, how can you, for some trifling fault, fear being expelled from the number of Christ's disciples? Has not Our Saviour said: "If any man will come after Me, let him deny himself, and take up his cross, and follow Me."[1] And this is what the faithful soul does, despite her aversions and repugnances. How, then, can she think that God will allow so many sacrifices to go unrewarded? "No," says St. Paul, "God is not unjust that He should forget your good works and your sufferings."[2] Persevere, faithful and tried soul! Your reward is before you. In you shall be realized the promises of Infinite Truth. Yet some few days of toil, and then an eternity of unending happiness, a foretaste of which you will very probably enjoy even in this life; for after trials God generally sends consolation, peace, and joy to the purified soul. This will be your experience, as it was that of the saints.

NINTH POINT.

We should not Pray God to Free us from our Sufferings and Combats. Should we do so, we must not Desire to have such Petitions Immediately Granted.

In spite of all these consoling truths, we must still confess that the state of repugnance and dryness is always hard to bear. Man is by nature an enemy to exertion and

[1] Matt. xvi. 24. [2] Hebrews vi. 10

self-victory. He feels keenly the conflict against self; and under this feeling he forgets what rich reward he can draw thence, what merit every victory secures him. In his desolation he turns to God for help; but for what does he pray? For an end to his trials, for freedom from his sufferings. If he finds that he is not immediately heard, that the Lord still afflicts him, he fancies his prayer useless, and that his petitions will not be granted. Disquiet, fear, and discouragement take possession of his heart. In this frame of mind he knows not how to pray; indeed, he hardly ventures to pray at all. Probably he says with Jesus: "My Father, if it be possible, let this chalice pass from Me;" but he takes good care not to add with his Divine Master, "nevertheless, not as I will, but as Thou wilt."[1] One must be deeply penetrated with the principles of faith before reaching that humble resignation which draws down the special care of Divine Providence.

Religion teaches that God so guides and leads His faithful servants that everything serves to His own glory and their true happiness. It belongs to God to determine how to dispose of men for His own honor, on what road to lead them to sanctity and bliss. Should the creature serve God according to his own humor and fancy, or should he prescribe to his Maker how he is to be guided,—that would be a manifest sign of foolishness. It would be to reduce human passions and errors to a rule of life.

Before God, subjection is man's duty. All that he has to do is to know the way upon which God wishes to lead him, and to follow it willingly and confidingly. It belongs to God to devise the plan, and to men, with God's assistance, to carry it out. The man who enters with these sentiments upon the way mapped out by God will certainly be led by Him most safely and securely to salvation; for the Lord, who has chosen the path by which to conduct souls to eternal happiness, gives them also special graces to walk uprightly and honestly in it. Pursue this path faith-

[1] Matt. xxvi. 39.

fully, and you will constantly correspond with the dispensations of the Divine Will over you; you may count upon the special protection of the Almighty, who cannot desert a soul that He sees in such sentiments.

When God wills to lead a soul to heaven by the way of trial, suffering, antipathy, and disgust, should she pray to the Lord to change His will and designs? She may do it, for we see that Christ Himself did so. Such a prayer has often been granted. If God allows us to wait long for a grace, it by no means signifies that He has refused it. A persevering prayer shall, indeed, be granted, and that at the moment appointed by the Lord wherein to show His mercy. But should a soul make deliverance from interior suffering the exclusive condition of her prayer, so as to become discouraged and dejected if God does not hear her, she would be very unlike to Christ and His saints. She would rather consent to the suggestions of the tempter, who is seeking to turn her from God, and withdraw her from the guidance of His providence.

The first and most desirable object of your prayer should be the virtue of perfect resignation to God's will, and the strength to bear with patience, fidelity, and love the state in which God places you for your sanctification. Be persuaded that you do not deserve God's particular favor; and that it is an act of His infinite mercy to receive the relapsing sinner, not as a child, but, in the words of the prodigal son, as the least of His hired servants. In the spirit of penance, then, accept your state of dryness, abandoning yourself wholly and submissively into the hands of the Lord, willing to endure as long as it may be conducive to His honor and glory. Such a disposition is the best means to obtain from God the cessation of a most painful trial.

You think God does not hear you because He leaves you in the state of disgust and temptation from which you wish to be freed. The principles of our holy religion declare you to be in error. Is your prayer resigned? Is it full of confidence? Is it persevering? Then, in accordance with the promise of Christ, it will be granted. Perhaps God may not give you precisely that for which you pray; but He withholds it only because it is less useful to you than something else that He has resolved to bestow, or because the bad use you would make of it would render it hurtful. Instead of the grace which in His mercy He denies you, He will send you others much more precious. He will give you graces that will support you in the combat, and render you capable of attaining to the perfection of Christian virtues, and by self-denial, mortification, resignation, and penance aid you to amass great merits for heaven; yet so that even when victorious you will feel your own nothingness, be convinced of your own weakness, and thus preserve Christian humility, the foundation of true virtue. You will by their help be vigilant over yourself, and keep up constant intercourse with God, whose assistance will appear to you ever more and more indispensable.

How wonderful does not the guiding providence of the Lord appear in St. Paul! Repeatedly did he cry to God to deliver him from the humiliating temptations that molested him. The Lord, however, permitted them in order to preserve his humility in the exalted revelations vouchsafed him.[1] Whilst refusing to free him, God addressed to him these consoling words: "My grace is sufficient for thee!"[2]

If, then, God refuses to shorten the sufferings of a tried soul, it does not imply that He is far from her, that He has not heard her, or that He refuses her petition. He has, we must conclude, other intentions over her. Though He does not see fit to deliver her, yet He is always ready to support her.

[1] II. Cor. xii. 7.   [2] II. Cor. xii. 9.

CHAPTER IV

Of Temptations.[1]

FIRST POINT.

Temptations are no Proof that God has Forsaken a Soul.

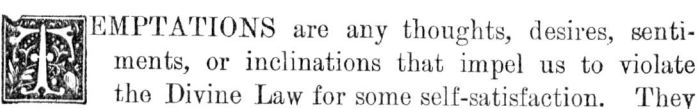

TEMPTATIONS are any thoughts, desires, sentiments, or inclinations that impel us to violate the Divine Law for some self-satisfaction. They should neither frighten nor discourage a Christian. Against two sorts of souls the evil one chiefly wages war: 1st, against those that, overcoming their passions and courageously following the path of virtue and perfection, truly serve God; and 2d, against those that, turning from their evil ways, shake from their shoulders the heavy yoke of sin. Against such souls the devil puts all his engines in motion to separate them from the love of Jesus Christ. The opposition of the Evil One, rightly considered, should rather be a source of consolation; for it shows that we are antagonistic to the enemy of our salvation, and that we adhere firmly to the will of God. A little firmness, and the victory is ours!

A soul anxious by nature, or one that God has led for a considerable time along the way of peace and consolation, easily fancies that He is angry with her—indeed, that He has utterly forsaken her—when He sends her temptations. She cannot think that God can find pleasure in one whose heart is filled with and vehemently agitated by sentiments so contrary to virtue. These artifices are the last efforts of the devil for the ruin of souls whom he failed to allure

---

[1] All the points of this chapter, with the exception of the Ninth, Twelfth, and Thirteenth, are taken from Father Michel's work on "Temptations." The Thirteenth point is from Fénelon.

by the enticement of sin. He seeks to rob them of that confidence which sustained them in the combat.

A soul that listens to such insinuations falls into the grossest errors. He who has even slight experience in the spiritual life and in God's guidance will not be surprised at the attacks he has to endure. Indeed, we know from Holy Scripture that the life of man upon earth is a continual warfare, and that he must constantly carry arms to defend himself both within and without. Within, against the enemies of his own household—his inclinations, passions, our self-love, which seek to seduce him under a thousand pretexts and artifices; without, from the influence of bad example, the fear of men, and of the hellish fiend, who in his jealousy has from the beginning sworn enmity against the happiness of mankind. Furthermore, the same Holy Scripture tells us that only through victory can we tread the path to heaven, and that no one will be crowned till he has, conformably to the Law, striven manfully to the end.[1]

St. Paul prayed to be freed from his temptations, yet he did not consider their continuance a sign of God's anger. The saints who, even in the desert, during the practice of the severest penance, were long and violently assailed by the Evil One considered their temptations as occasions of combat and merit, for they well understood the words of Scripture: "And because thou wast acceptable to God, it was necessary that temptation should prove thee."[2] This is, according to the principles of faith, the only just view of the matter. You should look temptation boldly in the face; then it will neither perplex nor discourage you.

Temptations are never a sign that a soul has been forsaken by God, for the Lord never wholly deserts man during his earthly existence. They are, for the most part, trials, or sometimes punishments. Divine Justice brings His creatures under the rod of correction for negligence in His service, for certain weaknesses, tepidity, and presumption, or for natural inclinations that the heart too keenly

---

[1] II. Tim. ii. C.   [2] Tobias xii. 13.

cherishes. But whether they be punishments or trials, they must always be accepted with resignation, and faithfully resisted. God is our most tender Father. With His justice He always couples mercy and mildness. To prayer and confidence He never denies His grace. He will not condemn us, although He may punish us in order to bring us back to Himself. Let no one, therefore, lose courage when he is tempted. God will pardon those that willingly accept the penance He imposes.

SECOND POINT.

Temptations are no Evidence of a Bad State of Soul.

Frequent temptations are, in general, a sign of the existence of violent passions, and a strong tendency to evil in the soul; but when we fight against them they are not proofs of a heart estranged from God. Since the sin of our first parents our inclinations have been corrupt; and not unfrequently this innate disposition to evil is strengthened by the influence of the senses upon the soul. It is this downward tendency which exposes us more or less to temptation, in proportion to the susceptibility of our senses. But as all this does not depend upon our own will, nor proceed from our own heart, so neither is it a sign that our heart is infected by any special vice. The heart is not rendered guilty by this liability of the senses to evil: it rather suffers under it. If it masters that tendency, and faithfully clings to virtue, then it is good, and remains such, however violent those inclinations may be.

The constant resistance of temptation is, on the contrary, the mark of a truly Christian heart. It is, on the one side, a proof of our love for God; and on the other, of the divine protection over us. This thought should console us, and increase our confidence. We are indebted to the divine mercy for our determined opposition to evil inclinations; and the greater the danger of a defeat, the more powerful and evident is God's assisting grace.

Your conclusion, consequently, is false when you say: "Were my heart and mind what they ought to be, did they really belong only to God, thoughts and feelings contrary to the love of the neighbor, thoughts against faith, purity, etc., would not rise up in me."

Indeed, if such thoughts and feelings depended on you, then the case would be quite different, and you might justly say your heart was turned far from God. But they depend not at all upon your will. They glide imperceptibly into the mind and heart, or they rush in suddenly with impetuous violence without questioning your will, and what is still worse, they take up their abode in spite of your efforts to dislodge them. They are not, therefore, an expression, an act of your free-will; it is not in your power to have or not to have them; and hence they prove nothing at all as to the state of your soul.

Only through the sentiments that proceed from reflection and free-will does the heart cling to an object. A soul may belong entirely to God in spite of the sentiments contrary to virtue that arise in her, provided they be involuntary and displease her. Yes, I go farther, and assert that the trouble the soul experiences in such attacks is a decided proof that she sincerely loves God and her duty, and faithfully adheres to both. Were your love of God and hatred of sin less strong, you would not be troubled; you would follow your natural inclinations and satisfy your desires. The infallible mark of our love for God is that which He Himself has given us, viz., firmness in combating our evil inclinations. The greatest saints, even the Apostle to the Gentiles, were not exempt from these trials, and yet they loved God most perfectly. Jesus Christ for our instruction would even allow Himself to be tempted. And what He, the Holiest of the holy, would suffer in His adorable humanity cannot be a sin; no, not even an imperfection, for He is as incapable of the one as of the other. We cannot, then, be either guilty or subject to punishment when we endure what He experienced and as He experienced it, provided we resist as far as our weakness permits.

THIRD POINT.

In Temptation we should Turn to God. He Sustains us in the Combat without our Perceiving it.

In those interior storms that so often break upon us we feel sometimes that the hand of the Lord is sustaining us in the contest, and we fight valiantly against our passions. The thought of the presence of God and the desire to please Him rouse our courage and confidence. But, again, God sometimes conceals Himself. He appears to sleep, as once before in the disciples' little bark, whilst the stormy waves threatened to destroy it. In this case the danger is greater, inasmuch as sudden fear easily takes possession of us and paralyzes our efforts.

But courage! Even in this critical moment there is nothing to fear, if you raise your eyes to the heights of heaven, whence cometh all our help. When the disciples on the lake saw themselves in danger of being submerged they lost no time in useless lamentation. They put forth all their energy against the violence of the storm, and sought refuge with their Divine Master, calling on Him for help. But He was asleep;[1] and yet, unknown to the disciples, He had Himself suggested all that they did to insure their safety. And precisely thus it happens. God sometimes hides Himself from our gaze, but He notes none the less carefully all that passes in our heart. We think at every moment we must sink, and yet we continue to brave the storm.

Whence the light that points out the right way and guides us upon it? Whence the secret impulse that animates us anew, that urges us almost unconsciously to choose the proper means and to put it into execution? Whence our courage, sinking apparently at every moment, and yet

[1] Matt. viii. 24.

in reality gaining fresh strength ? Whence that firmness which we oppose to the allurements of iniquity ? Whence all this ? From ourselves ? Could we, weak as we are, trust ourselves alone to oppose the enemy ? Is it not rather Christ who sustains us with His mighty hand, although hiding Himself from our eyes, concealing His sensible presence ? Is it not He who has promised that we shall never be tempted beyond our strength ? Yes, even when we think the Lord far from us, He is in the midst of our heart. We imagine that He has forgotten us, and yet He is thinking of us more than ever, since we then most need Him. He sees our struggles, He assists at them as He did at St. Stephen's; and if we do not lose confidence, He will accord us victory over all our enemies.

FOURTH POINT.

How one may Know whether or not he has Consented to Temptation.

What most troubles souls whom God leads in the thorny path of temptation is the fear they have of offending Him, and the doubt as to whether or not they have voluntarily yielded. The following instructions may help to clear up this doubt:

We are not perfect master of our mind and heart. We cannot prevent their being occupied with this or that thought, with this or that sentiment. Frequently they come upon us so suddenly that the mind is unconsciously carried after the suggestion. We are so absorbed that we neither hear nor see; we cannot even recall the precise moment in which such thoughts began to take possession of us. This remark holds good in regard to all sorts of thoughts and feelings.

Such a state lasts a longer or a shorter time according to the strength of the interior or exterior impressions from which they proceed, or according to the length of time they are allowed uninterrupted possession. It is only after their flight that the soul clearly and distinctly understands with what she has been occupied. Now if at the moment of awaking to self-consciousness she turns from the evil thoughts and feelings as quickly as possible, she may be reasonably assured that she has not sinned. The pleasure she experiences in being freed from such thoughts and feelings is an almost incontestable evidence that her will had no deliberate part in them. The mind, indeed, was occupied with the idea; but reflection, the voluntary consent of the will, did not step in. Every offence against God depends upon two conditions: the will on the one side must deliberately consent to evil; and on the other it must have the power to resist that evil. But neither of these conditions is possible in the absence of full consciousness; hence without that no sin can be committed. The prompt rejection of evil thoughts and feelings at the very moment the soul becomes aware of them is, moreover, evidence of good and pious sentiments. It proves that the temptation could certainly not have arisen, would never have been entertained, had she been conscious of its approach. She should, accordingly, behave as if the bad thoughts and sentiments began at the very instant she perceived them. At that point she should begin her examination of conscience, leaving unnoticed all that preceded. If one finds that he has resisted at the moment marked, he may and should be at peace.

The above-mentioned spiritual embarrassments often last a long time; as, for example, during prayer, in which involuntary distractions seize upon us and fetter the powers of the soul. That these distractions last long makes them neither voluntary nor deliberate; for it depends as little upon our will to cut a distraction short as to prevent it entirely. The distraction is, then, not sinful; since an evil thought that unconsciously absorbs us is not a sin. That we have dwelt long upon it does not make us amenable if we have not been aware of the fact; nor is it difficult to decide in cases of this kind.

It seems to me well to say a few words here of temptations to despair; for the impression they make, especially upon scrupulous souls, is so fearful, that one is often unable to form a correct judgment of them. Gerson says: "As violent temptations to blasphemy, to heresy and unbelief, or to impurity, do not render us guilty, neither should we accuse a soul of despair when, in consequence of fears and scruples which often play an active part in such temptations, she imagines and even declares herself guilty and damned." The holiest souls, St. Francis de Sales for instance, have had to struggle with this trial. Such thoughts often appear both determined and voluntary when, in reality, so far from being wilful, they are generally accompanied by interior opposition. This opposition rises from the secret confidence in God that dwells in the depths of the terrified soul without her perceiving it. When the violence of the temptation is over, ask her whether or not she really believes in God's willingness to forgive her if she humbly repents. She will answer you in the affirmative, adding: "I feared at first that I had yielded. My agitation rendered me no longer mistress of my thoughts. Now that the storm has passed, I would not for all the world have the misfortune to consent to feelings so dishonorable to the Divine Goodness." This answer is, according to Gerson, a sure sign that the tempted soul has not sinned mortally. "For there are souls," says he, "who from pure pusillanimity think they despair, whilst in fact they do not. They take the feeling of despair, experienced in consequence of exaggerated fears, for consent." This decision of a great spiritual guide is certainly very consoling. But, sorely tried soul, never forget the most secure means of salvation for you. Make frequent acts of hope, and your enemies will soon be silenced, or, at least, rendered harmless. Do not be disturbed that you feel the contrary of what you express, that your acts of confidence seem to you useless, hypocritical formulas. Practise faithfully this pious exercise in spite of apparent

Temptations.

opposition, and you will soon be cheered by wonderful results.

FIFTH POINT.
Passing Temptations.

Temptations are very different in point of duration. Sometimes they come suddenly and pass as quickly; in which case it is often difficult to decide whether the thought or emotion was a temptation or a sin. The soul turned from it; but so rapid was the passage of the tempter that she hardly knows whether the temptation was rejected at the beginning or not.

Under such circumstances, the usual dispositions of the soul, the ordinary course of action, must be the guiding test. When a soul faithfully and lovingly exercises the virtues opposed to the temptation; when she very rarely commits a deliberate fault against them; when she has voluntarily and courageously fought and conquered after a long endurance of temptation,—she may justly feel secure that those passing emotions were not sins, were indeed hardly temptations.

This decision rests upon the following basis: For a soul to act in opposition to good, settled principles, she must, in a manner, do violence to herself; and this cannot easily happen without her knowledge. Had, therefore, the soul habituated to good sentiments consented to temptation, she would undoubtedly know it; for even the passing impression would be sufficiently strong to attract at least some attention. In such a case let not uncertainty with regard to consent disturb the peace of a soul. The doubt here is equivalent to certainty; for had one really consented, he could not doubt.

All teachers of the interior life express themselves to the same effect on what concerns passing temptations. They tell us to despise them, to give them as little attention as possible; for experience teaches that they make no impression upon the soul, and that they rarely return when one leaves them unnoticed to occupy himself with other matters. To combat them violently, to pay too much attention to them by timorous examination of conscience, and especially to fear them, would be to call them back and strengthen them. Despise the temptation; and like a shadow or a flash of lightning it will vanish. If you pay it too much attention, the shadow will take form and shape; the lightning will create fire, which your pondering will steadily increase. Let these little temptations pass unnoticed; never recall them, but turn your attention to some useful occupation. If at the first instant of attack you raise your heart to God by a pious aspiration, particularly by an act of love, you will suffer no detriment.

SIXTH POINT.

Lasting Temptations, and those that Powerfully Affect the Senses.

All temptations are not passing. Many pursue the soul obstinately and violently; or if they grant a respite, it is for a time only. As they perplex both head and heart, anxious souls are easily led to believe that the oft-returning feeling must be sinful. But this idea and the uneasiness arising from it robbing the soul of the strength she needs, are much more dangerous than the temptation itself.

In long-continued temptations we are better able to judge of our behavior during them, and conclude whether or not we have anything with which to reproach ourselves. Above all, one should not allow himself to be overcome by unnecessary fear. He must hold fast to the principle, that the feeling of temptation is not free-will, but only a bait with which the devil angles for consent. He places before the mind some object, some evil thought, and then instils into the heart the pleasurable sensation naturally resulting from it. This sensation is stronger or weaker according to the temperament of the person, and the greater or less impression made upon him. But its strength or weakness depends not upon our will; for both precede consent.

That this consent should really follow, the will must freely embrace the feeling, approve and entertain it. A thought can occupy the mind and emotion agitate the heart without the will's having the least share in it. A soul may suppress good as well as bad sentiments, resist good as well as bad inspirations. Evil, like good, is not contained in first thoughts or sensations, which only present good or evil to the will and incline it to the one or the other. The moral worth of our actions depends upon the free choice of the will, which decides for good or evil, one or other of which it embraces with full consent.

If the soul has in the time of temptation earnestly implored God's assistance; if she has rejected the rising evil emotions; if she is horrified at the snares of the Evil One; if she has endeavored to turn her thoughts from them, and occupied herself with other good and useful things—she may reasonably assume that what she felt, however prolonged and violent, was only a temptation. She has not failed, although she may not be able to assert with perfect assurance that she was faithful during every single moment of the temptation.

Should it appear to a soul that in her excitement she only for some moments weakly opposed the attack, she may still believe she has resisted, and that the weakness of which she complains is more apparent than real; she may believe the same if she did not entirely yield, and if in her ordinary frame of mind she hates and abhors sin. Such an appearance of defeat is often an effect of the violence of temptation, which in a manner deprives our will of the knowledge that it has resisted. Even should this weakness be real, yet it would be hard for a pious soul to give that full consent which is necessary for mortal sin. In the latter case the soul must be fully conscious, and know for certain what she is about. God does not allow us to be tempted above our strength. He never abandons a soul that does her best to avoid sin. Now, when such a soul employs the means that religion and experience put into her hands, it is a proof that she is not guilty. She should hope that God, conformably to His promise, has preserved her from falls. These principles should be forcible enough to put an end to vain fears.

A temptation may be so violent as to exercise an impression upon the senses, but this should in no wise afflict us. What we have said of feelings applies also to sensual impressions and sentiments. They do not depend upon our will, which can neither hinder them nor set them aside, and which is, consequently, guilty neither of their existence nor their duration. Sensual impressions become sins only when entertained with pleasure. So long as they are considered a consequence of temptation, which we detest, and against which we make war, they cannot possibly give pleasure, they can cause no sin. Too much attention only strengthens sensual impressions; violent efforts to be freed from them produce the same result. Such impressions are not sins. No notice should be taken of them. The soul should aim only at combating the temptation from which they proceed, and withholding the consent for which they clamor.

SEVENTH POINT.

On Temptations that Retard us in the Practice of Virtue.

The foregoing principles impart courage and determination to resist the temptations that not unfrequently seek to impede our practice of virtue. The enemy of salvation dares not openly propose to certain souls to give up the practice of virtue and perfection; but he makes use of an expedient to check their progress in the spiritual life, to keep them through negligence in the lower walks. In ordinary affairs he leaves them in peace; but as soon as they begin their spiritual exercises, he fills their mind with a thousand exciting and frightful fancies.

Does he see them earnestly intent on leading a perfect life, and that neither human respect nor the thought of the continual violence offered to self can intimidate them, he adopts another course. He infuses secret vanity into the fulfilment of duty, he pursues them with these emotions until it appears that all they do is performed through self-complacency or the vain esteem of men.

Certain souls are so susceptible of this temptation that they soon grow weary and disheartened. They say: "The violence I do myself is, for want of a good intention, useless and worthless;" and discouraged by this thought, they resist the inspirations of God, they neglect their spiritual exercises, they lead a life filled with faults and imperfections. From the fear of temptation they omit the good inspired by God, and thus, by endeavoring to avoid a little danger, they fall into a greater. St. Francis de Sales gives us an apt illustration when he says: "One must pay no regard to the suggestions of self-love. When in the course of the day we have two or three times renounced them, we have done enough. We must not banish them violently, but gently and quietly. We must say no, and then remain in peace."

Are trifling or dangerous occupations, to which you devote yourself without a command from superiors, causes of temptation to you? Then by all means avoid them, that you may not wantonly run into danger. But from the fulfilment of your duties, from faithfully following the divine inspiration, the fear of temptation should never, never withhold you. Temptation is not a sin; but the non-fulfilment of duty and of what God expects is a sin. When you yield to fear and temptation, when you allow yourself to be diverted from your path, when you neglect your devotional exercises and omit the good which you could do, then you are unfaithful to the Lord: you rob yourself of the means of advancing in perfection, and you put into the hand of the Evil One a sure weapon against yourself. By degrees it will come to this, that you will fulfil not even your essential duties. The devil will make use of his power over you and the fear that he instils, to lead you to neglect your religious exercises, particularly the holy Sacraments. But how can you, in this weak and discouraged condition in which you do not venture to seek the true means—prayer and mortification,—resist the temptations with which the devil may perhaps the next moment attack you?

Neither must you fear temptations that would hinder you in the execution of good works. They are not sinful so long as your will is not in them. Should they last long, the best arms against them are acts of love and confidence; but if they are only passing, although very frequent, be not disturbed. Despise them, and drive them from your thoughts. Renew your intention of fulfilling the will of God in all things. If you do this, these temptations will not mingle the slightest imperfection in your good works: on the contrary, they will enrich them with greater merit by reason of their reminding you frequently to renew your good intention. Thus one turns evil to good, and the wiles prepared to ensure his condemnation serve to further his sanctification.

EIGHTH POINT.

One should not Parley with the Tempter. Means by which we may Turn from the Temptation.

There are passions which one will never master if he does not openly and vigorously declare war against them by doing just the contrary to what they suggest. To this belong all passions that spring from character, as long as they have not been ennobled by grace. Is one subject to vanity, to anger, to susceptibility, or to that folly which is called antipathy? He will overcome such emotions only by making use of every occasion to practise the contrary virtue. For one must not only suppress passion in its first attacks, but determine to mortify it till death. Should he be satisfied with avoiding only certain occasions, he would never succeed in uprooting the evil, and he will generally be overcome. Only by acts of humility, meekness, and self-conquest; only by the most polite, preventing, and amiable deportment toward those for whom we have an aversion,—can we with God's grace free ourselves from this passion.

All temptations whose source is in the passions enumerated above, should be often and freely combated. We must embrace every opportunity formally to oppose them, by courageously exercising the opposite virtue. The same mode of proceeding is not necessary with other temptations; and in this some souls greatly deceive themselves. Many, for instance, suppose that during the temptation they must think of and search out arguments for refuting the insinuations of the devil; and they would consider themselves as having failed if they had not acted thus. They allow themselves to analyze the passion that attacks them; and to justify such a proceeding, pretexts and excuses are never wanting. They thus become involved in a long and dangerous contest. Had they not entered into parley with their cunning enemy, they might perhaps have been freed in a moment. But instead of that, their want of promptitude causes them to endure pain and disquiet. It is particularly in temptations against faith, hope, and charity that such souls act in this manner. They wish to convince themselves of the strength of their virtue by opposing temptations with protestations and arguments to the contrary. This, however, not only gives rise to anxiety and trouble, but is also extremely dangerous; for one runs a great risk of succumbing, as soon as he begins to examine the temptation and enter into controversy with the tempter.

Temptation that enters the soul through the senses and holds up the prospect of sensual gratification, makes a strong impression. But the efforts by which we interiorly oppose it do not fall under the senses, do no harm to nature, and make far less impression. In this, faith can come to our aid; but if the soul is disquieted, faith has often little power to make itself felt, and but slight resistance is offered to the passion. To oppose it in such a way is to pay it too much attention, to keep it alive, and to provoke it to new attacks. Every movement under such circumstances brings with it the dread of yielding. By all this the soul is at last so bewildered that she can with difficulty view the matter clearly in her examination of conscience.

For such temptations there is no better remedy than fidelity to turn the mind from the evil and arouse pious sentiments in the heart. For although our thoughts are not all subject to our will, yet the will can force the mind to busy itself with other things calculated to divert attention from the temptation. For this purpose one need not make choice of the virtue directly opposed to the one attacked; for the evil is sufficiently disavowed by every pious emotion, every good thought, every act of virtue. Every soul must on such occasions do what she knows from experience to be the most useful. One has a particular devotion to the sufferings of Christ; the thought of them infuses into his heart a horror of evil. Another throws himself in spirit upon the Sacred Heart of Jesus, and implores His help and mercy. Others, again, to fly from sin, feel themselves especially drawn to venerate the Blessed Sacrament of the Altar. Another places himself in spirit before the judgment-seat of Jesus Christ, in order to awaken in himself a wholesome fear of the Evil One. Thus every one has some favorite truth of faith, which attracts him in a special manner and diverts his mind from present temptation. Acts of love toward Jesus, invocation of the Blessed Virgin, are under all circumstances an unfailing resource. Sometimes, however, indifferent matters, business affairs, a scientific question, a book lying at hand, are a still better means to divert the mind. Whatever may be of most use to us under the circumstances, that is the proper means. The only question is, How can we most effectually banish dangerous thoughts and sentiments?

The important point in the combat is to remain tranquil, to persevere with unshaken confidence in God, and at once to resist courageously the fierce attack of Satan. When the heart and the head are trembling with fear they know not on what to depend. Agitation never leads to a correct judgment of things. Daily experience shows the evil consequences of anxiety in spiritual, as well as in temporal matters. What does a man do when in a sudden danger, an unforeseen attack, he loses his presence of mind? He is blind to the help offered him; his weapons lie near him whilst he is seeking them in vain.

Receive the enemy with more confidence, look him boldly in the face, and you will meet on more equal terms. You will more quickly perceive the means of victory, you will grasp them more vigorously, and use them with greater success. And after all, why should you fear? The devil may, indeed, insinuate into your mind all that there is most hideous, but your consent he can never force. That depends solely on yourself, and not on him. Why, then, are you frightened by that over which you are sovereign ruler, and to which, with the divine assistance, you may always deny consent? Be firm. You have nothing to fear from an adversary who can conquer you only when you will it yourself. A discouraged soul is half overcome, for to her are wanting those special graces that God grants only to confidence. And how can they be given her since in her discouragement she does not even think of asking for them? Say not: "I have already experienced so often how weak I am in this or that temptation." You have been weak because you were wanting in confidence. For the future, act courageously, call upon God, and you will not be overcome.

Besides confidence in God, there is still a third point—particularly important in violent temptations; namely, you must carefully notice the first awaking of the passion, so as to stifle it at once. If by offering only slight resistance you permit the enemy to heat your imagination and fill your heart with evil, this first infidelity will weaken your soul's vigor, and the passion thus indulged will soon gain the upper hand. Prompt and energetic resistance on the first attack is doubly necessary in those temptations whose violence is strengthened by sensual impressions. If you allow such impressions to possess you, you will require a very special protection from above to preserve yourself from sin.

When one is inexperienced in spiritual matters he should in the very beginning expose his temptations to his confessor. He learns thus how to combat them, and how to help himself in the struggle. This act of Christian humility and simplicity draws very special graces upon the soul. A person following the call of the Lord, walking in the path of obedience, merits that God should take particular care of him in his sufferings. It frequently happens, also, that temptations cease as soon as they are divulged to the representative of God. But if, on the contrary, they are concealed in the hope that they will pass, time is given them to increase in violence, and they will be more difficult to overcome.

NINTH POINT.

How Temptations proceeding from the Imagination are to be Combated.

The most troublesome and sometimes the most dangerous temptations come from the force of the imagination. Fickle, nervous, and impressionable persons are particularly beset by them. On the melancholy, likewise, they exercise a tyrannical influence. With the first, they bear the character of change and inconsistency, which render serious reflection very difficult. A thousand thoughts flit through the mind, each producing its own strong, though fleeting, impression, and allowing no room for the cool, tranquil suggestions of reason. On the contrary, with the sad and the melancholy the imagination assumes a firm, reflective character. It sees everything in the darkest light, and is depressed by the thought of difficulty. **Trifles** that often have no foundation will make such persons think themselves the most unhappy beings in the world. They curse their existence, and sigh for death as the only remedy for the imaginary evil. Imagination is for all men a magnifying-glass, which enlarges a thousand and a thousand times the smallest occurrences of daily life and the trials and sufferings so dreaded by the soul. If it meddles with matters of conscience, it becomes an inexhaustible source of scruples, and with melancholy persons even a constant tendency to despair. If a soul accustoms herself to indulge the fancies of the mind, these fancies become fixed ideas, irrefutable convictions emancipated from the dominion of the will. Frequently these thoughts imperceptibly engross the mind for hours, producing, so to say, a species of insanity upon some points. St. Teresa, therefore, not inappropriately styles imagination "The fool of the house." If the evil is already thus far advanced, something must be said that will enable the soul to form a correct judgment of her state. The existence of such fixed ideas as, for example, a secret proneness to despair, some strong prejudice in our communication with others, does not render the soul guilty, so long as she cannot free herself from them. She should assuredly offer resistance, and it is extremely important for her to have a correct idea as to how she should resist, and what she may gain over herself by such resistance; otherwise, she would by ill-directed exertions increase the evil instead of diminishing it.

The imagination is an enemy not to be openly defied. Not violent efforts, not prolonged disputes with their endless subtleties, can conquer it; for it has most frequently the devil for accomplice, and he is one with whom argument is not to be held. The safest means to fight against a lively imagination may be summed up in these four words: *anticipate, despise, bear patiently, divert the mind.*

1. ANTICIPATE.—Here, above all, the maxim applies, "Nip in the bud!" Do you perceive that one or other of your stereotyped fancies is rising to excite you? Close in-

stantly the doors of your heart, give it no entrance. This you will be able to do when you faithfully and conscientiously banish the unbidden thoughts that solicit your attention. Raise your heart to God; offer the dangerous gratification to Him as a sacrifice; deny yourself every deliberate reflection, every wilful return of thought in that direction; occupy your mind with something useful, agreeable, and edifying, that the excited imagination may be diverted. Instead of this, what is your general custom? You open windows and portals with pleasure to the temptation. You welcome it. It is agreeable to your inclinations, because it finds in your own soul a sympathetic chord. In the twinkling of an eye you have made with it a tour round the world, and in spirit written a romance that twenty volumes would not contain. By the disquiet and excitement, the painful feelings now experienced as the natural result of what has preceded, you will recognize, though late, what a dangerous enemy you have admitted within your walls. You would now like to expel him, but it is too late. The dam is broken, the stream rushes with full force, the overflow will cease only when the water has run off. Or, to speak less figuratively, your excitable imagination has broken loose from the restraint of the will; and its frenzy will cease only when weariness or some chance accident steps in, so to say, to interrupt it. Nothing, then, remains for you but to be patient, and guard against your will's taking any part in what it cannot prevent. How this may be done, I shall now explain to you.

II. Despise the Temptation, be Patient, Divert your Attention.—Is the imagination over-excited? Then, as has been said, it is no longer possible, by open resistance to master its fantastical images and representations, or the impressions they produce. Only by despising them, by enduring them with patience and a certain indifference, can you resist the current, presupposing, of course, that your free-will does not become an actor in the scene, does not give consent to the ridiculous, if not sinful thoughts that fill the mind. Yes, in spite of the various, extravagant fancies of the imagination; in spite of sinful sentiments and impressions, which are the natural consequence of such fancies, if your will still remains subject to you, such interior disturbances amount to nothing. The struggle has its difficulties, which are all the greater in proportion as you have allowed yourself to be frequently mastered, and thereby strengthened the power of the Evil One. But by the aid of grace, which will never be wanting, you can and should keep your will free from the bustle and excitement going on in your interior. Do nothing but rise above your disordered imagination, remain passive, ignore the storm, wait patiently till its fury is spent. You must act as one attacked by a violent headache or fever. He gives such ills no nourishment, he guards against strengthening them by indulging in what has produced them; but he knows also, it would be useless to oppose them violently or to protest against them. Have you a stone in your hand, and do you wish to be relieved of it? Do not resort to any extraordinary effort. Merely open your hand, and the stone will fall of its own weight.

The frightful pictures which the imagination sometimes places before us, are in reality of no account. They gain no ascendancy over a firm, determined will that passes them by unnoticed. On the contrary, excessive fear deprives the soul of presence of mind and power of defence. The timid warrior, like the turkey in the fable, loses his head in the contest and falls into the snares of the enemy. The deceitful pictures of the imagination are like the shows of strolling players. They exhibit their wonders to their gaping spectators; and the more attention they receive, the more they exert themselves. But when that is withheld they put up their chattels, and move off. Notice and indignant replies exasperate an abusive scoundrel, whereas the opposite course reduces him to silence. If you have been accustomed to attend to the delusions of your fancy, so that they have grown into fixed and incontestible prejudices, then to treat them with patience and contempt will be more difficult, but none the less necessary. Here, as in all other cases, it is still true that free-will can deny consent. It is as if you were in the presence of an immoral picture and your eyes forcibly opened upon it. You would be compelled to behold what could only fill you with disgust. Would you sin by this unwilling glance as by a deliberate one? Certainly not. It is precisely the same with the imagination.

Another illustration will, perhaps, show more clearly that contempt, patience, and diversion of mind, serve as excellent means in this struggle. Picture to yourself a madman crying: "Fire! Thieves!" Terror seizes the whole family. All rush to extinguish the flames, to expel the thieves, when some cool-headed person quietly says: "O it is only the fool screaming!" Instantly the excitement subsides. The terrifying scream may, perhaps, have produced in some one a violent headache, but he pays no heed to it. He laughs and goes about his ordinary affairs, if not without indignation, yet without alarm. This is a true picture of what takes place in many souls tormented by the insane fancies of their imagination. Never forget that the imagination is the fool of the house. It is not the soul, the free, rational soul whose actions alone concern the conscience. You will be frequently obliged to listen to the noise and shouts by which the fool tries to mislead you. But you need not take part with him, you need not scream with him, much less shape your actions by his dictum, nor silence him by long arguments. Say to yourself: "No. Although forced to listen, I shall give no heed to the fool and his ravings. To silence him is not in my power. I shall not even attempt it. Patience, then! When he is wearied, I shall have rest. In the meantime, I shall attend to my duty as well as possible. It will serve as a salutary distraction, and I shall be better able to endure the tiresome struggle." Behold the manner of comporting oneself in a situation certainly far from pleasant.

TENTH POINT.

Of Frequently Recurring Temptations. In Time of Peace Prepare for War.

When a soul is exposed to frequent temptations, she must in time of peace prepare for the attack and gather strength for resistance. He who awaits the moment of assault to arm himself, will be surprised and conquered. In time of peace prepare for war. This well-known maxim must also be observed in the spiritual life—the more so, as here every defeat entails incalculable loss, since it robs us of an eternal kingdom.

Preparation for temptation consists in a truly recollected interior life. A dissipated soul pays no great attention to what passes in her interior, and a temptation may have made great progress before she is able to offer any resistance. A soul that occupies herself with frivolous things will find it difficult to consider the great truths of religion, which alone can hold the balance against the violence of passion. On the contrary, one that carefully preserves interior recollection by occupying herself with God and holy thoughts, sees the enemy's approach from afar. She hastens to guard against him, and soon comes off victorious. A mind accustomed to revolve the great truths of our holy religion and a heart to which virtue has become sweet, will rarely be carried away by the deceitful bait held out by passion. The persevering exercise of prayer, the protection of the saints, and particularly of the dear Mother of God, who is to be invoked in every danger, open the treasures of heaven and obtain those special graces of which a dissipated soul is unworthy, and for which she does not even ask.

If to an interior, recollected life is added the frequent reception of the Holy Sacraments, then is one doubly secure. Although sometimes overcome by temptations, one should not for that reason turn away from those holy means of grace, but rather receive them still more frequently. The Holy Sacrament of Penance was instituted not only for the remission of actual sins, but to impart special grace for avoiding possible ones, and to strengthen the soul against her passions, the cause of her former falls. To live apart from the Holy Sacraments, is to rob the soul of grace. The oftener one approaches the Holy Sacrament of Penance, the greater horror will he have for sin. All learned theologians agree in saying that a Christian who has had the misfortune to commit mortal sin should not delay to extricate himself from his sad condition. And this so much the more if he experiences within himself a strong inclination to that particular sin; for once separated from God, he is exposed to imminent danger upon the return of the temptation, and he will surely relapse into his sins. The greatest injury he can inflict on his soul, is to withdraw from the Holy Sacrament of Penance.

Holy Communion, when received with due preparation and proper dispositions, is a powerful safeguard against temptation. Here is received Jesus Christ Himself, the Saviour of our soul. He gives Himself entirely to us. How, then, can He refuse grace necessary for fidelity to Him? The Council of Trent says of the Divine Eucharist: "Jesus Christ left us this Divine Sacrament as a spiritual nourishment for the preservation and strengthening of the life of grace in us, and as a protecting means that purifies us from daily faults and preserves us from mortal sin." Session XIII., chap. 2. But when does the soul most urgently require a special grace that confirms her in good, strengthens her against the enemies of salvation, and preserves her from mortal sin? Assuredly, in the time of temptation. In the days of trial this Heavenly Food of the soul, this powerful means of protection, is more necessary than ever. Voluntarily to deprive one's self would be to yield to one's weakness. Again, a soul that worthily receives the Holy Sacraments, occupies herself with the sentiments she should carry to the Lord's Table. She ignores the temptations that pursue her, and feels strongly impelled to keep aloof from all that could place an obstacle to divine grace.

A further preservative against temptation is the practice of penance. Penance obtains many graces, humbles the understanding, weakens the passions, satisfies for sins and imperfections, renews holy fervor, and arouses vigilance. It should not, however, be used immoderately. Every Christian should do penance, should mortify himself, but only to a certain limit. Whatever exceeds this, is excessive; and again, Christian prudence commands us to take care of our health. Penance is for most people a sure remedy against evil inclinations; yet there are some to whom, on account of a certain peculiarity of character or temperament, it may become extremely hurtful. Such persons should never undertake anything of the kind without counsel and permission.

ELEVENTH POINT.

Of the Advantages of Temptation.

Many grieve over temptations, because they do not view them in the true light. They look only on their danger and the evil to which they incite, forgetting the advantages they procure and the spiritual benefits that may be gained by them. Many, either because they do not know their worth, or do not reflect upon it, draw little or no benefit from their temptations. May the following instructions help all such souls to endure more patiently and overcome more easily!

In temptation a Christian soul can practice the solid virtues and accumulate great merit for heaven. What a consolation for us that even the snares of our enemy may procure us the greatest advantages for eternity; and that the evil spirits, if we but will it, may promote our happiness and salvation! How greatly does this thought strengthen and encourage us in the combat! Listen to the words of St. James: "My brethren, count it all joy when you shall fall into divers temptations. Knowing that the trying of your faith worketh patience. And patience hath a perfect work; that you may be perfect and entire, failing in nothing."[1]

Generally, man reflects but little upon self, knows himself but imperfectly, and dives reluctantly into his own heart, because he fears the discovery of faults that would cause his self-love to blush. His whole aim is to extenuate his shortcomings and to rejoice in his own good qualities. From this foolish inclination originate the sensitiveness and irritability of his self-love, the vain self-esteem that exposes him to so many dangers, and the self-complacency that makes him prefer himself to others. Pride, the mainspring of all his evils, blinds him to his faults. Even pious souls are not always free from self-seeking. Glancing upon their virtues, they fancy themselves to be something, they strive to have their good qualities recognized; even their holiest actions are infected by this secret passion.

The infallible remedy for this dangerous evil and its bad consequences is temptation. Temptations reveal to man his whole heart. They show it to him as it is. When left to himself, he can no longer conceal himself from himself, or palliate his defects. Temptation is the light by whose dull gleam he sees the full extent of his weakness, his misery, and his perversity. Anger, envy, jealousy, hatred, revenge, and the still lower and more humiliating passions attack him one after the other; and thus assaulted, he arrives at the conviction that by nature he is not superior to others.

The first fruit of self-knowledge in a Christian soul is humility, such humility as stands in correct relation with her misery. The soul finds in herself subjects for humiliation only. She may notice some good qualities; but the tribute of praise that they might exact soon dwindles before the numerous evil inclinations with which she has constant-

[1] St. James i. 2.

ly to contend. She is, in her own eyes, what she would be before men, were her heart with all its passions unveiled to them. She feels no other sentiment for herself than contempt; therefore she constantly humbles herself before God and exacts nothing from men. We know what sterling advantages self-knowledge animated by a religious spirit brings with it.

A soul to whom the whole misery of her heart has become clear stands confused before God; and such confusion is most beneficial to her, since by it she is preserved from vain self-esteem.

The knowledge of our own perversity as imparted to us by temptation has still another result, which may very much contribute to our perfection. A soul that, in spite of her temptations, would still work out her salvation, must unite herself more closely to God and be more watchful over herself. Close adherence to God and watchfulness over self are two excellent means to make rapid progress in the way of holiness. Such a soul, as soon as the enemy begins to stir, raises her eyes to the holy mountain whence cometh help. The more he molests her, the more closely she clings to God in prayer, as a child in the midst of danger holds on more and more tenaciously to its father's hand. She is watchful to guard against the danger in advance, and she avoids everything that could in the least excite former temptations or give rise to new ones. He that has learned from daily combating, that his wicked inclinations must be subdued at their birth, will detect the evil emotions of his heart at once, and will never be taken unawares.

TWELFTH POINT.

Devotion to the Ever-Blessed Virgin Mary is an Excellent Remedy Against Temptations and a Means of Preserving Interior Peace.

We do not undertake to speak here in detail of the goodness and power of the ever-Blessed Virgin and of devotion to her. The whole volume would not suffice for that. We wish only to remind souls in a few words how powerful is Mary's assistance for the preservation of interior peace. Among the honorable titles conferred by Holy Church on the Mother of the Redeemer, we find that of Queen of Peace —*Regina Pacis*. How aptly does not this apply to her! She is, indeed, the mother of the true Solomon, the King of Peace. According to the expression of the Holy Fathers, she is prefigured by that sign of peace given by God after the Deluge; viz., the rainbow.

Mary is the dispensatrix of all divine gifts. In her hands, therefore, lies that most precious of all goods, interior peace that surpasses all understanding. To her we must turn for this, as well as for all other gifts. St. Bonaventure says: "Our eyes should ever be raised to Mary's hands, to receive good things from her." From whom shall the child seek rest and help if not from its own dear mother, who so faithfully and solicitously watches over its happiness? Mary is our Mother by her love, and by the last testament of her Divine Son who, on the cross, gave her to us as a Mother. The bonds that unite us to her are stronger and holier than the ties of nature. The blessed servant of God, Father Nieremberg, assures us that the united love of all mothers for their children, is only a shadow compared with that of Mary for each one of hers. Mary loves us more than all the angels and saints together. She proved this when, for our salvation, she consented to the shedding of the blood of her Divine Son. St. Bonaventure applies to her these words which St. John wrote of God the Father: "For God so loved the world, as to give His only begotten Son."[1] What could she deny us after such an offering? And how could we on our part place limits to our love and confidence in her? "They can never be lost," says Blosius, "who humbly and ardently persevere in devotion to Mary."

St. Bonaventure says that not without reason does Holy Church call Mary our hope: "Although He should kill me, I will trust in Him."[2] God so created Mary that no one can fear her. Not justice, but mercy alone belongs to her. The Lord has endowed her with goodness and compassion so great that she can despise no one fleeing to her for help; she can deny assistance to no one pleading for it. God gave us Mary for a support in our weakness, a consolation in our sufferings, a help in our dangers, and a refuge in our sinfulness. Even crime cannot prevent our having recourse to this Mother so full of tenderness. When in danger of losing peace, let us flee at once to Mary. It is, however, in the hour of temptation that we must take refuge near our powerful, our good Mother. The mere invocation of her holy name, strengthens us against the attacks of the tempter. "Glorious and wonderful is thy name, O Mary!" cries out St. Bonaventure. "He that invokes it with confidence, has nothing to fear at the hour of death; for the devils can not hear it without fleeing from the soul that invokes it."

"Therefore," says St. Thomas of Villanova, "As little chickens at the sight of the hawk fly under the protecting wing of the hen, so should we flee to the protection of Mary's mantle as soon as the tempter attacks us." Mary herself once said to St. Bridget: "If even my sinful children flee to me for protection, I feel impelled to save them, like a mother at the sight of a sword raised above the head of her son."

We shall, then, always be victorious in our combats against sin, if we have recourse to Mary. Calling upon her holy name during temptation, is the best evidence that we have courageously opposed the enemy; and this is particularly the case in temptations against holy purity. Her name is, indeed, the buckler of perfect purity. The names of Jesus and Mary should be inseparable in our heart; in temptation they should constitute our firm support. To these holy names is associated a third, inseparable from them in our prayers upon earth as it is in heaven. It is the name of Joseph, the virgin spouse of Mary, the foster-father and protector of Jesus, of whom St. Teresa says: "In all things, I choose him for my protector. I never remember having asked anything of God through his intercession without having been favorably heard. Never have I known any one who invoked him without making signal progress in perfection. His power with God is of wonderful efficacy for all that turn to him with confidence." The people of Egypt, pressed by famine, begged their king to aid them. They received for reply the words: "Go to Joseph, and do all that he shall tell you." And, in like manner, Jesus Christ, our Divine King, sends tried souls in their disquiet, temptations, and sufferings to His foster-father, to him who protected His childhood, who guided Him in all things, and to whom He confided the management of His household. Yes, to us He says: "Go to Joseph, and do all that he shall say to you."

THIRTEENTH POINT.

Means Against Sadness.

Here are two rules that seem to be of the utmost importance here. The first is that you make use of the natural means offered you by Providence, in order to shake off sadness. Do not overburden yourself with laborious occupations, spare your corporal and spiritual strength; reserve for yourself some leisure hours in which to pray, to read, and to enjoy good conversation. Cheer your soul with thoughts of eternal happiness, and shake off depression by spiritual and physical diversion taken in the Lord.

Seek also a discreet and trusty friend to whom you can pour out your heart. To such a one disclose everything that is not the secret of another. Perfect confidence enlarges and enlightens the mind. A sorrow long concealed oppresses the heart. Speak out, and you will discover that you have made the matter over which you are grieving much more serious than it really is. Nothing so quickly dispels gloom as the simplicity and humility with which, at the sacrifice of self-esteem you reveal discouragement and dejection, and seek light and consolation in the holy communication that ought to exist between the children of God. Confine yourself to those of your acquaintances whose conversation is cheerful and recreative. It is not necessary that your circle should be large, nor must you be too fastidious. Be ready to converse with all peaceable and reasonable people. Again, whenever you feel sadness creeping over you, read, work, or take a walk. Change occupation, that weariness may not attack you. In short, do whatever your frame of mind may suggest, provided there is nothing sinful in it. If you feel that, in spite of these helps and rules, sadness still asserts its reign, then follow the second rule: Endure patiently. Interior desolation carries the soul more speedily forward on the way of pure faith than all exterior exercises could do. But do not let yourself be held back by it. Do not indulge in relaxation which will aim at usurping possession of your interior. One step when in this state is always a giant stride, and is of more value than thousands when the soul is in consolation. Despise your dejection and go on quietly, for this state of soul is more useful, more meritorious to you than gigantic, heroic strength and courage.

O how deceitful is that sensible courage that finds everything easy, undertakes all, suffers everything, and unhesitatingly attributes all to self! Ah, it nourishes self-esteem and confidence! It pleases the world; but to the soul it is a refined poison.

A soul that, like Christ in the Garden of Olives, is sorrowful unto death, and with her crucified Lord, cries out: "My God! my God! why hast Thou forsaken me?"[1] is much more purified, much better fortified in humility than the valiant one who rejoices in peace over the fruits of her virtues.

[1] Mark xv. 34.

CHAPTER V.

On Prayer.

FIRST POINT.[1]

For What we should Pray.—We Must Persevere in Prayer.

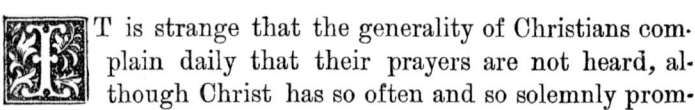

IT is strange that the generality of Christians complain daily that their prayers are not heard, although Christ has so often and so solemnly promised to grant the fulfilment of all our petitions. We cannot ascribe this result to the nature of the thing for which we pray, since in His promise Jesus excepts nothing: "Therefore, I say unto you, all things whatsoever you ask when you pray, believe that you shall receive, and they shall come unto you."[2] Nor can we attribute it to the unworthiness of the petitioner, for Christ gave His word to all without exception: "For every one that asketh receiveth."[3] Whence comes it then that so many prayers remain unheard? Perhaps, because the greater part of men are so immoderate, and impetuous in their demands. They seem to aim at forcing the Lord to yield to their wishes. Do their rudeness and impetuosity render them troublesome? No, nothing of all this; and I am convinced that one reason why we receive so little from God is, that we desire so little, importune so little.

Jesus Christ, on the part of His Heavenly Father, has made us the promise to give us all things; consequently, the greatest as well as the least. But He has also prescribed the order we should observe in our petitions; so that if we do not follow His directions, we may hope in vain to receive.

---

[1] This point is taken from Father de la Colombière.
[2] Mark xi. 24.   [3] Matt. vii. 8.

He expressly tells us: "Seek first the kingdom of God and His justice, then shall all else be added thereto." We are not forbidden to wish for riches and whatever else appertains to the maintenance and enjoyment of life; but they must be desired in their order only. If desirous of having our wishes fulfilled, we must seek first the absolutely necessary, and to them shall be added the less important.

Holy Scripture furnishes us an example of this in Solomon, the Wise Man. When God left him at full liberty to ask whatever he wished, the pious king craved only wisdom wherewith worthily to fulfil his regal duties. He chose neither treasures, nor earthly glory. He aimed only at embracing so favorable an occasion to obtain true and lasting goods. By this wise procedure he received not only what he had asked, but even more than he had desired. "Because thou hast asked this thing, and hast not asked for thyself long life nor riches, nor the lives of thy enemies, but hast asked for thyself wisdom to discern judgment. Behold, I have done for thee according to thy words, and have given thee a wise and understanding heart. Yea, and the things also which thou didst not ask: to wit, riches and glory."[1]

Since God acts thus, we need no longer wonder that we have hitherto prayed without effect. I must say that I have often been moved with compassion at beholding the fervor of certain persons who have had novenas offered, who have given alms, made vows, performed fasts and pilgrimages in order to succeed in earthly undertakings. "Blind men!" I exclaimed to myself, "how much I fear that you pray to no purpose! These vows and sacrifices should have been brought to the Lord to obtain perfect conversion, patience, contempt of the world, detachment from creatures. After taking this first important step, you could have begged for health and temporal blessings, and God would have granted all your desires over and above."

When the most important petitions are not made first,

[1] III. Kings iii. 11, 12, 13.

God often denies the temporal; since without the spiritual, they would prove not only prejudicial but even injurious. We murmur and complain that God is cruel and unfaithful to His promises. But let us remember that our God is a good Father, who would rather endure our complaints and murmurs than quiet and console us with pernicious gifts.

What has been said of prayer in regard to temporal things, applies also to prayer for the averting of temporal evils. For example, some one says to me: "I do not long for riches. I should be content, if I were only freed from my vexatious embarrassments. Gladly would I leave fame and celebrity to those that desire them, could I only avoid the shame which an enemy's calumny is preparing for me. Freely do I resign pleasure and enjoyment; but the pains from which I suffer, I can no longer endure. I have already prayed so long and implored the Lord to smooth matters for me, but He remains inexorable," etc., etc. I reply that I am not surprised that God is deaf to your petitions. You suffer from interior ills which are much greater than the exterior ones of which you complain. Why do you not rather pray to be freed from the former? Had you prayed with this intention only half so much as you did to be delivered from temporal sufferings? God had long since set you free from both. Your poverty serves to humble your naturally proud spirit; the calumnies, which trouble you so much, are necessary for you, because you cling so tenaciously to the world; that illness is a check upon your impetuous seeking after pleasure. God would give you a proof not of love but aversion, if He removed this cross before you are in possession of the virtues necessary for you. Did God perceive in you an ardent longing for these virtues, He would give them to you, and you would have no need to ask for other things. You perceive, therefore, that we receive nothing, because we ask for so little. God cannot circumscribe His infinite munificence without injury to us. But observe, I do not say that it is not permitted you to pray to God for temporal things. The prayer for temporal blessings is sufficiently purified when the condition is added: "In so far as it is not contrary to Thy honor and my salvation!" But as it seldom redounds to God's greater glory or furthers the soul's salvation to be heard in such petitions, I repeat that you run the risk of receiving nothing so long as you do not ask for the higher gifts.

Shall I tell you how to pray for temporal happiness and in such a manner as to force God to hear you? Say to Him once for all and with your whole heart: "O my God! either give me wealth sufficient for my desires, or else infuse into my heart such contempt for riches that I may no longer desire them! Either free me from poverty, or make it so lovable that I shall prefer it to all the treasures of the world. Either put an end to my sufferings, or grant that they may become to me a source of pleasure and contentment.

"Thou canst take from me this cross, or Thou canst make it light and sweet. Thou canst extinguish the fire that consumes me, or without extinguishing it, Thou canst make it serve to cool me, as did the flames of the fiery furnace the young Israelites. I implore Thee for the one or the other. What matters it in what way I attain happiness? If by the possession of earthly goods, I shall be eternally thankful; if by their privation, it will be a miracle still more glorious to Thy holy name, and one that will lay me under greater obligations." Such a prayer is worthy a true Christian. And what will be its results? First, come what may, you will be perfectly contented. Can they who languish most for worldly treasures, desire more? Secondly, you will infallibly receive not one alone of the coveted graces, but become a sharer in both. God will bestow upon you riches and the spirit of detachment, so that you may possess the former without danger. He will take away your sufferings whilst infusing into you such a thirst for them that, without the cross, you will gain the merit of the patience of the cross. In a word, He will make you happy here below, whilst at the same time causing you to feel and understand the nothingness of earthly happiness. In this way, your happiness here on earth cannot contribute to your misery in the other world. What can you desire more? So great a good certainly deserves the asking. It is worth importunity and perseverance in prayer. The reason that so little is received is not only that we ask so little, but also because we rarely pray aright for the little we do ask.

Do you desire that your prayers be infallibly heard? Would you constrain God to fulfil all your desires? I say to you, above all, never weary nor waver in prayer! He who ceases to pray soon loses humility and confidence; and therefore deserves not to be heard. An ancient Father of the Church says: "Pray not in an imperious tone, as if you would be heard at once. That would seem as if you expected from God instant obedience to your commands. Do you not know that He rejects the proud and gives His grace to the humble? What! your pride revolts when you are constrained to repeat the same petition! Does it not evince a want of confidence in the Divine Goodness, so quickly to despair of obtaining what is asked, or to regard the least delay as a refusal?"

Christian souls, learn a truth which I would deeply imprint upon your heart! A proper idea of Divine Goodness will never allow a person to think himself rejected, he can never believe that God will rob him of hope. For my part, I avow that the longer God permits me to pray for a grace, the more my desire for it increases; neither do I consider my past prayer lost, unless it has been discontinued. But if, after a whole year's fruitless entreaty, I go on as fervently as when I began, I have not the slightest doubt of the fulfilment of my desires. Far from becoming discouraged at the delay I rejoice, convinced that the longer God permits me to pray, the more perfectly I shall be heard. Had my first entreaties been utterly fruitless, I should not have had the grace to repeat them and my confidence would not have remained unshaken. But since my perseverance has not faltered, I may justly hope to be richly rewarded. Not till after sixteen years of prayers and tears, did St. Monica obtain the conversion of her son, St. Augustine. But O, what a conversion! What a consummate change of mind! How much more than the pious mother had dared to hope! Augustine was shackled by the chains of sensual pleasures and unbelief. All that Monica desired was to see the licentious youth happily united in the bonds of holy wedlock, and God gave her the joy of seeing him embrace the highest counsels of the Gospel. She desired only that Augustine should be a Christian, and God appointed him a shepherd of His flock, a priest, and a bishop. Had this mother, after one or two years' prayer, allowed discouragement to seize upon her; or had she, seeing the evil she deplored ever on the increase, after ten or twelve years, ceased to supplicate for her son's conversion, what an injury would she not have done him, of what consolation deprived herself, of what treasures robbed future generations!

One word now for pious souls who plead at the foot of the altar for those priceless spiritual goods, for which God is so pleased to be petitioned. Happy souls, who in the light of the Lord have understood the value of earthly things —courageous souls, who groan under the yoke of passion and implore deliverance from perverse affections—fervent souls, inflamed with the desire of serving God holily and perfectly,—pious souls, who implore the conversion of a beloved husband, of sons, or friends;—I beg you, in God's name, not to weary! Never leave off praying. Be indefatigable! Be persevering! To-day God denies, to-morrow you shall receive! This year you have been unsuccessful, but next year you shall superabound. Do not consider your labor lost. God numbers your every sigh. You shall receive according to the measure of your supplications. You are collecting for yourself a treasure which will suddenly be yours and amply fulfil your desires.

Behold, again, the loving mystery of the Lord! Supposing that He refuses your petition. He dissembles only to inflame you with new fervor. Recall the history of His treatment of the Canaanite woman. He would neither see nor hear her. He treated her as a stranger—yes, He even treated her sternly. One would think that He would have become impatient and indignant, that the importunity of the unfortunate creature would have exasperated Him. But no! He is filled with wonder at her confidence and humility. They rejoice His Divine Heart. It is for the same reason that He appears to reject you, that you, too, may repeat your prayer. " O disguised Goodness that assumes the appearance of cruelty!" cries out the Abbé Guerric. " With what tenderness dost Thou reject those to whom Thou dost intend to grant the most!" Be not led into error, Christian soul! Implore the more earnestly, the more God seems to reject you.

Do like the Canaanite woman. Arm yourself with the same weapons against God as He Himself uses against you. Say to Him: " True, Thou wouldst throw the bread of children to the dogs, wert Thou to let me share it. I am wholly undeserving, nor do I expect it in virtue of my own merits. It is through those of my Saviour only that I ask. Ah, Lord! take less account of my unworthiness than of Thy promises! Be not unjust to Thy own mercy by treating me so justly! Were I more worthy of Thy favors, the conferring of Thy benefits on me would honor Thee less. It is, indeed, not just to bestow favors on an ungrateful recipient; but I implore Thy mercy and not Thy justice." Remain firm, happy soul! You who have begun to wrestle so well with the Lord, let Him not go free. He is pleased when you do Him violence, for He desires to be conquered by you. Distinguish yourself by your importunity. Become a marvel of perseverance. Force the Lord to show himself to you unveiled. Entreat His mercy until filled with astonishment He says to you: " Great is thy faith: be it done to thee as thou wilt."[1]

[1] Matt. xv. 28.

SECOND POINT.[1]

Various Instructions on Prayer and on the Dryness often Experienced in it.

As soon as certain souls cease to experience pleasure in prayer, they are not unfrequently tempted to pray no more. To discover their error they must consider that perfect prayer and the love of God are one and the same thing. Prayer does not consist in emotions of sweetness, in pious imaginations, in vivid mental illuminations, nor even in the consoling consciousness of contemplating God. These are only externals. Without them the love of God may be the purer in us ; because as soon as deprived of all such additions, it is more directly and exclusively united to Him alone. But such a love of pure faith deprives poor nature of comfort and support. We deem all lost by such despoilment, whereas all is gained.

Pure love resides solely in the will. It is not an effect of the feelings, and the imagination has no part in it. It acts without sentiment just as blind faith believes without seeing. You must not suppose love to exist in the conceit of the imagination. Not at all. True love lives in the will separated from the imagination. The more intellectual the interior operation, the greater its efficacy, the higher the degree of perfection that God desires for us. The operation of our will is, therefore, much more perfect when it is purely spiritual ; for by it faith is proved and humility preserved. Then is love chaste and sincere. Then the soul loves God for Himself, no longer depending upon sweets or consolations. She follows the Lord, but not because of the multiplication of the bread.

" What !" some one replies, " does piety consist in mere union of our will with the will of God, which union is, perhaps, more imaginary than real?" I answer : " If this union of the will with God is not confirmed by fidelity on

[1] Taken from Fénelon.

important occasions, I shall indeed believe it chimerical; for a good tree brings forth good fruit. A good will, although co-existing with those little weaknesses that God leaves in the soul for her humiliation, should make us attentive to fulfil the Divine Will. If she is conscious of her daily faults, she may feel sure of possessing that uprightness of will that entitles her to a place among the 'men of good will.'

True virtue and pure love are found only in the will. And is it not a great deal for one always to incline to the most perfect as soon as he knows it? to retrace his steps when he remarks that he has deviated from it in the slightest degree? never deliberately to will anything that God does not will? and finally, in a spirit of entire renunciation and self-sacrifice, to be perfectly ready to surrender all, and that even when every species of consolation is wanting? Do you count as nothing self-examination, the retrenchment of self-love, the habit of acting in naked faith, the rejecting of useless returns upon self? Does not the old man die more quickly by these means than by the beautiful reflections of self-love and the numerous exterior exercises by which we seek to prove our progress?

It is an infidelity against pure faith for a soul to wish to know for a certainty that her state is good, and for that purpose to aim at knowing exactly what she does. We shal' never know it, for God wills that we should remain ignorant of such things. For this reason, to reflect so much upon it simply means to lose time in walking by making considerations on one's gait. The safest and shortest way is that of self-abnegation, self-forgetfulness, and abandonment to God. Self should not, except through necessity, receive a thought.

The best prayer is no other than the love of God. For this not many words are necessary. God has no need of our words. He knows our most secret sentiments. You truly pray when your heart prays; and the heart prays by its desires. To pray means also to desire, but to desire what

God wills we should desire. Conformably to this principle St. Augustine says: "He that loves little prays little; he that loves much, prays much."

The heart that is animated by right desires and true love never ceases to pray. The love that lies concealed in the depths of the heart, prays without intermission; for though the thoughts are not turned directly to God, He knows them. God sees in our souls the desire which He Himself has infused, the desire of which you yourself are not always conscious. This desire, which is your determined frame of mind, touches the heart of God; it is a secret voice which incessantly brings down His mercy upon us; indeed it is itself that "Spirit which asketh for us with unspeakable groanings."[1]

This love implores God to give what is wanting to us, to regard our weakness less than the uprightness of our good intentions. We know not for what we should ask, and we would often long for what would be injurious to us. We would aim at special graces, pious sentiments, and shining virtues, fitted only to nourish nature and self-confidence. But pure love prepares us for all the secret designs of God. It leads to unreserved abandonment to His will and renders it at all times eager to allow Him to do in us His will, what He wills and as He will.

In this happy state, whilst willing nothing, we actually will all that happens to us. What God gives us is precisely what we would have wished; for we wish all that He wills, and only what He wills. This condition includes in itself every species of prayer. It is a disposition of the heart that contains in itself every desire; for the Spirit asks in us what the Spirit Itself will give us. Even in the midst of exterior occupations, even when the circumstances in which Providence has placed us are such as to occasion dissipation, we carry within our breast an inextinguishable fire that is constantly uttering its silent prayer, like a lamp ever burning before the throne of the Lord; "I sleep, but my

[1] Romans viii. 26.

heart watches."[1] "Blessed is that servant whom his lord finds watching."[2]

To preserve this spirit of prayer, and consequent union with God, we must observe two rules in particular. First, that we nourish it ourselves; and secondly, that we avoid everything whereby we could lose it.

What nourishes the spirit of prayer in us? Regular spiritual reading and meditation; frequently looking up to God during the day, a retreat from time to time, and the reception of the Sacraments.

Everything by which we might lose the spirit of prayer should fill us with fear and rouse us to greater watchfulness. Therefore we must avoid too great distractions and worldly society. We must renounce all pleasures that too greatly excite the passions; we must ward off everything that could re-awaken love for the world, or our former vicious inclinations.

We might multiply these points to infinity, but we can here give only general rules, for every soul has her own special needs.

In order to nourish the spirit of prayer one must choose for spiritual reading the books that instruct on duties and failings, that teach us the greatness of God, that tell us how we are in duty bound to serve Him, and that point out in what we have failed. There is no question here of the reader's heart being roused to violent emotion as if by a touching drama. "The tree must bear fruit."[3] Life in the root is proved by the fruitfulness of its branches.

The subject of meditation should neither be choice nor subtle. The best are those simple and natural reflections that spring directly from the truths of faith. Consider few of them, but do so profoundly, leisurely, tranquilly, without aiming at high thoughts and glorious visions. Above all, strive to show forth in your daily life what you have learned in meditation.

With regard to the manner of meditating, experience

[1] Canticle v. 2.   [2] Luke xii. 37.   [3] Matt. vii. 17.

must be the guide. He who finds a fixed method good, should keep to it. But he who cannot subject himself to such, ought not on this account to contemn what is beneficial to many other souls, and what is so highly recommended by spiritual men of great piety and experience. Every method is intended to help the soul and not to hinder her. As soon as it becomes useless or a hindrance, we must abandon it.

In the beginning it would be well to use a book, closing it at the point that strikes us, and reopening it when food for meditation is exhausted. As a general rule, those truths that are the more attractive are the more useful for us; for God makes known to us through them, His particular impulse of grace. By this means also we can peacefully follow our inclinations. "The Spirit breatheth where He will; so is every one that is born of the Spirit."[1] "Where the Spirit of the Lord is there is liberty."[2]

By degrees consideration diminishes, whilst pious emotions, quiet contemplation, and holy desires increase. The soul has been instructed and sufficiently convinced; the heart now begins to enjoy—it is nourished and inflamed.

Prayer, at last, becomes by a simple and clear intuition more and more perfect, and the soul no longer needs so many subjects, no longer multiplies reflections. One word may afford sufficient matter for long prayer and consideration. We turn to God as to a friend. One has, at first, a thousand things to say, a thousand things to ask. Gradually, however, the conversation begins to flag, though without detriment to the enjoyment of the interview. All has been told, all has been discussed, there remains nothing more to be said. But the sweetness of being together, of gazing upon each other, of sitting side by side, is still theirs, they still taste the happiness of a sincere and intimate friendship. Though silent, they understand each other: they feel that they are intimately united, that both

[1] John iii. 8.   [2] II. Cor. iii. 17.

hearts are but one, and they pour without reserve one into the other.

So should prayer become a simple, confidential union with God, a union that transcends all human conception. But God Himself must raise us to this prayer. To aspire to it ourselves would be dangerous presumption. One must be conducted step by step by an experienced guide, who, first by thorough instruction in spiritual things and then by urging on to perfect self-denial, secures a solid foundation for the edifice about to be raised.

As to the exercises of a retreat, and the reception of the Holy Sacraments, the soul must be guided by the judgment of the spiritual director. The particular needs of the soul, the effects of the Holy Sacraments on her, together with many other personal details should be taken into consideration.

PART IV.

OF SCRUPLES.

CHAPTER I.

What is to be Understood by Scruples.—The Difference between the Scrupulous and the Truly Pious.—Certain Characteristics by which Scruples may be recognized.

A SCRUPLE is a doubt as to what is or is not lawful. It may have little or no foundation, although it sometimes assumes the appearance of conviction, and throws the conscience into great confusion.[1]

Whoever is frequently disquieted by doubts of this kind, whether on one or several points, may be called scrupulous. This word has a contemptible signification, and as the most scrupulous are often erroneously reckoned the most pious, the scorn attached to the epithet frequently falls upon devotion itself. This is most unjust, for true piety is always coupled with light. Ignorance and doubt spring from spiritual darkness alone.

Neither must true piety be judged by the false ideas which scrupulous souls form of it. Two great masters of the interior life have in a few lines sketched their own high ideas of it. St. Francis de Sales says, "We must do everything from love, and nothing through constraint. We must love obedience more than we fear disobedience."

[1] Vasquez in 2. 2 disp. 67, Art. 2.

And the celebrated Archbishop of Cambray adds: "Woe to those trifling, self-entangled souls that are always in fear, whom fear leaves no time to love and make generous progress! O my God, I know it is Thy will that the heart which loves Thee should be broad and free! Therefore, I shall act with confidence, as the child playing in the arms of its mother. I shall rejoice in the Lord, and shall seek to make others rejoice. I shall enlarge my heart in the assembly of the children of God, and I shall strive to acquire the child-like sincerity, innocence, and joy of the Holy Spirit. Far from me, O my God, that miserable and over-solicitous knowledge which is ever consumed with self, ever holding the balance in hand to weigh every atom! Such lack of simplicity in the soul's dealings with Thee is truly an outrage against Thee. Such rigor imputed to Thee is unworthy of Thy paternal heart."

Scrupulosity is not perfection, it is failing. It is a weakness for which the soul, far from glorying, should humble herself before the Lord. To wade in conjectures, and to discover sin where sin does not exist, is a mental defect wholly irrational. Such a fault is as fatal as it is ridiculous, and is justly numbered among the greatest dangers to which a soul can be exposed. "A narrow, scrupulous conscience," says Gerson, "has often worse consequences than one that is too broad; for it is a way without an end, it wearies without leading to the desired term—eternal salvation! Discouragement, and too often despair, are its result."

According to Father Alvarez de Paz, the following are the chief characteristics of scruples, and by them a scrupulous soul may be known:

1st, and chiefly (and upon these signs should one most depend), when your director assures you of the fact.

2d. When you persist in thinking that you have confessed mortal sins, though your confessor assures you that there is either insufficient matter for absolution, or at mos only slight venial sins.

3d. When you have asked an experienced director's

What is to be Understood by Scruples.

advice on your doubts, and his answers have left you as comfortless as before.

4th. When you often propose questions upon trivial, insignificant matters which might apparently be easily settled.

5th. When with excessive care and anxiety you try to avoid certain imperfections over which the most pious souls pass lightly.

6th. When you are doubtful about things that do not disturb even the most anxious souls.

7th. When you are sad and dejected about past sins; when you muse over former confessions, and are worried about a thousand ridiculous thoughts which you persist in regarding as sins, although your will had no share in them.

8th. When you imagine your confessor does not understand you sufficiently to guide you, and when under this pretext you obstinately determine to oppose his decisions and commands; for instance, when in confession you refuse to adhere to the points he has prescribed to you, or to go to Holy Communion. Whoever, guided by his own judgment or that of his director, perceives in himself one of these signs, must admit that he is scrupulous. He should mistrust himself, renounce the direction of his own conscience, and confide himself to better hands, as the sick man leaves to the physician all the wisdom, judgment, and foresight necessary for his case.

CHAPTER II.

General Causes of Scruples.

WEAKMINDEDNESS.—A very common cause of scruples and unfounded doubt is the natural weakness of a mind upon which everything makes an impression, and which a trifle is sufficient to rob of peace.

This mental weakness may prevail in a greater or less degree. Existing in the highest degree, it trammels free-will and sound reason, and even entirely destroys them. But of such mental debility I speak not here, for its victims call for compassion and not for advice. The mental weakness here alluded to, is a natural defect which may be united with the greatest candor and virtue. It consists in the facility of being easily disquieted without the power of afterward deciding how far consent has been given.

2. A PERPLEXED BRAIN.—There are souls to whom it would be a great relief to be able to express themselves freely. They would speak openly if they could clearly and intelligibly understand the cause of their own trouble. But their brain is confused. They can declare nothing with certainty, and their words are naturally as confused and unintelligible as their thoughts. The director thinks, at first, that he has understood them; but a moment after a different version of the story is related. He may succeed in calming the soul for the time, but soon follow interminable questions and endless explanations.

This confusion of thought often arises from an exaggerated subtlety of the understanding that is ever ready to rack the brain, that in its vagaries outstrips the limits of common sense. A sound, healthy mind accepts reliable evidence, and with it remains in peace; but a crafty one with a head screwed to concert pitch, finds doubt where none exists, has its second thoughts, its sharp points with which to torment itself and others. It never accepts the decisions given it. He who gropes along this way instead of following the path of Christian simplicity, enlightenment, and knowledge, buries himself ever more and more deeply in darkness. He is wanting in humility, the only road that leads to light: "If you become not as little children," says Our Lord, "you shall not enter into the kingdom of heaven."[1] But children are docile, they hearken to their master's words. In all simplicity they receive instruction, their mind becomes gradually enlightened, and their judgment formed. It is precisely in this particular that anxious souls should allow themselves to be guided by their spiritual directors; otherwise they will never possess that interior peace which is so little in harmony with vain cavillings.

3. AN UNBRIDLED IMAGINATION.—A flighty imagination which welcomes every fancy and chases after every novelty, is a fertile source of scruples. This is the more true, by how much the more the imagination tends to exaggerate and to view everything in a distorted form. If moreover, stubbornness of character is added to such an imagination, then the resistance of one who would rectify it only embitters its possessor and confirms her in her own ideas. The imagination excites the senses to such a degree that one can hardly distinguish whether the will takes part in the matter, or upon what side it stands. Such a state is in the highest degree deserving pity. Yet this fault is not inconsistent with sincere piety; for piety has its seat in the heart, whose recesses are inaccessible to the imagination so long as the will bars the entrance.

They that confound imagination with their own being, that look upon it as part of self, should be taught that this faculty of the soul is, to a certain degree, a stranger, something outside of themselves over which they possess no

[1] Matt. xviii. 3.

other power than that of not allowing themselves to be ruled by it; that its silly conceits cannot be accredited to them as faults, since they are accountable only for the movements of their heart. This latter, even in the midst of a thousand impure imaginations, remains innocent so long as it takes no pleasure in such fancies. Finally, let the tried soul know that there is no better means to banish such temptations, or at least to lessen their attacks than to regard them with cool contempt. Fear increases their violence and obstinacy; scorn puts them to flight. The spirit of impurity especially has, for those that despise it, only the strength of a child; but it is a giant to those that fear it.

He who is tormented with a strong imagination, must learn not only to distinguish it from the will, but also to bridle it. Fénelon says: "You think, perhaps, that to curb your imagination does not depend upon you; but I beg leave to assure you that it does depend very much upon you. When one puts an end to deliberate emotions, the indeliberate are at once diminished. The less one yields to excitement, the greater his chance of becoming habitually calm, the greater his power to control his heated imagination. A pebble falling into the water, causes it for a time to play in ripples. So, in the beginning, you may not have been able to prevent some little emotion; but cease to agitate the water, and it will of itself gradually return to rest. God will guard your imagination if you cease to excite it by scruples, reflections, inquiries. . . . Turn away from long entertainments with your disorderly imagination. Control your day dreams, but do not use violence, for that would be like attempting to restrain a rushing stream. When you find that your imagination is growing excited, is conjuring up dangerous pictures before your mind, turn quietly to God, and aim not at offering determined resistance to its vain phantoms. Let them pass unmolested and busy yourself with some useful occupation."

4. IDEAL PERFECTION.—Many souls of perfectly sound

mind and moderate imagination, suffer notwithstanding from scruples, because they create for themselves an ideal virtue quite incompatible with man's condition in this life. They do not think of the evil consequences of original sin, which remain in us after our justification; they are astonished at the opposing elements, the contradictory inclinations and sentiments they discover in themselves. They know not how to distinguish between what must be improved and what endured; between what renders them guilty and what is left them for their humiliation; what is deliberate and what is not. They do not understand their real duty. They desire to uproot what ought to remain as a trial of patience. They are, consequently, ever uneasy, ever making anxious efforts that only serve to weary them, to rob them of interior peace, to plunge them from discouragement into despair; since it is impossible for them to reach their unreasonably pursued ideal.

The guide of such souls should teach them, that to sigh over one's misery and complain of it to God, is the ordinary prayer of the just; that the spirit is willing, but the flesh is weak; that the old man continues to live in us together with the new; that man's free-will is redeemed from sin, though concupiscence remains; that the senses and imagination are opposed to justice; that we carry the precious treasure of salvation in a frail vessel of dust, verily, in a body of corruption and death; that we must struggle to the last moment of our life; and that, finally, according to St. Augustine, "Our perfection here below consists less in not committing faults than in bewailing those we do commit."

5. IMPERFECT KNOWLEDGE OF RELIGIOUS PRINCIPLES.—Many souls know very well all that has just been said; yet they are consumed with pangs of conscience, because they are wanting in an adequate knowledge of the great principles of religion, and because they have no right idea of the hidden connection between certain moral truths that appear to be in direct opposition to one another.

Such persons fix their eyes upon one truth to the exclusion of all the others, forgetting that one may perhaps modify another. They know the unselfishness and necessity of almsgiving, but they know nothing of wise economy. They are prepared to pardon, but they will not admonish. They tremble in holy fear of God, but their hearts remain closed to the consolation of confidence in Him. They understand the dangers of speaking, but not those of keeping silence. They love prayer and the practice of penance, but they are wanting in the moderation which understands how to harmonize works of devotion with those of penance.

This exclusive attention to the acquisition of a single virtue exposes souls to a thousand doubts. Their one-sided manner of looking at a thing, in order to determine their mode of action, leads them to commit a hundred vagaries, which their sound reason does not approve, but which their conscience imperiously demands. They would regard as a great fault the sacrifice of inward agitation to exterior decorum, although they know well that on more than one occasion the former has led them too far.

To quiet such souls we must explain to them that the virtues are all connected, all in harmony with one another; and that they must never devote themselves exclusively to one.

In like manner, must they be instructed on the difference between the Counsels and the Commandments; between small faults of frailty and mortal sins. Every soul should endeavor to know the exact line of her duties. Not that such knowledge should prevent the striving after higher perfection or lead to the neglect of acts of virtue beyond this line, but that she may embrace such acts and such perfection magnanimously and heartily, a proceeding absolutely necessary, and yet quite incompatible with the overstrained fear of sin.

In connection with this, St. Antony gives us two rules of conduct, which will make the fulfilment of duties easy, and which we recommend souls to weigh maturely:

I. "When a precept admits of two interpretations, one

rigorous the other mild, we should, other things being equal, prefer the latter; for the Commandments of God and His Church have not been given to rob us of interior consolation, though a scrupulous and too anxious interpretation of them would necessarily produce such an effect.— Thus, for example, the command to fast does not hold good for all Christians; for the weak as well as for the strong, for the sick and for the healthy, with the same force. It is binding, in proper time and measure, only upon those who can fast without any notable prejudice to their health.

II. "Neither God nor the Church would command us anything impossible; for reason teaches that no one can be forced to do what he is not able. But the literal meaning of the word of the New Testament, *'impossible'* appears to me to be *'hardly possible,'* by reason of too great difficulty, —for otherwise how could even the Lord say: 'My yoke is sweet?' Thus the commandment enjoins us to pray devoutly though not with an uninterrupted, effective attention which human weakness does not always admit. But it imposes upon us that obligation only as far as is possible. Such fervor and attention really existed at the commencement of your prayer; but now it is implied in your good intention, so long as you do not by wilful distractions deliberately retract it. Of such distractions, however, a scrupulous soul would very rarely be guilty."

III. To these two rules of the holy divine, on the unanimous consent of all theologians, a third may be added: "A scrupulous soul, on account of her weakness, is not bound to watch so carefully over her conduct as others. Moderate care is sufficient for her."

It is, however, highly important for such souls to have a true idea of God; for practically, at least, they almost always consider Him as a hard, exacting master; as an inexorable judge whom nothing can soften; and, shall I say it? —almost as a spy who lays traps for them, who waits to ensnare them in a fault. Is this to honor the Lord as He wills to be honored? Is He not the most tender, the most merciful of Fathers, the Shepherd who gives His life to save His unfaithful sheep, the God whose tender mercies are above all His works?[1] Would one think of an honest man as such souls think of God? It is easy to understand how an idea so false and cheerless of God's disposition toward men must alarm and confound souls, and how necessary it is for such erroneous judgments to be rectified.

6. TOO MANY REFLECTIONS UPON SELF AND ONE'S OWN INTENTIONS.—Excessive self-examination and inquiries into one's intentions, end in uncertainty. The more closely one considers himself, the less he learns to know himself. One must be at a certain distance from an object in order rightly to distinguish it. If he stand too near, it appears, if seen at all, just as indistinct as if at too great a distance.

This thought must be placed clearly before souls, pious and fervent, but who do not understand the weakness of human reason, nor how easily it is confused and dazzled when it views an object too long and steadily. They will learn to know themselves much better if from time to time they view self at a certain distance; for a correct view maintains one in a happy medium between the two extremes of never reflecting upon self, or of doing so too frequently.

7. HOW DIFFICULT IT IS TO JUDGE ONE'S SELF JUSTLY.—It is very hard to judge one's self justly. The case in point concerns us too nearly and for this reason our judgment is always to be suspected. One is too indulgent; whilst another, from fear of this fault, is too exact. One shuns self-knowledge; the other thinks he knows himself only when he condemns himself.

The golden mean is for every one to render to himself a faithful account of his good and bad deeds; not to bury the gifts and talents received from God under his misery; nor to abuse them in order to conceal the same misery. Let

[1] Ps. cxliv. 9.

him sigh and thank. He should not excuse the bad, nor yet put an evil interpretation on the good.

Be as just and reasonable toward yourself as toward your neighbor. Be humble, but be also straightforward and simple. To avoid pride do not render yourself guilty of ingratitude. Prefer interior peace which stimulates you to confidence and warmer love, to that suspicious disquiet which keeps you always in fear, and leads at last to discouragement.

This golden mean, however, is not easily found; therefore it is more prudent to defer one's judgment of himself to a clear-sighted guide. The latter is disinterested and free from prejudice and all that could perplex the mind; hence, it is reasonable to prefer his intelligent decision to our own confused and suspicious ideas.

8. THE DIFFICULTY IN DISTINGUISHING THE THOUGHT FROM IMPRESSIONS, AND THE IMPRESSIONS FROM CONSENT. —If one were dealing with theory only, he might more readily leave the judgment of such matters to others. But most scruples do not relate to temptations of mere passing thought; they are those that dwell in the mind for some time, and produce upon it an impression more or less lively.

Here the discrimination must be made as to whether consent has been given and to what extent; whether the free-will approved that in which sensuality found pleasure; and whether what came into the mind tarried there, or was deliberate in its beginning or progress.

The imagination is so closely allied to the heart, and so near to the understanding, that it is very difficult to distinguish the action of each, which difficulty occasions a thousand doubts in otherwise well-instructed and often very innocent souls.

If those to whom the foregoing state of disquiet applies, had to decide the same matters for others, their judgment would not, in general, be expressed so severely as is that upon themselves. Not unfrequently they would counsel a friend to despise what throws themselves into fear and doubt; for in the former case they judge things by the light of truth and not according to feeling. The impression made by evil thoughts perplexes the mind of the one beset by them; and yet in the case of another, he would be perfectly clear-sighted.

Ask such souls what they would do if another laid the same difficulties before them. They would certainly not judge at random. They would make accurate comparisons between the bad thoughts and the ordinary actions of the person, between the impression produced by the temptation and the soul's actual wishes and sentiments, between the unavoidable effect of evil representations and that dependent on free-will. Not till after such comparison would they clearly distinguish temptation from consent. Then they would declare that, although the temptation might have been strongly felt, yet free-will had no part in it, and consequently no consent had been given.

The director must persuade such souls to follow, in their own case, the same moderate and secure principles; and to question others less, since they themselves are so capable of imparting wise and reasonable advice.

Learn to distinguish between the feeling of sin and consent thereto. The former is a fire enkindled in the heart, not easily extinguished, and it often produces sinful impressions; but the latter is a free act of the will, by which the soul chooses to sin. The former leads to the border of the abyss, but only the latter can precipitate into it. Without the will, feeling can never render the soul guilty. Do not say: "If I have not explicitly consented, still I fear, on account of the length of the temptation, that I may have indirectly consented." One may struggle long without being conquered. Not by the continuance of the temptation, but by the resistance of the will, must we judge whether or not we have consented.

Gerson says: "We do not commit mortal sin because bad thoughts come to us; for we only sin when we give free consent to these thoughts, that is, when our will favors them and finds satisfaction in them. We have nothing to fear so long as our will disapproves or hates the evil. Without its consent the most filthy pictures sully the soul less than the hideous face of some horrid monster would blur or cloud the surface of a mirror into which he glanced. On the contrary, temptation increases the soul's merit. Conscience has to deal only with the free, rational will which belongs to the superior part of the soul, and which can preserve its horror of forbidden pleasures even when the gross sensuality of perverse nature most violently experiences the sting of evil. These last impressions, it may here be remarked, are often so strong that a scrupulous soul will not only imagine that she has consented, but even that she is in a sort of hell, in which she is rejected by God on account of her past sins. She hovers on the brink of despair. The foregoing instruction shows how unfounded are such fears.

9. A TENDER, TIMOROUS CONSCIENCE.—A tender conscience may easily become anxious, and how far may not this fear extend when there is question of eternal salvation!

The director should combat scruples on the principles from which they proceed. He should tell anxious souls how much they are opposed to true piety, and what a hindrance they are to perfection, which is founded upon love and confidence.

"Nothing," says Fénelon, "is so contrary to Christian simplicity as is scrupulosity. It conceals, I know not what, double-dealing and falsehood. The scrupulous soul imagines her trouble and anxiety to proceed from her tender love of God, whilst in reality she is only disquieted about self. Natural motives and self-love make her jealous of her own perfection. . . . It is not God who infuses such anxiety and returns upon self. When He shows us our faults, He does it simply and mildly. He reproaches and consoles at the same time. He humbles without confusing;

He arouses in us the deepest shame, though mingled with unruffled peace. The Lord is not in the whirlwind.

"The remedy for this fearful condition is to despise all such unfounded fears. Some one has justly said that the imagination is the cradle of scruples, whilst sound common sense is their tomb. When scruples arise, the soul should turn to God and let them pass unheeded. Occupy the mind with other thoughts. A scrupulous soul that reflects and takes counsel with herself will always find cause for groundless anxiety. One should deal with scruples as with a servant whom he allows to go in and out without exchanging words."

Lanspergius adds: "Despise all these ridiculous and impure thoughts. Let them pass like a flock of young geese, that deafen us with their cackle. When a dog barks at you, you certainly do not stand to dispute with him. Act in like manner with your scruples. To despise them will soon rid you of them; to bandy words with them is only to impress them more deeply on your mind; neither must you fear nor violently oppose them, if you wish to avoid similar or even worse consequences."

10. THE MALICE OF THE DEVIL.—The devil, who knows better than we the evil consequences of scruples is, in his cunning, always inventing new material for them; and, with exquisite malice, seeks to keep their dangerous effects alive within us.

He, the enemy of all tranquillity, is ever intent on disturbing peace of conscience. He, condemned to eternal despair, finds consolation in shattering the hope of others. He, robbed of eternal bliss, would make the means of salvation useless to others by inspiring them with unfounded fear and terror. He is consumed with envy against those that advance in virtue, therefore he labors to retard their progress by a thousand hindrances. Obstinate and hardened in his darkness and pride, the adversary endeavors to prevent scrupulous souls from obeying, so that they may prefer the judgment of their own benighted mind to that of their director, and proud and rebellious persistence in their own views to peaceful humility.

This is an alluring temptation. Under a hypocritical mask it conceals artful malice. The unveiling of it should suffice to create the greatest horror of it, and lead a soul earnestly intent upon her salvation to obedience and subjection. This point is, however, too important to be disposed of lightly. It shall be treated more fully in the following chapter.

CHAPTER III.

Dangerous Consequences of Scruples.

Obstinate persistence in one's own pride and conceit is generally the secret source of scruples. The way of God is simple and direct for the humble, and for the pure and upright heart. Roundabout ways and solicitude proceed only from want of light, and still more from self-love, which is inexhaustible in its nice reasoning. It cannot take a step forward without looking back to regard itself. It very reluctantly loses sight of self, and it is this preference for self that is expressed in scruples. A scrupulous soul squanders her own time as well as that of her spiritual director; and with this useless loss she burdens her conscience.

Scruples turn the attention to trifling things instead of directing it to more important subjects. It pursues butterflies when it ought to be reflecting on those truths that furnish solid food for the soul's nourishment.

Scruples weary the heart and mind by endless and fruitless musings; so that neither energy, freedom, nor courage are left for undertaking and prosecuting any good work.

Scruples make piety a burden, for the scrupulous soul finds in it only torment and difficulty.

Scruples lead the soul, at last, to fear all devotional practices; for none brings consolation; each becomes a wearisome labor that ends in the reproach: "I have committed only faults in its performance!"

Scruples pave the way to negligence and tepidity; for it is not possible to endure long what is not loved, nor love long what brings only suffering. This exaggerated conscientiousness leads to the opposite extreme, viz.: a soul once unable to bear in herself small or even imaginary imperfections, now falls into actual and inexcusable faults.

Scruples consume the fervor of the soul. The sources of fervor are spiritual joy and consolation; but such sentiments die out when the heart is tired and weary. Sadness conceals all that is greatest, most elevating, and consoling in religion. The dejected soul sees only its terrifying aspect.

The Wise Man admonishes us to express toward God such sentiments as accord with His infinite goodness, and the Holy Spirit invites us to taste and see how sweet is the Lord. But instead of following this precept, the scrupulous soul sees in God only an inexorable judge. She avoids His glance instead of seeking it, and she flees from Him, forgetting that He is her highest Good, and the God of her heart. She turns His threats upon herself and makes over His promises to others. She distributes the words of Holy Scripture, unjustly retaining for herself those only that inspire terror.

Thus, scruples that conceal themselves under the cover of zeal for justice' sake, are, in reality, enemies of justice; for they rob the soul of the support she needs to maintain herself firmly in good, they give rise to dangerous temptations against faith and holy purity, they cast the soul into that gloomy sadness which serves the devil as a mask and renders it easy for him covertly to enter hearts.

Finally, scruples holding the soul chained, as it were, in the narrow prison of her own misery, she lives only for herself and her sufferings. Jesus Christ is a stranger to her. A solid and enlightened piety would impel her to live wholly for her Redeemer, to conceal herself in His Sacred Wounds, there to forget self and to seek in His justice and holiness remedies for the evils of which she is always complaining and which, alas, she never amends!

CHAPTER IV.

Universal Remedy for Scruples.

In the chapter on the cause of scruples in general, may be found in brief words a remedy for them. But so important is this matter, that we must here speak of several cures for the malady, before treating singly of each and its particular remedy.

I. OCCUPATION.—It is owing to an over minute self-examination that some are constantly worried with anxieties of conscience. It would be more advantageous to them to occupy themselves in other things. Gerson says: "The heart of the idler is like a mill in continual motion, and which acts upon itself when it has no more corn to grind." Manual labor, particularly when it is painful and very humiliating, often affords a better remedy for scruples than the most learned treatises.

Earnest study produces the same result if one has the talent for it. The dry study of languages so difficult and thorny, particularly at the outset, is a salutary means of distraction. The translation of a difficult author is also very useful for this end; and the corporal works of mercy turn the mind from its own musings, to occupy it with attractive matters.

II. CHEERFULNESS.—Melancholy is a natural cause of scruples; therefore, the soul must preserve herself from it or seek a remedy for it. She must labor earnestly against self, in order to become mistress over the spirit of sadness, which frequently holds sway over melancholy temperaments. It reduces the soul to a state of relaxation, weariness, and anxiety, by which the Evil One is able to retard her advancement on the path of virtue. The scrupulous soul must work herself out of this self-made trouble, must resist sadness energetically even when she believes herself almost overcome. She must take part in conversation and amusement, however burdensome such a proceeding may be to her; and she must never follow her inclinations for retirement, that she may more freely indulge her gloomy thoughts and fancies. Conversation with pious and spiritual persons is interesting, and exerts a healthy influence on the anxious soul. St. Teresa desired to see her spiritual daughters always bright and cheerful, because by such a demeanor they impart fervor and devotion even to others: "My dear sisters," said she, "if only God is not offended make your intercourse amiable to all. Be friendly and cheerful as far as you can, that your neighbors may covet your happiness for themselves, and that your virtue may not intimidate or frighten any one. The holier the sisters are, the more cordial and unrestrained should be their manner of acting. However sad and troubled you may be, you should never avoid recreation and intercourse with your sisters. We must earnestly strive to make ourselves lovable to all who come in contact with us, but particularly to our sisters. Lay this truth very much to heart: God pays no attention to a thousand trifles over which you often worry and fret."

III. HUMILITY AND CHILD-LIKE SIMPLICITY.—Among the virtues which the scrupulous should especially endeavor to acquire, the following are recommended: humility, child-like simplicity, and obedience; the renunciation of their own ideas, the desire of dependence; a fear of self-direction and secret attachment to liberty of opinion; fidelity to prayer; fervor and punctuality in the fulfilment of the duties of one's state.

The scrupulous on experiencing dryness, disgust, and other temptations, at once fancy God has abandoned them. If they hear fervor spoken of, they must immediately analyze the difference between fervor of feeling and fervor of will. The former is not demanded of them; the latter, which is far more pleasing to God, and far more lasting, is to be had for the asking. A soul possesses sensible fervor when, borne on the wings of divine grace, she advances with joy and gladness in the way of salvation. Then, like the Spouse in the Canticles, she runs after the delicious odors of God's sweetness. This state is, assuredly, a very blessed one; but it is to be feared that the soul finds too much satisfaction in it, that her fidelity is a little selfish, that she loves the gifts of God as much as God Himself, and that she is already receiving here below a part of her reward in the joy that springs from the practice of good.

On the contrary, fervor of will is purely spiritual. Its effects are to draw the soul nearer to God, even when she appears to be turning from Him. She feels the whole burden of the cross, and yet she carries it patiently. Every moment she stumbles over obstacles, but in the depths of her heart live a courage that is not presumptuous, and a holy strength that overcomes every obstacle. She, indeed, possesses not the tenderness of devotion, but she has the determination to practice it. This state is, undoubtedly, painful; but it is more perfect than that of sensible fervor, for it renders the soul more conformable to her Crucified Jesus. She enters more deeply into the knowledge of her nothingness and misery, and her love of God is never greater than when deprived of nourishment. In such a state, she, so to say, supports herself ; and, in spite of coldness and darkness, life glows brightly in the interior of her heart.

How well St. Teresa understood this ! For twenty years God led her by the way of interior suffering. She never asked Him to release her, but only to bear with her. Once, when in great interior dryness, the cry escaped her for one drop of the dew of heavenly consolation, she reproached herself for it as a want of Christian humility and perseverance.

It is, therefore, this fervor of the will that tried souls should regard as the highest virtue. When they find themselves in spiritual dearth and perplexity, let them believe that God sends this state to His elect, though not as a sign of reprobation. Let this thought calm them. Fidelity to duty—this is the solid virtue that God requires of them.

IV. CONSCIENCE CONSIDERED IN THE TRUE LIGHT.— Conscience is that interior voice which tells us what is good and what is evil. Its judgments relate partly to what we have already done, and partly to what we are about to do. In the former case, its importance is far less than in the latter. Conscience is in the latter case guided by reason and can not undo what has been done, whilst it influenced the moral worth of the act before its commission.

For example, I believe at the time that such an action is lawful. If later on I discover that I have erred, and that my action was a forbidden one, my discovery does not render me guilty, since such was not the case when I committed the deed. But if, at the moment of commission, I consider the act wrong, and yet commit it, the later discovery of my mistake does not render me less guilty. It is my own perverse will that renders me guilty.

Conscience is the natural rule of man's actions, and when united with truth it is always to be followed. Yes, even an erroneous conscience is to be followed as long as the means of setting it right are wanting. In such a case there is no other rule of action. But when a person can correct his erroneous conscience he should make use of the means in his power; for wilfully to follow a guide suspected of falsehood is to expose one's self to the danger of sinning. But if one is uncertain as to how he should judge of an action, since sufficient reasons are not wanting either for or against it, the matter assumes the form of a doubt, and he should seek light from another; for in such a case one is virtually without direction. But if he is in the impossibility of taking counsel, because of hurry or some other hindrance, he can act as he thinks best. The protestation of the will, "I would not do that if I knew it to be a sin," suffices to place the conscience in security.

The foregoing remark is very important for scrupulous persons, as they are often in doubt and do not always have some one at hand to enlighten them. Often, too, they have the very best reasons for considering their actions as not sinful; indeed, they may have a moral certainty that would justify any reasonable person in acting confidently. But their miserable propensity to analyze everything, and the cunning of the fiend who abuses their weakness, prevent their resting on these lawful principles. They give themselves up to a thousand useless and frequently ridiculous fears, which cloud the true light they once possessed. Their mental anguish rests only upon weak and deceitful possibilities undeserving of notice. The doubting soul should not refrain from action on the strength of such considerations, which, far from being the true voice of conscience, are only illusory sounds.

A scrupulous person does not act contrary to his conscience when he despises unfounded anxieties, or even when he is deaf to well-founded doubts. He must, however, as we have said above, renew his good intention. He should, moreover, subject the judgment of his false conscience, though to him it may appear to be true, to the authority of his spiritual guide. Such a proceeding is in accordance with his true conscience, which prescribes the rightful authority of spiritual directors rather than his own personal views; for the scrupulous are always wanting in the light necessary to pass judgment upon their own actions. Mayhap the scrupulous will call this "acting contrary to conscience." We reply that we shall not dispute about words, but merely say that it is not only allowed, but even necessary, so to act; for the true maxim, that one must not act against his conscience, cannot be applicable here.

From what has been said we may easily understand what is meant by the words "forming a conscience." To form a conscience means to establish, with the help of general principles, what we may call a practical rule for those occasions of doubt upon which one cannot directly decide. For

Universal Remedy for Scruples. 287

example, imagine two points in question, one of which you must absolutely choose. It is Sunday. Shall I remain with a sick person and miss Holy Mass, or shall I go to Holy Mass and set aside the care of the sick? A well-instructed person knows that his duty is to remain with the sick. We now take it for granted, however, that you are not well instructed, and that without sin you can find no way out of the difficulty. In such a case you need not decide the question, since you are not prepared to do so. You must call settled principles to your aid, saying: "There is no sin committed from necessity; for free-will is an indispensable condition of sin. This freedom is wanting to me, for I am forced to do one or other of two things which appear to me to be alike sinful. I must either neglect the sick, or remain from Holy Mass." Acting upon principle, you may conclude that on whichsoever course you decide, you cannot commit sin. Therefore, on similar occasions, form your conscience from the general principle: "Sin presupposes free-will." The safest plan is always to act on the authority of the confessor or director. Although your own sense or convictions are in opposition to his decision, yet you will always be safe in following it. Yes, the only right thing to do is to subject yourself to it.

V. THE NECESSITY OF DEPENDING UPON ANOTHER, AND OF FOLLOWING HIS ADVICE.—It is for scrupulous souls indispensably necessary to follow the advice of another. They must, indeed, act; but in their actions they cannot follow their own unreliable judgment; hence, God makes obedience a duty for them. A scrupulous soul, then, acts directly contrary to the will of God when she guides herself according to her own discernment, instead of following the counsel which God gives her through another.

To free the soul from her scruples, we must tell her that she has no choice—she must obey her confessor's directions. But to attain to this blessed state of obedience she must not think it is enough to desire this virtue and understand its necessity: even the most stubborn are capable of such desires. She must submit her sentiments and impressions to the scrutiny of her spiritual guide. His reason and not hers must prevail. He must conquer her resistance, she must follow his decisions; in one word, she must desist from self-guidance. This is a sacrifice bitter to pride, but humility knows how to sweeten it. Is not self-guidance the way of scrupulous souls? They do, indeed, follow their spiritual director; they have a thousand little things to ask him, though clinging all the while to their own preconceived notions. They follow their own judgment as obstinately after his decision as before. They do not trust him fully. They imagine that he makes the way to heaven much too broad and easy for them. They, in short, subject themselves to his decision only in so far as it pleases themselves. Hoping to find more discerning guides, they wander with their difficulties of conscience from confessional to confessional, like an anxious invalid that consults every physician but puts no trust in any. Nothing so impairs the peace of the conscience as these unending consultations. A sick man needs but one physician, and each soul but one confessor. To run from one to another increases interior suffering, and gradually engenders aversion for the reception of the Holy Sacraments. "Woe to you that are wise in your own eyes and prudent in your own conceits!"[1] says the Lord. On the contrary, submit. "Lean not upon thy own prudence."[2] Silence your self-love, which hinders you from submitting your judgment to your father-confessor or director, and you will experience in yourself the truth of this other promise: "An obedient man shall speak of victory."[3] Interior peace is the fruit of obedience. This was true even in St. Bernard's time. This saintly abbot, hearing that one of his monks through scrupulosity no longer said Holy Mass, said to him: "Go, brother, on my word, and say Holy Mass!" The monk obeyed, and his scruples vanished forever. God rewarded his obedience by restoring to him interior peace. And now a scrupulous

[1] Is. v. 21.   [2] Proverbs iii. 5.   [3] Proverbs xxi. 28.

soul says to me: "Indeed, I too should be obedient if I had a guide possessed of the piety and enlightenment of St. Bernard. But when I think of the comparatively little penetration of my father-confessor, I hardly dare confide to him my conscience and eternal salvation." Whoever you may be that reasons thus, we reply: "You are wrong. You should resign the care of your soul into the hands of a guide, not because of his piety, learning, and wisdom (although it is generally good to make choice of one possessed of these precious qualities), but because he is appointed by God to reconcile you with Him in the Sacrament of penance. To him, therefore, the divine power is granted. Hence you should obey him not as man, but as God Himself, who speaks to you by His mouth." And not unfrequently is this faithful obedience so much the more meritorious and pleasing to God, when he to whom you render it for the love of God, through lack of personal qualities, merits your confidence less. To act differently, then, would be to proceed in a purely human manner. It would be to imitate heretics, who believe and do what they think to be right without subjecting themselves to any one. Assuredly they are not worthy models for souls that would pass for devout!

We shall conclude in the words of a clear-sighted, intelligent, spiritual man: "I am firmly persuaded that all remedies against scruples are only useful for those that are obedient to their director—for those that let themselves be guided by him. A scrupulous person wanting in confidence in his guide will never under any conditions be cured. He must be considered an invalid of whose recovery one despairs till he resolves to resign himself to subjection and confidence in God. All theologians agree in making obedience a strict and unconditional duty for the scrupulous.

VI. SACRIFICE OF ONE'S OWN DOUBTS.—Choose, then, for yourself a guide esteemed for learning and intelligence that you may unhesitatingly prefer his judgment to your own: but once you have made your choice do not change or again resume the direction of yourself. Accept the decision of your director instead of your own, at least for some time, and study which of the two is the more conducive to your peace. Hearken no longer to yourself, or at least to yourself alone; for your past decisions have only thrown you into greater perplexity. Take to heart these words of Fénelon: "As drink increases the thirst of a dropsical person, so scruples multiply when they are noticed. The scrupulous deserve this punishment. The only remedy is to enforce silence upon your tongue and diseased understanding. And since you needs must be anxious about everything you do, it is better that it should be in obedience to another than to your own self-judgment. God will bless your first humble efforts of submission; and you will perhaps feel so relieved when freed from the yoke of self-direction that you will guard against retaking so heavy a burden upon your shoulders."

The interior conviction of the scrupulous soul that she would sin in doing what she is told must by no means serve as a pretext for not obeying. This conviction, which she falsely takes for conscience, should and must be relinquished. In obedience to her guide she should do even the contrary to what her erroneous conscience demands. This is the secure way—yes, according to the unanimous opinion of theologians, the only way—to accomplish God's designs and attain life eternal. When she acts contrary to her tiresome and erroneous convictions she gradually succeeds in destroying all that is opposed to interior peace. In vain would she object that she dare not act against her conscience, for this principle has no longer any application to her. She turns it, on the contrary, against herself; for the true conscience of the scrupulous, against which they are not permitted to act, is not the origin of their ridiculous fears of sinning, but it brings before them forcibly the knowledge of their duty to submit in obedience to spiritual directors. This authority is truly divine, since Christ has promised His priests: "He that heareth you heareth Me:

and he that despiseth you despiseth Me."[1] The scrupulous soul who, despite her anguish, follows the advice of her director, obeys God Himself; and who would dare to say that in obeying God one acts against conscience? He, on the contrary, who prefers self-judgment to obedience, follows his own inclinations, and pursues a way equally dangerous and foolish against the authority of God. "He who would be his own teacher," says S*t*. Bernard, "becomes the pupil of a fool."

[1] Luke x. 16.

CHAPTER V.

Various Kinds of Scruples, and their Remedy.

THE foregoing dissertation on scruples might, in general, be considered all-sufficient; but we deem the matter so important as to require some words on each separate species.

We shall strive to recall briefly some of the most usual and best known scruples; for it is not possible to follow all such wandering imaginations. Besides, it is our intention to confine these remarks to the most important only.

I. SCRUPLES ABOUT FORMER CONFESSIONS.—Has the confessor reason to believe that the previous confessions were valid? Has a general confession already repaired the defects of past confessions? Has the general confession been repeated even many times? If so, there must be no question of further repetitions.

The belief that justification depends upon the exactness of our accusation is an error. The detailed confession of our sins wipes them out as little as the reckoning of a debt cancels it. It is unquestionably necessary that the penitent accuse himself of all that burdens his conscience. But by this self-accusation he does nothing more than acknowledge himself a debtor. Whoever reposes all his confidence in the minute accusation of sins is unconscious of the greatness of his insolvency. The blood of the unspotted Lamb of God is our indemnity, our justification. In Jesus Christ alone we hope; and the sinner does little toward his salvation by reiterating his acknowledgment of sinfulness, and expecting more from his own memory than from the saving death of the Lord.

Various Kinds of Scruples, and their Remedy.

The constant repetition of confessions, then, is not only useless, but also dangerous.

It is dangerous, first, because the long examination preceding the confession brings up before a lively imagination pictures that may be the occasion of new sins and temptations. It is calculated to revive the remembrance of certain sins that should forever be forgotten. Thus the best remedies frequently bring death to the sick when taken indiscreetly or unseasonably. Explanations often most dangerous, and which some desire constantly to repeat, were not necessary even in the first confession; and now there should be still less question of them.

In the second place, the continual repetition of confessions perplexes the scrupulous soul, since it furnishes the imagination with nourishment and the mind with new subjects of torment, to which we have already seen more than one soul succumb. A scrupulous soul eagerly grasps at a general confession; but when will she end it? There have been instances in which such a confession has lasted a whole year when the confessor had to bring all his courage and determination to bear in order to effect a satisfactory termination. And what came of it? In what did it result? In more difficulties and disquiet than before. All has not been told, matters have not been explained as they are, important circumstances have been omitted, certain sins must be repeated. Suppose the confessor is weak enough to permit it, then new trials arise, the penitent has had no contrition; fresh embarrassment! How shall one extricate himself from such a labyrinth?

II. SCRUPLES OF ORDINARY CONFESSIONS.—Some souls are at peace in regard to the past, but the present is for them an exhaustless source of trouble. According to their ideas they are never clear enough in confession; they are always ready to repeat their sins; they torture their memory not to omit anything. Some new point is always recurring to them about which they must interrupt the confessor's instructions. It presents itself even during the absolution, and rouses fresh anxiety. It leaves them no peace at the Lord's Table, and impels them afterward to return to the confessional, not from necessity, but only from a desire to relieve their anxiety. They have so often yielded to this, that now it entirely rules them.

Such trifling is unworthy our holy religion, and it generally proceeds from an imperfect knowledge of it. There is a time for the examination of conscience, another for the confession of sins; a time for humiliation and docile attention to the admonitions of the confessor; and, finally, a time for performing the penance imposed, and another for thanksgiving after the grace of absolution. These periods should not be confounded one with the other. Things should be done systematically. The fruit of one action is lost by busying one's self inopportunely with another.

The penitent must accustom himself to make a clear, decided, and concise accusation, after which he should think of nothing but of what the confessor is telling him, and of preparing for the devout reception of absolution. This over, no further accusations are to be made. The faults of even the just are so multiplied that they could never be enumerated in detail. The most important of these details are often hidden from their gaze, so that the fault appears quite different in the eyes of God from what it does in their own. The validity of confession depends neither on the degree of self-knowledge,—always limited,—nor on the retentiveness of memory, but upon uprightness of heart and sincerity of sorrow. To these important and essential points one must chiefly attend. The Lord God Himself makes little account of those small faults that would have been confessed had they not escaped the memory either in the examination of conscience or even in the act of accusation, and which may easily be mentioned at another time.

On this subject St. Francis de Sales says: "One must not be alarmed when in confession he cannot remember all his faults; for it is not conceivable that one who frequently examines his conscience should forget a grievous sin. He must also not be so trifling as to wish to confess every little imperfection. An act of humility, a pious ejaculation, suffices for this without confession. . . . You must not be too anxious to tell everything, to run after your superior, to make much ado over the trifles that annoy you, and that will, perhaps, have passed in a quarter of an hour. You must learn to bear such things courageously. We cannot get rid of them at once; for they are, in general, the consequences of our imperfect nature. That your will, feelings, and desires are so fickle; that you are at one time moody, at another cheerful; that you are pleased or displeased in speaking or in keeping silence, and a thousand similar occurrences,—are matters to which we are naturally prone, and to which we must remain subject as long as this transitory life endures. . . . It is not necessary to accuse ourselves in confession of the little thoughts that like gnats swarm about us, or of the disgust and aversion we experience in the observance of our vows and devotional exercises. We are not obliged to include them in our confessions; for all these things are not sins, but only disagreeable and burdensome difficulties. . . . The time after confession is not to be employed in reflecting whether everything has been rightly expressed. The penitent should rather remain peacefully near the dear Lord with whom he is again reconciled, and thank Him for His great mercy. Let not what you may have forgotten disturb you. . . . Do not torment yourself because you have failed to discover all your little faults in order to confess them; for you frequently fall without even perceiving it. Besides, do not the Holy Scriptures say that the just man sees or feels that he daily falls not only seven times, but seven times seven? And yet he rises again without stopping to notice either his fall or his rise. Be not, therefore, solicitous, but go on declaring honestly and humbly what you have remarked. What escapes your memory leave to the sweet mercy of Him whose outstretched hand supports those that fall without malice, in order that they may not hurt themselves; and who so gently and promptly sets them on their feet again that they neither observe their fall nor their rise."

To this salutary teaching of a great saint we add the opinion of a grave theologian.[1] In answer to the question as to whether a scrupulous soul, by not confessing certain sins, of the lightness or grievousness of which she is ignorant, or because she is doubtful as to whether or not she has already confessed them, would run the risk of really committing grievous sin by not fully explaining matters in her confession, he says that she would not thereby render herself guilty, for the scrupulous are not bound to such exactitude, since such an obligation would evidently keep them in a state of the most painful anxiety and cruel interior torture. Still greater would be the prejudice done the soul if other and graver spiritual trials pressed heavily upon the mind. These latter, according to all theologians, are quite sufficient to dispense from such exactitude.

Collet adds: "Confession was not instituted to torture the conscience, but to set it at peace. Hence the scrupulous must despise all inquietude regarding the validity of confession and the exactitude of examination. They should simply practise that blind obedience which is the most efficacious remedy for scruples."

One word in conclusion on a few special circumstances connected with scruples. Anxious souls sometimes imagine that they must contrive to relate in the confessional the whole matter of their accusation. They go into the minutest details, whilst it is sufficient merely to mention the sin. When there is question of thoughts, which are often only temptations—and in this case one is not obliged even to speak of them—the scrupulous think they must fully explain them; they must describe everything, however immodest, exaggerated, or impossible, that an excited imagination can picture. They fancy also that they must make the confessor see, as in a panorama, all that passes within

[1] Reginald, De Prudentia Confessarii, Lib. II. s. 131.

them; and since the impossibility to do so, as well as a sense of shame, revolts against these imaginary obligations, they regard their confession as incomplete. The more they say, the more, according to their ideas, remains to be said; and yet there is in reality nothing easier than the accusation of such sinful thoughts. The penitent should simply mention what virtue has been violated, and only in some very extreme cases is it needful to add one word upon the particular tendency of these thoughts, namely, if it changes the nature of the sin. Then he says whether or not he has really consented. If in doubt about the consent, it suffices to mention this doubt in general; as for instance: "I know not for certain whether I yielded or not to this or that evil thought. I fear that I was negligent in banishing it." In such cases, indeed, perfect silence on the point may be maintained—a course very advisable if the penitent is scrupulous. Anything more is superfluous, especially in the case of holy purity, where endless explanations are more dangerous than useful, since they recall the temptation with double peril. The above are just principles. How far remote are they from the erroneous ideas of a scrupulous conscience! And how much sweeter and easier is the yoke of the Lord than that which man, in his littleness, imposes upon himself!

We give here three instructions, which if followed may prevent many scruples.

First. The penitent that has harbored feelings against his confessor, or who has made him the subject of unfavorable criticism, complaints, murmurs, evil speaking, and the like, is not obliged in his accusation to say that the confessor was the subject of them. It is enough to confess the faults in general, without naming the person. The same holds good in the case of any aversion or natural affection that one may feel for the father-confessor.

Secondly. The penitent can say to his confessor regarding the neighbor everything that the former ought to know, in order that he may be able to solve the difficulties, to advise, and to console. The seal of confession protects the good name of the party concerned.

Thirdly. A lie in confession renders the sacrament invalid only when the penitent thereby conceals what he is bound, under pain of mortal sin, to confess. Except in this case, the penitent is not obliged, when later on he confesses this lie, to state that it was told in confession. This rule applies to other venial sins that one may commit even in the confessional, such as suspicions, murmurings, impatience with the confessor's directions, and the like.

III. SCRUPLES ON SINCERITY OF CONTRITION.—*Good Resolutions.*—Certain souls are particularly solicitous about the essential points of the Holy Sacrament of Penance. They think they accuse themselves without true sorrow and a sincere resolution of amendment, because they perceive no decided change in their life, and continue to bring the same faults to confession. Such souls must know that their conclusion would be just were there question of dealing with crime; but of that there is here no mention, since we are dealing with scruples.

The sorrow of the just for daily faults may be deep and true without its perfectly curing souls of their weakness. God knows the desires of His faithful children. He hears them, but only at the right time. It is more important for God-loving souls to be well-grounded in humility than to be freed from defects; therefore the dear God often leaves them for a long time struggling in vain, merely that they may become truly humble. The contrition of the righteous for their faults cannot be measured according to the same rule as that of great sinners for their crimes. The faults of the former do not affect the essence of the Christian life. Nay, through the Divine Goodness they not unfrequently become the occasion of the most sublime virtues, and a protection against great dangers. One would form an erroneous judgment were he to conclude from relapses into faults that he loved them, or that his repentance was insincere. St. Francis de Sales says on this point: "God has been pleased on some occasions to perfect sinners all at once, as St. Mary Magdalen, who in an instant, from an outcast, a corrupt creature, became a pure, untroubled well-spring of perfection. But in the disciples the Lord left after conversion many traces of former evil inclinations, and this was for their real good. We confine ourselves to St. Peter, who after his first call stumbled more than once, and by his threefold denial at last fell miserably.

"A soul that, after a long slavery to passion, should become in a moment perfect master of it, would be in great danger of falling into pride and vanity. We must proceed gradually, step by step, to victory. The saints spent decades of years in acquiring such conquests. Be kind, then, and have patience with all, but above all with yourself.

"You complain that, in spite of your desire for perfection and the pure love of God, you still perceive imperfections in yourself. We reply, that in this life we can never quite divest ourselves of self. We must continue to bear it about with us till God takes us to heaven. As long as we must drag the burden of self, we are dragging something very worthless. Patience, then! You cannot lay aside in one day all the bad habits acquired by a long course of spiritual negligence. Fix your eyes upon God, and then turn them upon yourself. You will never behold Him apart from His goodness, nor yourself destitute of misery, which you will thus look upon as the object of the divine goodness and mercy."

Fénelon says: "Formerly you were wanting in light to discern the emotions of your perverse nature, which are now so plain to you. The more light, the better one sees that he is worse than he thought; but, for all that, he must not be discouraged. You are not worse than you formerly were: on the contrary, you are much better. But as your evils decrease, the light that discovers them increases."

Let what has been said reassure the doubting of the sincerity of their contrition, although they may relapse into faults of frailty. And now, a word to those that fear for the sincerity of their sorrow, since they do not experience sentiments of grief so lively as those that are felt upon the loss of relatives or property. Such souls for long hours seek to awaken this feeling, but generally without success. And then, what anguish of heart in receiving absolution! We cannot better advise such souls than by telling them to reflect upon the following words of St. Francis de Sales:

"You desire to know," says he, "how in a short time you can make a good act of contrition. I tell you for this no time is necessary. You have but to prostrate yourself in the spirit of humility and sorrow before the Lord for the offences against Him. In God's eyes you are capable of much, if you are capable only of willing. You already have contrition in desire. You do not, indeed, feel it, but neither do you see nor feel the fire under the ashes, although it is there."

IV. SCRUPLES ABOUT DEVOTIONS OF OBLIGATION.— The devotions to which duty binds are to many the cause of a thousand anxieties, whilst those they have freely chosen themselves are often better performed and with much less disquietude. The reason of this is, that the soul is not tormented in the latter case by the fear of performing them badly.

Men, in every other respect intelligent and enlightened, often allow themselves to be ruled by this excessive fear. They become a burden to themselves and useless to others, because they have acquired the unhappy custom of fearing in everything and of finding difficulties in all the duties of their state.

The necessary intention is to many an inexhaustible source of scruples. For example, they think they have not performed the penance imposed by the priest, unless they have previously spent a quarter of an hour,—what do we say?— an hour, and even more, protesting in all conceivable forms

Various Kinds of Scruples, and their Remedy.

that they now really wish to perform the penance imposed by the confessor on this occasion, for this purpose, etc., and that they assuredly had no other intention in it! If these poor, tormented souls would say simply the prayers prescribed, or read the chapter given them, without all these ludicrous precautions, and also without the least concern about their *intention*, the *right* intention would certainly not be wanting, and they would more perfectly, more easily, correspond to that of the *confessor*.

It is very important that, when undertaking the direction of a soul, the confessor should energetically combat such weaknesses in the penitent; for it might lead to fatal consequences, and indeed to it many have sacrificed sound reason.

Such scrupulous souls should never be allowed to repeat their prayers of obligation—for instance, the Divine Office. Disobedience in this point is a very great fault. Nothing so exposes us to distractions as the thought that we may repeat our prayers after having said them badly. Let such a practice be begun, and it will soon become habitual, since the repetition will be attended by no better success than the first attempts. Thus the prayers that can never be finished become at last an insupportable yoke, which exaggerated punctiliousness will end in throwing off altogether.

No man can entirely avoid distractions in this life; but they can injure our prayer only when they are voluntary or neglected. The best means of overcoming them is to pay no attention to them, but to revert quickly to our former train of thought, without inquiring how or by what we were for some moments diverted from it. The most importunate distractions, when displeasing to the soul, become prayer. To repeat or omit devotions in consequence of distractions means to yield to them.

St. Teresa herself admitted that frequently she was unable to finish a *Credo* without distractions. We also must submit humbly to our fate. We must not exact more of ourselves than does God, to whom our humility and obedience are a thousand times more pleasing than our vain efforts to reach an unattainable end.

V. SCRUPLES ABOUT MOTIVES OF WELL-DOING.—From actions let us proceed to motives, on whose account so many are troubled. They know, on the one hand, that the holiness of an action depends upon purity of intention; and on the other, they fear that all they do is tainted with secret pride, human views, or motives of vanity.

Undoubtedly every good action should be vivified by the love of God and the desire to please Him. The fear that the depravity of our heart should mingle with our good works and rob them of their merit is also reasonable. An intrinsic part of devotion consists in this holy fear, which is inseparable from love. There is certainly no more secure means of determining whether an action is done from pure love, or whether other motives are mixed with it. The heart is unfathomable, unknown to ourselves; but it would not be so were we sure of its love. We should know "whether we are worthy of love or hatred"[1] if we knew what kind of love rules and directs us. We could then do what St. Paul would not venture to do, namely, judge ourselves.[2]

But it is precisely the uncertainty that conceals from us the interior depths of our being which should furnish the best consolation to those who torture themselves about their imaginary bad intentions. Whence know you that your actions do not proceed from the grace of Jesus Christ? Has He given you a special sign by which to recognize its effects in you? May not one deceive himself in this way, as well from false humility as from presumption? Can you distinguish exactly the gifts of God from those that spring from self, and thus discover the extent of your misery? Fear you not to abuse God's grace in ascribing the good which it aids you to accomplish to the malice of the Evil One? And you who are so much troubled lest

[1] Eccles. ix. 1.   [2] 1 Cor. iv. 3–5.

pride should taint your works,—do you not deem it pride when, instead of being grateful to God, you complain?

But such persons will answer: "How can we conceal from ourselves that vanity and other evil motives corrupt most of our good works, since we are sensibly alive to their impression? These impure motives besiege us! They mingle in all we do, and, like shadows, follow us everywhere. In spite of all our efforts, we cannot cast them off."

You take pains to be freed from them—you are troubled that your efforts are not crowned with the desired success? Ah, then, you are not so much to be pitied as you imagine. That you are troubled is a good sign. We fear not for you, since you are watchful.

One more question: "Do you never perform any good work in silence? Do you always seek witnesses? Can you never be silent about an alms, a prayer, or a mortification?" You answer: "It is my greatest consolation to do good secretly, for then pride has to sacrifice what publicity would have granted it. O that we might live without witnesses! Then we should be in peace, or at least should easily conquer our enemies."

You now see that appearances are not, as you thought, entirely against you. You have given evidence that you flee temptation, you love concealment, and that at heart you are humble, or at least desire to be so.

Concerning the importunate attacks of pride, we are not anxious for their cessation. God is the master of them, and He has not promised that they should ever cease. He stands by, to assist in the combat; but the struggle will last as long as it pleases Him, and very often even to the end of life.

Temptation must not, however, be confounded with sin. Pride surrounds us on all sides. But it is not on this account in our heart, which, despite of the fierce and persevering attacks of the enemy, remains closed. If it does not yield to the impressions that pride makes upon the imagination, the noise is outside only, and conscience preserves its purity.

A very fitting comparison will illustrate this fact. Your shadow follows you everywhere, and yet it is no part of your person. It imitates all your movements and actions, though it is not the cause of them. You cannot escape from it or chase it away; and yet it does you no harm. It is exactly the same with the importunate attacks of pride. Contrary to our will, it follows us everywhere, anxious for as great a share as possible in all our intentions and actions; but so long as we refuse our consent, its importunity cannot affect us. Instead of losing time in fighting flitting shadows that escape our blows, or in vain efforts to flee from the demon of pride, we have only to refuse these admittance into our heart, and keep our glance fixed on Jesus Christ, who alone has power to conquer.

The foregoing instructions are comprised in the important admonitions of St. Ignatius to the scrupulous in his "Spiritual Exercises." He says:

"When a devout soul wishes to say or do anything that deviates neither from the customs of Holy Church nor the traditions of the Fathers, and which she considers calculated to promote the honor of God our Lord; and the thought, or temptation comes from without (i.e. from the enemy) not to say or do it, because she might be guilty of vain complacency, or some other fault, let her raise her mind to her Lord and Creator, and if she sees that this word or action will tend to His honor, or, at least, not be contrary to it, let her do what is directly opposed to the tempter's suggestions, saying with St. Bernard: 'I have not begun for you, nor shall I stop for you!'"

VI. SCRUPLES ABOUT DUTIES SUPPOSED TO BE ESSENTIAL.—Scruples founded on the foregoing captious argument are the more difficult to cure when they relate to duties supposed essential, but which one has not had the courage to fulfil. Such scruples are, unquestionably, more torturing than most others. We cannot conceal from ourselves, on the one hand, the apparent duty; and, on the other, we cannot resolve to comply with it. We then reason thus: "I surely do not love God above all things. I cannot be pleasing to Him, I cannot save my soul if I do not change my frame of mind; but of this there is little prospect."

Many lines would not suffice to relate in detail all the obligations that some, with more ingenuity than perspicuity, impose upon themselves without, however, being able to fulfil them. It is the duty of the confessor to give these disquieted souls an insight into themselves, and to solve their doubts; but they should submit everything to his judgment. They should never forget that what would often be a duty for persons possessed of interior peace, is not so for those who, from excessive fear, are to a certain extent deprived of the free use of their soul's powers. They are incapable of complying properly with certain obligations; consequently, they are dispensed from them. This is the case, for example, in regard to fraternal correction; for timorous or restless souls can scarcely comply properly with this injunction. They may, therefore, take silence as their rule when in doubt as to whether they should or should not administer such correction.

VII. SCRUPLES WITH RESPECT TO HOPE, THE SOUL BELIEVING HERSELF IN A BAD STATE.—"I should gladly hide from myself my tepidity and cowardice," says many a soul sad unto death; "but how can I deceive my own conscience, my own eyes? My works witness against me, my life is passing in vain desires. I see the good I ought to do, and I do it not. I feel for it an interior, secret aversion that time does not diminish. My slothful, drowsy heart cannot awaken from its weakness and lassitude. I rise only to commit new faults. My will is not only weak, but absolutely bad, and I catch myself in repeated infidelities toward God whom, in a certain way, I try to deceive by my exterior, whilst my real sentiments are in total opposition to His Law. All this fills me with doubt concerning my salvation, and often deprives me of hope. I know very well that this unhappy feeling of despair does not remedy the evil, but that, on the contrary, it fills up its measure. But how can I resist it, since it is evidently founded on reality? The Gospel holds no promises for a coward like me. It condemns relapses, and my life is a chain of them. It demands fruits of penance, and I produce none. All the good of which I read bears testimony against me, because I am so far removed from what it teaches; and although I still make my act of hope, yet I do not know whether my heart's sentiments correspond with the words I utter."

We permit this desolate soul to pour out her sorrow. It relieves her, and consoling words more easily penetrate the heart that has discharged its bitterness. Now, however, we shall confront her with her own words!

Granting, we answer her, that your misery is as great as it appears to you,—yes, we shall even suppose it greater than you have represented,—do such sentiments portray one wanting in virtue, one that has no love for virtue? Are not hunger and thirst for justice favorable signs of salvation? Are not the tears that even the most just shed over themselves a proof that justice is not perfect in this life?

In what, then, do your faults consist? They rank among those that even the just cannot avoid. Good! Now, what would you think of yourself if you committed no faults at all? if your pious desires were all at once crowned with success? if you feel so drawn to good that its practice cost you no effort? if you were always as patient and gentle as you would desire to be? if, in a word, you suddenly became so perfect as to be a subject of astonishment to others and amazement to yourself?

"Ah!" you answer, "I should tremble at such a state. If God did not give me the humility and gratitude of the blessed spirits, I should importune Him to reserve for me till the next life a perfection of which the present is unworthy; for its glare would certainly dazzle me more quickly than it did the fallen angels and our first parents."

You see, therefore, how necessary humiliation is to humility. Do not, then, consider the imperfections God leaves you as a sign of His anger, but as a proof of His loving designs over you. By them He will make your cure certain, and preserve your virtue from the inroads of pride.

Bewail your misery, but thank God that you know it and feel it; for it might have been coupled with blindness and hardness of heart. His mercy has not left you like so many others in blind indifference. Recognize your own due in the punishment of others, and be very grateful that the goodness of God has preserved you from the number of those who live in peace and presumption in their sins.

Do not ruminate on what is lacking to you; rather admire the goodness of God in conferring so many graces and benefits on one so unworthy. With the Canaanite woman gather the crumbs that fall from the table of the children of God, instead of complaining that you are not like them seated at the table. Like Ruth, be satisfied with gleaning, and murmur not that you are prohibited to gather at will. Your complaints are secret murmurs that place obstacles to the fulfilment of your good desires. Become more grateful and humble, and in similar proportion you will increase in spiritual riches. You have been accustomed to regard only your wants and not your unworthiness. Learn henceforth to unite both. You are, indeed, in want of many things, but nothing is due you. You should desire all and hope for all; but without Jesus Christ you have no right to anything.

You are inconsolable that your will for good is so sluggish, your heart so wanting in straightforwardness and sincerity before God, whilst you perceive in yourself a sort of double-mindedness and falsehood that seem to give the lie to your good works. But do you not know that your goodwill comes from the grace of Jesus Christ, and that Christ is our Redeemer chiefly because He delivers us from the perversity of our own will? Can you give Him anything that you have not received from Him? Have you sought first your Saviour, and loved Him first? You see all that He has done in you. Why do you not hope that He will perfect His work? In His goodness He began it when you did not even desire it; will He now desist when you so ardently implore Him to supply what is wanting? Do you not know that He Himself inspires your prayers, that He is the cause of your sighs? How can you think that He despises His own gifts, that He does not hear your prayers, that He is indifferent to your tears?

Your slothful, tepid life saddens you. But do you consider it a good remedy to allow hope, the fountain source of fervor, to sink? Does one advance quickly when he runs haphazard, or says to himself that every step is useless? Does one set his heart upon what he considers the property of another, or, at least, intended for another? Can he retain sufficient strength to reach the term, when he is prepossessed by the idea that he will never arrive at it? Hope alone grasps at a good, looks upon it as intended for itself, and takes all possible measures to attain it. Let hope, therefore, be something living and active within you, and you will nerve yourself to overcome your sluggish nature.

As a last plank for discouragement, you allege that you are wanting in fervor of penance. But from what has been said, you should be convinced that it is only from the want of hope and confidence that you feel so little strength to lead a penitential life. Patience in affliction, and the desire to suffer, to be crucified with Christ, spring from the well-founded expectation of eternal goods, and from the perfect conviction that if we suffer with Christ we shall be glorified with Him. Hence there is no better remedy for all your temptations than confidence.

VIII. SCRUPLES THAT MAKE US SEE IN EVERYTHING A PUNISHMENT FROM GOD.—Some souls regard every adversity that happens to them as a punishment from Divine

Various Kinds of Scruples, and their Remedy.

Providence. Such a view renders patience in suffering more difficult, and deprives them of the greatest advantages of the Cross.

Such souls should reflect that, during this life everything may be rendered conducive to salvation. If God takes from us something that we considered useful to our perfection, He does it only to lead us thereto by a more secure way. Nothing is more necessary to us here below than obedience to His divine dispensations, nothing more truly beneficial than His grace. We do not lose, on the contrary, we gain a great deal when God Himself takes the place of those of whom He deprives us. Were we alone in the world with Him, we should possess in His goodness an inexhaustible source of strength.

No one knows whether or not he belongs to the number of the predestined; but all are commanded to hope it, and to believe that the various designs of Providence tend to what is best for us. The Lord does nothing that is not for the salvation of the elect. For them alone does the world exist, and it shall be destroyed when the last of the elect shall have attained perfection. Verily, if the whole world were subjected to a universal upheaval, that general destruction of existing things would have for its object only the greater good of the elect.

Timid, or imperfectly instructed souls, very frequently misunderstand the assertion that there is a certain measure of grace beyond which God grants no more. If, therefore, they experience new difficulties in the practice of virtue, or think they have fallen into a more considerable fault, they fancy they belong to the number of those to whom only limited graces are imparted, and that they can hope for no more.

This interpretation of the doctrine of the measure of grace is utterly false. Holy Scripture bids the sinner hope till his last breath. The Church robs no soul of this precious gift. She is convinced that the dying are never exhorted to penance in vain, although death-bed conversions are often doubtful. The time of patience and mercy ends for us only with our last breath, and until then we must never consider the source of grace closed. Just as little dare one regard the foregoing teaching as general maxims of faith, or apply them to individual souls; for it is evident that, even if the general principle be true, yet it would always be presumptuous, and a fault against Christian hope to apply them with certainty to one's self or others.

IX. Scruples that make us consider Little Faults an occasion of greater ones.—Some anxious souls always see in their little faults occasions of greater ones. They persuade themselves that God punishes them by permitting them to fall into greater sins. They usually support this assertion upon Holy Scripture, in which they read that less faults lead to greater, that one imperceptibly falls into the latter by neglecting the former, and that imperfections to which little attention is paid may often lead to the gravest faults.

This, rightly understood, is true; but one goes too far in asserting that trifling faults of frailty are the proximate occasions of great sins.

The Holy Scriptures nowhere say that faults of weakness are punished by the commission of more considerable sins. If such were true, what would become of the just man, although he falls seven times a day? Does he not persevere in his righteousness? Has not the Beloved Disciple said, in the name of all: "If we say that we have no sin, we deceive ourselves, and the truth is not in us. If we confess our sins, He is faithful and just to forgive us our sins, and to cleanse us from all iniquity." [1] God's threats refer only to the despising of little faults: "He that contemneth small things shall fall by little and little!" says the Wise Man. [2] Indifference will be punished, for it is allied to pride. Impenitence excites the anger of God; for it shows contempt of His mercy, which is not invoked, as also of

[1] I John i 8.   [2] Ecclus. xix. 1.

His justice, which the sinner neglects to appease. On the contrary, the Holy Scriptures furnish the most consoling promises for the humble and faithful soul whose weakness impels her to greater watchfulness, and who neither loves nor excuses her faults of omission or impetuosity. This is the correct interpretation of the foregoing text, which, falsely understood, is the source of many scruples.

But let us suppose that the faults which occasion such scruples are not merely of inadvertence, that the heart clings to them, that they are not avoided as they should be, nor sufficiently atoned by humble penance. In spite of all this, one would commit an error in considering them as proximate, that is ordinary and inevitable occasions of transgressions. No part of Holy Scripture or tradition tells us this. To make such an assertion would be to anticipate the decrees of the Almighty, which we are not allowed to fathom. If this were true, the most pure, the most innocent souls might be cast into despair; for they, above all others, judge their faults most severely, in the fear that they are wilful or not sufficiently effaced by heartfelt sorrow.

It is precisely to such discouragement that the enemy wishes to lead souls, showing them in a magnifying glass their fault and its consequences. So long as they are at peace he does not venture to present to them manifest evil; but if he succeeds in disturbing them, after some imperfection, he can attack them more boldly. He knows full well that confidence in the divine assistance and the humble conviction that God will not cast them away for slight negligences and sins, will serve as a protection against his assaults; hence, he endeavors to deprive souls of such sentiments by recalling to their mind all the denunciations they have ever heard against negligence and tepidity. They become thereby their own tempters; and by looking upon their damnation as inevitable, actually cast themselves into the abyss.

This hellish snare seems, indeed, so openly laid as to be easily detected; nevertheless, as experience shows, it often proves dangerous. Souls that would have been invulnerable had they preserved confidence in God's help, are often wounded and sometimes brought low, by falsely imagining that little faults in the beginning have caused them to be abandoned by God. They would have preserved with holy jealousy the precious treasure of innocence, had they but known that its possession was still theirs. Every means must be employed to put an end to such scruples; for they degenerate into temptations, and through vain fear, lead to great sins.

X. SCRUPLES WITH REGARD TO FAITH.—DOES ONE REALLY BELIEVE OR NOT?—Our faith should be active and living. Supernaturally, it should be to us what the senses are to the things around us. St. Paul calls it: "The substance of things to be hoped for, the evidence of things that appear not."[1] Anxious souls not finding their faith possessed of these elevated qualities, doubt as to whether they believe or not. If, in addition, they read in the Epistle of the same Apostle that the faith of Moses was so great as to make the invisible God present and visible to him, they become sad and discouraged because they are far from experiencing anything similar. Such souls will find consolation in the following instruction:

First. Faith can be real and even very strong, though unaccompanied by any lively feeling, not even by the consciousness of its possession.

Secondly. It is with regard to faith, as well as to every other virtue, desirable that, in addition to its possession, one should have an actual perception of it; for this supports the soul in difficulties, consoles her in suffering, raises her above the purely sensual, and fills her with holy joy.

Thirdly. If the sentiment of faith is weak, or even appears to be entirely extinct, the soul must not be disturbed; for spiritual dryness produces tepidity, strengthens temptation, and impels the soul to seek in exterior things the consolation of which she is interiorly deprived. Still let sorrow

[1] Hebrews xi. 1.

be calm, let it never disturb the soul's peace. God often permits this trial for our good.

Fourthly. The lively sentiment of faith is not regained by disquiet and agitation, still less by useless exertions that wear out body and mind. Humility, prayer, punctual fulfilment of duty, and the sacrifice of all human consolation alone can restore and strengthen it.

Fifthly. God, for reasons well known to Himself, leaves us in spiritual darkness; therefore, we should humble ourselves without disquiet. Fidelity in this state is a great evidence that God, though concealing His presence and His gifts, dwells in the heart by faith or the ruling of His Holy Spirit.

Sixthly. It is extremely important to devote but little attention to the loss or acquisition of what can be given or withdrawn without detriment to our true sentiments. The essence of piety does not consist in these unstable things which are independent of our will. Be grateful when you possess them; humble when you lose them; but, at the same time, and in spite of the unevenness of the way, seek always to advance steadily in virtue.

Seventhly. It is extremely dangerous to judge the state of one's soul by signs that may have a double significance, or that do not bear directly on the immediate relations of faith and love. Such judgments lead only to presumption or discouragement; and they are, for the most part, without foundation.

Eighthly. Nothing is more opposed to the spirit of faith than that longing after certainty; that desire to feel, to experience; that grasping, as it were, everything with one's hands. This would be to found religion upon experience and sensible perceptions, to require of God an account of His doings, to ask Him to spread out before us the treasures of His grace, and to make known to us the amount of His riches. It means that, if God does not give us in the present sensible feeling as a pledge of the reward in store for us, we will withdraw our confidence in His word and promises. And, finally, it means submission to His direction only on condition that He appoint us judges of His proceedings.

All that has just been said may be given in answer to those who complain of the want of sensible feeling; and who think that they have no faith, because it is for a time concealed in the depths of their heart, though, after all, its root may there be found.

To labor in the darkness of night, in which everything seems to vanish from us, is, on the contrary, the sign of firm, solid, and meritorious faith. "Because thou hast seen me, Thomas, thou hast believed: blessed are they that have not seen and have believed!"[1] But that faith dwells and acts in these anxious souls, is shown in their life, proved by the thousand actions they daily perform in obedience to the Divine Law, and which can have no other source than faith. Their anxiety is itself the best evidence of this; for it would not be conceivable that religion could be in their eyes a mere fable.

For the rest, the foregoing principles may be applied to a much wider field. They are a remedy for the scruples of all who believe themselves destitute of certain necessary virtues, because their feelings are contrary to their desires.

XI. SCRUPLES ABOUT TEMPTATIONS AGAINST FAITH.— Besides those enumerated above, there is another species of scruple concerning faith. It consists in thoughts and doubts purely indeliberate, for the most part confused and uncertain; but which likewise very often openly and directly attack faith in its entirety, or in its individual articles.

This temptation troubles, and at the same time perplexes, anxious souls. They distinguish with difficulty how far the thought or doubt has gone. The impression of it remains, and they suspect secret unbelief to be the root of the temptation; or, at least, they fear that these frequent and importunate attacks will, in the end, weaken their faith. They

[1] John xx. 29.

ask themselves whether, in these combats, they always do their duty, and if they will continue to do so in the future.

To every soul thus tempted we reply: "We will be responsible for the good and pious sentiments of your heart, and for the sincerity of your faith. We assure you that the storm rages only around you; and by God's grace it will even serve to confirm you in faith."

Such souls make far too much account of these attacks, more importunate than dangerous. By their excessive fear, they strengthen the thoughts from which simple contempt would have freed them. God, by this temptation, merely wishes to admonish them to pray for humble, simple, child-like sentiments. If they do this they take from the devil all hope of success; for how could faith be weakened by a temptation that is employed as a remedy against pride.

These souls should never interrupt their occupations, still less their prayer, to combat and cast off such doubts against faith. Were they to do so they would fulfil the intention of the enemy, who tempts them only to disturb their devotions. "To such attacks no answer should be given!"

The sign of the cross on the forehead, mouth, and heart, is a powerful weapon against the enemy, and the name of Jesus puts him to flight. The mere thought of Christ's death, His victory over hell and unbelief, will suffice to restore peace to the soul.

The tempted soul may also say from time to time: "O my God, I believe! Help Thou my unbelief! Give me a faith more worthy of Thee! Do Thou rectify my imperfect faith! Increase faith in me! Do Thou Thyself preserve in me the gift of faith! Thy grace has made me believe. May it preserve to me this faith that overcomes the world, and the prince of this world!" They may say also: "I unite myself to the faith of Holy Church. I assent to all that she believes. With my whole heart I acknowledge as true everything that has been revealed to her."

To despise temptations, and to divert the mind from them are the most effectual remedies against them. If one makes use of professions of faith, which should not be done frequently, the shortest and most simple are decidedly the best and most efficacious. "I believe all that the Church believes! Ask me no more." Above all, beware of contending with the fiend. One should guard against replying to doubts; for, in default of proper solutions, such a procedure might lead us still deeper into spiritual darkness —yea, even to perdition.

The director should say to such timorous souls: "The Lord knows the sincerity of your heart. He heard and understood you, even before your petition ascended to Him. He appears to sleep, and yet He is with you in your labor and fatigue. One word upon His awaking, and wind and waves will be calm. Attend more to Him than to the surging billows and the rolling of the fragile bark. With Him shipwreck is impossible!"

XII. SCRUPLES ABOUT TEMPTATIONS TO BLASPHEMY.—If there is one attack more fearful than another, but one that nearly always remains extraneous to the will of the tempted, it is that of blasphemy. We need not here enter into detail concerning it. He that is visited by this heavy trial, knows best in what it consists; and it would be dangerous to excite the imagination of others with pictures whose inherent vileness must needs produce a strong impression.

The spirit of darkness is ever intent on making piety wearisome and hateful to some. Whilst he leaves in peace those that follow their passions and live without thought of eternal salvation, he unceasingly endeavors to disturb those that seek to live in interior recollection and purity of heart.

His most successful attacks are generally concealed, and they are such as best harmonize with our natural inclinations and the remains of the old man in us. Vanity, self-love, desire of earthly happiness, impurity, are the ordinary weapons he successfully uses.

God does not always permit the adversary to employ against the just the cunning of the serpent. He often suffers him to make his attacks only amid the less dangerous roaring of the lion. The devil then spreads fear and confusion, though creating more noise than damage to the soul. He displays his deformity too openly; consequently, his temptations bear on their front the name of godlessness and blasphemy.

God then establishes the heart in security. He leaves to the enemy only the exterior fortress of the senses and imagination, and they serve him to no purpose. He closes to him the temple and sanctuary. He permits him to enter the courtyard only,—not, however, to reign therein, but that he may, by his profanation of it, excite men's hatred against himself and show to them what a monster he is, to what abominations he impels, how frightful his company, to what terrible despair he is condemned, how powerless is his rage against God; and, finally, what gratitude we owe Jesus Christ who by his death has rescued us from the lion's jaws.

Therefore, devout souls should not be concerned, still less discouraged, or think they are abandoned by God when attacked by thoughts of blasphemy, be these thoughts apparently ever so abominable, ever so degrading to God and the saints, or opposed to faith or purity.

It is best for such souls to reflect as little as possible upon these involuntary pre-occupations, to pay no attention to them still less to protest energetically or vehemently against them. Here again, a contemptuous turning away from the thoughts, is the most efficacious remedy; for, according to Gerson: "One overcomes temptations to blasphemy, as well as all others of thought, most easily by despising them, never reflecting on them, and turning the mind from them to occupy it with other matters. It is dangerous to contend with them directly, or to oppose them violently." Souls sorely tempted in this way, may either seek distraction in cheering occupation, or entertain themselves with pious thoughts, sing Psalms or spiritual canticles, among which let them choose those that awaken hope and love. Almsgiving, also, has great power in driving away the spirit of darkness.

XIII. SCRUPLES UPON AMBIGUOUS POINTS SUGGESTED BY THE IMAGINATION.—We know not whether to attribute it to the Evil One, to a diseased imagination, or to both together, that sometimes spiritual reading and vocal prayers assume a double meaning: true and serious on the one hand; comical and criminal on the other.

If this phenomenon is of short duration, the soul is astonished by it though not disturbed. If it frequently returns, it exerts a saddening influence and the soul grows restless; but if it becomes a custom, prayer and reading are abandoned as the cause. The victim of such temptations questions himself as to whence proceeds this tendency of thought which even religion is not able to master. He becomes solicitous about the state of his soul, and thinks that in himself lies the cause of so sinful a turn of mind.

To act thus, is to pay far too much attention to such thoughts and, worse still, it is to yield to a temptation which should be met with sovereign contempt. Indeed, such attacks of the Evil One should confirm in the soul a love for reading and prayer, as it proves how much the devil hates such exercises. During the temptation they should be performed with all the more fidelity and perseverance, even when apparently useless. We should at this time humble ourselves at the sight of the perversity and corruption of our imagination, acknowledging before God our powerlessness to bridle it, and recognizing in the trial a just punishment of the many and deliberate revolts of our will against His commands.

What is indeliberate is not sinful. Christ Himself says: "What does not come forth from the heart cannot sully the heart." Now, what man cannot prevent, is not deliberate. In the painful trial just spoken of, one ought to be particularly intent on grounding himself in confidence in God and tranquillity of mind; in studying how to preserve these precious treasures, and in setting at nought the plans of the tempter. By so doing, the temptation will soon cease.

XIV. SCRUPLES CONCERNING CHRISTIAN LOVE OF THE NEIGHBOR.—The duties of Christian charity or love of the neighbor, are to certain souls an inexhaustible source of scruples. This arises from want of insight in judging correctly of their feelings, words, and actions. We cannot here enter into details; but we shall mention, at least, some of the principal maxims that may solve many doubts.

In sentiments contrary to charity, one should draw the proper distinction between what proceeds from natural feeling and what from free-will. To the former belong particular aversions founded upon the disagreeable humors of others, their physical defects, tone of voice, deportment, manners, and a thousand trifles that do not admit enumeration, that fall under the class of those things of which one can hardly render an account to one's self. Whatever may be the cause, the effect remains the same: one finds no relish for the object of his aversion, and unavoidable association with him becomes sometimes a real torture. It is extremely difficult, often even impossible to overcome such an antipathy. Nor is this necessary, since it is not deliberate, and does not at all concern the conscience. No Commandment of God or of the Church obliges us to find every one according to our taste. A person need not be disturbed, then, if he finds such feelings continue, despite his efforts to overcome them. It is good to oppose them by praying for the object of antipathy, by being preventing in his or her regard, and by embracing every opportunity to be useful and pleasant to him. Rarely are these means unsuccessful in overcoming our antipathy. But conscience requires nothing more than that we should not regulate our conduct by our natural aversion, and that our deportment toward the persons in question does not betray the indeliberate and guiltless bitterness within. In this way, such a temptation, like all others, will become an occasion for acquiring merit.

In addition to these natural antipathies, there often exists in souls an aversion toward those who have offended them. These occasional antipathies are more dangerous than the former; for they are generally accompanied by a motive of revenge which it would be wrong to indulge. Whoever experiences anything of this nature, must be on his guard not to allow himself to be led into actions opposed to charity. The remedies given above for natural antipathies, are still more necessary here. But if, in spite of them, we do not succeed in their destruction, we should not be disquieted; for he that faithfully resists has not to reproach himself with what he involuntarily experiences.

Others scruple that feeling of regret which they sometimes experience at their neighbor's prosperity, as well as the incipient desire that some evil might befall them. Such feelings are assuredly sinful when they proceed from hatred, envy, or a desire of revenge; but they may likewise proceed from a motive of charity, of justice, or some other virtue, and consequently be most innocent. Thus we may, in order to deter others from sin, wish punishment to a malefactor; or misfortune to a sinner which may convert him, or deprive him of the power and riches that he uses for the oppression of others, or to lead them astray. For the salvation of souls, we may even desire the death of those who are detrimental to the spiritual welfare of others; and, surely, we may regret that important offices are intrusted to unworthy men. In all this, there is nothing contrary to charity. The only evil that we are never allowed to wish our neighbor, is that absolute evil which can produce no advantage whatever either to himself or to others; viz., the loss of God and supernatural graces, or eternal damnation.

Unfavorable judgments about the neighbor are, likewise, for timorous souls, an oft-recurring source of disquiet. Every unfavorable opinion of our neighbor is not a rash judgment. A simple uncharitable thought that passes through the mind, without our deliberately dwelling upon

Various Kinds of Scruples, and their Remedy.

it, is as little capable of sullying the conscience as any other passing temptation. But if the thought is not rejected, if it be entertained by reflections upon the conduct of the party concerned, and if it is to a certain extent cherished, though without its culminating into a decided judgment, there it is only a grave suspicion, which, too, may be amenable to punishment, as we shall presently show. When we go so far as to decide that the thing really is as it appears to our mind, it is only then that, properly speaking, we form a judgment. Whether or not this be the case is best proved by an unhesitating and decided answer on the point in question.

Not every unfavorable judgment, not every suspicion, is criminal, but only those that are not well-founded. Such are those in which the actions judged do not agree with the certainty of the judgment. Such alone are prohibited under the name of rash judgments.

Consequently, no judgment, however unfavorable, if it rests upon a moral certainty, is a sin. How could there be evil in such a judgment when it is as clear as daylight? As to what regards mere suspicion, undoubted certainty is not required for its justification, but only a greater or less degree of probability arising from appearances. It is sinful only when our consent exceeds the degree of probable evidence; for a suspicion is capable of many degrees of modification, and each may correspond to the rules of prudence proportioned to the importance of the motive. As to the rest, suspicions, even when rash, rarely exceed a venial sin.

The same holds good in regard to rash judgments when the object in question is of little importance, when there is hesitancy, or when the necessary reflection is wanting; for to commit mortal sin, full knowledge of the evil and entire consent of the will must unite.

To prevent all scruples we shall add, that to form an unfavorable judgment on sufficient grounds is not a sin, although it would be more perfect to refrain from judging of the actions of others when it is not our duty to do so. It is, in general, best to interpret the actions of others favorably as far as possible ; but this praiseworthy simplicity must not exceed the rules of prudence. Prudence requires, in order to prevent scandal or danger, that the person harboring suspicion should act toward the suspected party as if he were, in reality, as bad as he appears to be. In such a case it is sufficient to suspend judgment, but at the same time act as if it were unfavorable.

Another source of scruples for timid souls is the duty of fraternal correction, of admonishing and warning the sinner, of preventing backbiting and other faults, which is to be understood, of course, when the erring party is neither a parent nor one in authority. Such fears are quickly dispelled. The scrupulous are simply to be told, that the rules on this point are intended only for those that are in a state to exercise them reasonably, without detriment to their interior peace. But Christian correction is not a duty for such as cannot practise it without disquietude ; and who, by their imprudent proceeding, make matters rather worse than better. How can he, that is incapable of directing himself, direct others?

We cannot further enlarge on Christian charity, but we hope that the instructions here laid down may bring peace to troubled souls. We advise them, in spite of the clamors of their own unreliable conscience, to adhere firmly to them.

XV. SCRUPLES ON HOLY PURITY.—There remains now but one species of scruple—one, however, that is most frequently brought forward—viz., scruples concerning holy purity.

There is no question here of what is really hurtful to this holy virtue, for we are speaking not of sins, but only of scruples ; that is, of doubts that trouble innocent souls unnecessarily, or upon very slight foundation.

But what anguish of heart seizes the soul upon the slightest doubt that arises on this delicate point! And how can we, in a virtue that concerns both soul and body, distinguish the separate co-operation of each? How can we know what was or what was not deliberate? How decide what was nearly so?

The distinction is here, indeed, difficult. Think of a highly susceptible soul, as the scrupulous generally are. The ardent imagination, heated by the fear of temptation, is full of the most indecent, the most extravagant pictures, whose impure and lasting impressions affect even the senses. At the same time, the evil tendencies of perverse nature strongly impel the soul to yield to sensual gratification, whilst the rational will is violently stormed to consent to the evil desires of the lower passions.

By so fearful a combat, the soul becomes quite confused and dejected. "The noise which," according to St. Francis de Sales, "rages around the strong fortress of the will, whilst all the other powers are already in the hands of the enemy, reduces her to extremity. She almost loses the consciousness of resistance, although the superior part of the soul still renders evidence of its presence. But this superior part is so delicate that, in the interior darkness which surrounds her, it almost escapes the spiritual eye." These words enlighten us upon the anguish of a soul during and after such a temptation; for it is, indeed, difficult to render to one's self an exact account of what passed in the innermost sanctuary of the soul.

It is for the most part impossible for a soul thus tried to decide for herself. She should, therefore, submit all to the judgment of her spiritual director. The following principles may be of assistance to souls thus tempted, provided their anxiety leaves them sufficient calmness to apply them; though, at the same time, it must never be forgotten that obedience and subjection to the confessor will always be their first principle and highest law.

I. Purity of soul is not to be taken for granted from the fact, that the imagination and senses experience no impressions contrary to the holy virtue. The soul may be almost continually at war in its defence, and yet possess this virtue in a very eminent degree; and, on the other hand, she may have very little love for it, although rarely assailed by temptations against it. As true heroism is shown upon the battle-field, so the purity of a soul never shines with greater lustre than when stormed by the most violent assaults. Holy purity dwells principally in the heart. It is the love of this virtue that makes us pure. Our purity is measured by our love for it. Struggles strengthen and inflame that love; whilst peace renders it sluggish and effeminate. The soul may be happier when not tempted; but that is not pronouncing her purer. The doubts of a soul whose peace is rarely disturbed generally deserve more notice than those of one in almost constant war; for when our weapons have been long out of use, we are much more liable to receive slight wounds than when they have been well exercised in the combat.

II. Nothing, without the consent of the free-will, can harm holy purity. The most shocking temptations, let them recur as often as they may, are so many victories, if the will adheres to what is good. All the efforts of the enemy, though united to the most violent allurements of passion, serve only for the purification of the soul if, amid such attacks, it preserves in its heart the precious treasure planted there by grace.

We may even say that impure thoughts are so much the less to be dreaded, the more exaggerated and horrible they are. They are snares too gross, too rudely laid, for a soul that treasures in her heart the fear of God and the desire of her eternal salvation. Hence, the masters of the interior life say rightly that temptations of self-love, pride, self-will, and complacency in good works, are far more dangerous to a devout soul than all the attacks of impurity, blasphemy, and ungodliness that could be presented to her by a fantastic imagination or by the gross insinuations of the demon. The soul may say to herself: "The more violently I am attacked, the more surely may I hope that I am in a good state." No such noise is made to break into an open door. When the cannonading is no longer heard, it is a sign that the besieged city has either capitulated or been taken by storm. But if the siege continues, it is an unmistakable evidence of the city's strength and power of resistance. It is precisely the same with the tried soul. Had she, with cowardly and sinful satisfaction opened her heart to the insinuations of the enemy, he would no longer molest her, he would suffer her rather to rest in her apparent peace. Were he ruler of her heart, he would make no further efforts to enter it; for says the "Following of Christ": "Sinners whom the devil possesses without resistance, he does not tempt." Resistance and combat are, therefore, a positive proof that consent has not been given. Had the soul, as she fears, yielded to impure imaginations, would she stop at more sinful actions? In her state of desolation, her good-will alone joined to the assistance of divine grace, can preserve her from evil deeds; for this state naturally impels her to seek consolation in the indulgence of passion. So long, therefore, as one has not to accuse himself of an exterior fault against purity, he may believe in the innocence of his soul.

III. The best means to close most securely the avenue to scruples on holy purity is, at the very onset of the temptation, to comport one's self as should be done in every other attack of the enemy; namely, to resist dangerous thoughts, emotions, sentiments, or feelings from the very first. On forbidden matters, one should refrain from curiosity. He should not be carried away by certain inclinations produced by the novelty of these thoughts. He should not allow them to begin by so capturing and enchaining him that afterward he will with difficulty free himself from them. Finally, by his negligence, he should not give occasion for painful examination of conscience as: "How far did the temptation extend? What consequences had it? What share had the will in it?" Watchfulness and earnestness in the early struggle spare much after disquiet and anxiety.

IV. Want of watchfulness and fidelity in the beginning, are assuredly, faults; but I do not mean to say that every carelessness in this matter is a grievous sin. Our frailty is great; and God, who knows it, does not judge it so rigorously as we think. Little faults always remain little faults. God pardons them, though He does not wish that we should excuse or repeat them.

V. Too much anxious foresight courts the temptation, and makes everything an occasion for it. Preserve, therefore, freedom in those things in which God leaves you free. Do not substitute painful constraint for wise reserve. Do not confound what is lawful or indifferent, indeed even necessary sometimes, with what is unnecessary or dangerous. Do not forbid yourself certain things innocent in themselves, because your unbridled imagination finds in them, I know not what kind of temptation. Do not, under the pretext of conscientiousness, set aside prudence and reason. Attend carefully rather to avoiding evil than to seeking it everywhere. Do not select for your line of conduct your own vague and uncertain apprehensions; for you would thus fall under the category of the unjust and perverse to whom, according to the words of St. Paul: "All things are clean to the clean: but to them that are defiled, and to unbelievers, nothing is clean: but both their mind and their conscience are defiled."[1] This point is, without doubt, the most important for you; hence, you should very specially take it to heart.

VI. Neither foresight nor seclusion, mortification nor prayer, can prevent the attacks of Satan or hinder him from employing against us the sting of a body not yet in perfect subjection. God alone is able to check him, and to forbid his molesting the saints; but God often sees that a humiliating temptation is, even for His elect, a counteracting necessity, that they may not be puffed up on account of their high gifts. He allows them to feel their own weakness, that this feeling may more perfectly confirm in them the kingdom of His grace, for nothing is truer than this

[1] Titus i. 15.

Various Kinds of Scruples, and their Remedy. 327

saying of St. Augustine: "Love is the protectress of virginity, and humility is the throne of love."[1]

It was in this way that the Lord subjected even the Apostle Paul to the most humiliating temptations of the flesh. Thrice did the saint implore to be delivered, but each time he received for answer: "My grace is sufficient for thee!"[2]

We see, also, how St. Jerome in his desert amid the most frightful austerities, and St. Augustine at the period of his greatest fervor, complained of these impure temptations. Yes, they acknowledged that, waking or sleeping, there passed before their mental gaze pictures of which holy modesty would not permit them to speak. Judge now for yourself, devout soul, whether you have reason to despair, to think yourself abandoned by God, when you experience something similar to that by which these great saints were tried. Attacks of this nature are, besides, often connected with purely natural causes and, indeed, they are not rarely the result of a too great dread of them. Cool self-possession joined to thorough contempt, are sovereign remedies against them.

We shall conclude with some extracts from the letters of St. Francis de Sales. He writes: "You are quite right, my poor, dear daughter. You have within you two men . . . and these are in conflict. The good-for-nothing one is so malicious that very often the other has great difficulty in keeping his stand. Then he thinks himself conquered, and that the evil man is more valiant than he. But no, my daughter, the Evil One is not stronger than you, though he is more perverse and obstinate. When you begin to weep, he rejoices; for then much time is lost. He is already well satisfied with your losing time on his account, since he cannot induce you to lose eternity.

"Courage, dear soul! I repeat with the greatest emphasis, and in the name of Jesus Christ. Courage, dear

---

[1] De sancta virginitate, cap. ii.   [2] II. Cor. xii. 9.

soul! So long as one can cry out resolutely, though without feeling, 'Live Jesus!' there is nothing to fear. Tell me not that you appear to say it without strength or courage, in a manner forced and violent, as it were. O my God, this is precisely that holy violence which bears away the kingdom of heaven! See, my daughter, this is the sign that the enemy has taken the citadel, though not yet the unapproachable, invincible tower which can be lost only through its own fault. I mean your free-will, which resides in the highest point of the soul; which depends only on God and itself; and which, when all the other powers are in the hands of the enemy, alone remains master of itself, able to refuse its consent.

"The soul is troubled, because the adversary continues his clamoring and knocking at the entrance. One can hardly distinguish what the higher point of the will says and does, though its voice is clearer and louder than that of the lower will; but the latter is so rough and coarse that it drowns the clear tones of the former.

"Mark, in conclusion, that as long as the temptation is displeasing to you, there is nothing to fear; for why should it displease you, except that you do not will it? . . .

"Do you know how God acts on these occasions? He allows the malicious fabricator of such wares to offer them to you for sale, to give you an occasion of proving by contempt of them your love for divine things. And should one be alarmed, should he change his position for another? O my God, no! It is only the devil, turning everything into confusion, putting everything into disorder, moving about in all directions to find an open door. Should one be vexed at this? Let the enemy prowl in vain; but do you keep the avenues well closed. He will in the end grow tired; and if he does not, God will Himself raise the siege and force him to lay down his arms.

"Neither your present disquiet nor your other fears surprise me. Thanks be to God, no harm has befallen you! Be not disturbed, then, beloved daughter. Stand firm.

One must not allow himself to be carried off by the storm, or swept away by the current. Let the enemy rage and howl at the door. Let him knock, stamp, cry, bark, and do as he will. We know that he can enter our soul only by the door of our consent. If we keep it fastened, and often give an eye to its being well secured, we need have no concern for the rest. Nothing is to be feared."

CHAPTER VI.[1]

Conclusion and Summary of what has been said of Scruples and the Remedies for them.

NO thought, not even the most heinous, as long as it is displeasing to us, can render us guilty. "Look at the mirror," says the celebrated Bishop of Belley, in his "Spiritual Combat," "it reflects perfectly the object held before it; but this object is not in the mirror. It is precisely the same with our heart. It is a mirror . . . in which the devil, in his cunning, can depict things in an abominable, shameful, and terrific manner; but our will alone can open the door to evil and admit these horrors into the soul. The tempter may practise his juggling as long as he pleases; he may present to your heart the most impure pictures; he may pour into the ears of your spirit the most horrible blasphemies, the most criminal and wicked suggestions—yet all this cannot render you guilty."

"And should these attacks continue your whole life long," says St. Francis de Sales, "they would still not be able to soil you with the least stain of sin."—"Yes, but I fear my feelings." . . . To this we answer with all theologians, who are certainly more reliable than your fears, that it is not less impossible for doubt and consent to be entertained at the same time, than to make certainty and uncertainty agree. Consent presupposes submission so entire and resignation of the soul so perfect, that doubt cannot possibly exist. The surest sign of the soul's not consenting is that very doubt as to whether or not she has consented. Mortal sin consists in the resolve of the will, and its malice

[1] This chapter is from Boudon's "The Holy Way of the Cross," Book III chap. 5.

leaves no room for a moment's doubt.—" Yes," you reply, "as many temptations and as many crosses as God may send me, if only I do not offend Him!"—But is it, then, possible that you do not perceive that you are merely trying to escape suffering? In this, self-love plays a great part, and artfully deceives you. Humble yourself before God, and acknowledge that He knows better than you what is needful for you.

According to St. Louis of Granada, most scruples of this nature proceed either from the incapability of distinguishing temptation from consent, in which case obedience is the only remedy, or else from a lack of due appreciation of the Divine Goodness. The tempted soul, in question, dreams not of the ardent longing of God for her salvation; she sees in Him not a father, but only a stern judge. In such a case, the admonition of the Holy Ghost should be followed; sentiments worthy of the goodness of an all-merciful God should be awakened; and the Lord should be sought in all simplicity. The scrupulous indulge ideas of God that would be very derogatory even to an honorable man. It appears to them that He is intent only upon their destruction; and yet, the mercies of the Lord are infinitely greater than can be imagined!

Scruples sometimes proceed from a melancholy temperament. Lawful diversion and medical prescriptions are then necessary. Again, they may spring from some defect in character, in which case they are with difficulty cured, and submission of judgment is the great desideratum. Scruples may also proceed from the reading of unsuitable theological works; for example, such as treat of predestination, or others that exaggerate serious truths. For such scruples there is no other remedy than the absolute sacrifice of such reading and the reflections to which it gives rise. The books in question should be given up, conversations upon them avoided, even deliberate thoughts of them banished. Rashness here entails much unhappiness and suffering, for experience shows that such inquisitive souls live in constant disquiet, and never arrive at perfect peace. Sometimes scruples are a special dispensation of God to purify and humble the understanding. In this case, patience and resignation to God's will are the best remedies. To some other souls scruples come from the Evil One, who seeks to perplex and discourage them, and thus render devotion insupportable. Finally, an inexperienced and undecided confessor may either give occasion to scruples, or he may increase them where they already exist. In such a case, the penitent should unquestionably change him without delay.

But from whatever quarter scruples arise, the following rules are intended for souls whom they concern :

I. General confessions are of no use whatever to the scrupulous, if one has already been made. Such souls fancy the repetition of their general confession will quiet their mind; but they are greatly deceived. St. Francis Xavier says very justly : " Unnecessary repetitions, instead of putting an end to scruples, increase them tenfold. There is no blessing upon such confessions; for, in spite of fine pretexts to the contrary, self-love and self-gratification are the sources whence they spring. They displease God, and should, therefore, be forbidden. Even annual confessions are not good for the scrupulous; neither should they confess twice before the Holy Communion, a proceeding to which they are often impelled by the thought that their last confession was not a good one. They must not return to the confessional, not even if they think they have forgotten a sin; for it will suffice to mention it the next time they approach the Sacrament. They must, making no account of their difficulties, communicate whenever their spiritual guide thinks proper.

II. A fundamental rule for the scrupulous is to omit all doubtful sins. Others may confess such sins; but timorous souls (as there is no obligation in the matter) should not do so. If they would follow this rule, how soon their endless confessions would finish; for they can scarcely accuse themselves, with certainty, of one sin. It is no use for them to plead that they do so for the sake of greater security: for, on the one side, God does not require it of them; and on the other, it is not suitable to their spiritual condition. Such accusation springs from nothing else than self-love. As to temptations, they may confess them only when they can swear upon the Holy Gospel that they have consented to them. The scrupulous should not too greatly prolong their examination of conscience. Their state requires but a very short review, since they already have their sins too constantly before their eyes. Oh, if they would remember that confession was not, as some teachers of error have asserted, instituted to distress and torture the conscience, but to alleviate and console it! All that God exacts of us is, that far from wilfully and deliberately concealing anything necessary to be told, we frankly and honestly declare the sins that come to our mind after a careful and reasonable examination. Sins forgotten are pardoned along with those that are confessed. If this were not so, souls possessed of an imperfect memory would be burdened with an impossible duty. All the rest one should quietly submit to the judgment of an intelligent confessor; and were it to happen that even he erred in his decision, yet the obedient soul may rest in perfect security. You think, for example, that your general or ordinary confession was invalid. Your confessor tells you the contrary. Suppose, now, that he is wrong and your confession was, in fact, as you fear. Even so, if you remain obedient, you will neither be responsible to God nor less pleasing to Him.

III. Above all things, a scrupulous person should avoid persistency in self-judgment. He should renounce his own ideas and give up his own false notions. It devolves not on the patient to choose his remedies, to decide upon his medicines. This choice is never left to the sick. Even physicians consult one another when indisposed; and the most expert lawyer advises with others of his profession in questions involving his own interests. Entire submission is absolutely necessary for the scrupulous. They gain more by simple obedience than by a thousand instructions, penitential works, or other devout exercises. Once, when St. Ignatius was tormented by scruples, he fasted eight entire days, without taking any nourishment whatever, to move the Divine Mercy to grant him deliverance. But all was in vain. Nothing but simple obedience to his confessor freed him from the torture. God desires submission of mind. Do what we will, without such submission all will be useless. But, when the scrupulous imagine that they do not explain themselves properly, that the confessor does not understand them, and does not rightly know their state, they must thoroughly despise such suggestions as the pure effects of self-love. Say sincerely what passes in your interior. Say it as well as you can. To more you are not bound. It is the confessor's business to examine whether or not he understood you rightly; yours to obey implicitly.

Finally, you must generously oppose your scruples. If they call upon you to repeat your Office, or the penance imposed in confession, or to assist at a second Mass on Sundays or holy-days, on the plea that you have not fully satisfied the obligation, disregard the suggestion precisely on that account. If the thought comes that you commit a sacrilege by receiving the holy Sacraments, or that certain innocent things are mortal sins, rise above it, act courageously in spite of your fears and difficulties. You say: "But it would be a sin for me to do something, although good in itself, but which, to my false conscience, appears sinful." We reply: In such a case, others might possibly sin; but with you it is quite different. Your confessor has assured you that it is not sinful; hence, you not only do not commit a sin in acting contrary to your own judgment, but you do something very pleasing to God. A priest was once on the brink of despair. He thought he committed a sacrilege every time he celebrated Holy Mass, and transgressed, besides, in nearly everything he did. Divine Providence sent him a holy and enlightened man, who said to him: "Father, rise above this imaginary sacrilege.

Do with hearty good-will what your scruples represent to you as a gross sin, but which, in the just opinion of sensible people, is no harm at all." The priest obeyed simply, his feelings to the contrary notwithstanding; and thus he was freed from his mental torture. We once knew a person who made several general confessions, in order to repair some former ones that were really invalid. But in vain did she seek peace of conscience in these repetitions. She resolved, then, to prepare again with very special attention for another general confession. She spent much time in the examination. With incredible attention she wrote her accusation in its fullest details; and then confessed in a private chapel thus to be subjected to fewer distractions. But after all this labor, she was more than ever disquieted. She obtained peace only by submitting her judgment to that of her confessor and giving up general confessions; although the last, like those that had preceded, was in her own opinion equally invalid. She gained in the end, but only by submission, marvellous peace, not won, however, without a hard-fought struggle with self, and not till she could make up her mind to desist from repeating her supposed unworthy confessions. God infused it into her soul as a reward for her obedience, without which she would, despite her anxiety and efforts, have still been disturbed and disquieted.

CHAPTER VII.

Examples of the Danger that attends Self-willed Persistence in Scruples.

IN conclusion, let a frightful example serve to convince the scrupulous of the necessity of obedience. This example is found in Martin Luther of wretched celebrity. This heretic spent the first part of his life in the exact fulfilment of the rules of his Order; but, ever disquieted by scruples that he would not overcome by humble obedience to superiors, he succumbed to temptation, and ended in those lamentable errors that are only too well known. We extract the following particulars from the excellent work of Cazalès:

"Luther," says one of his biographers, "was in the highest degree what the directors of souls term scrupulous; and herein lies, according to my opinion, the explanation of his later doctrine on justification, and his revolt against the authority of the Church."

A writer of his own party gives us in the following extract an insight into Luther's state during the first period of his life:[1] "Though naturally frank and cheerful, yet in the cloister Luther was always sad and disquieted. This sprang in the beginning from the thought of his father's dissatisfaction at his embracing the religious state. His violent expressions on that head greatly disturbed Luther, who was, besides, anxiously longing for some certainty as to the pardon of his sins; and in nothing that he did could he find consolation. . . . One of his spiritual directors at this period said to him: 'My son, what do you want? Do you not know that God has commanded us to hope in

[1] Walch, Luther's Works, vol. xxiv.

Him?' When John von Staupitz came to Erfurt, Luther complained to him of his misery. He confided to him the fact of his being tormented by frightful thoughts. He was firmly convinced, as he said himself, that he alone had such temptations and combats, and that neither Staupitz nor his other spiritual guides knew or understood anything concerning his case." Here one clearly sees the stupidity of a scrupulous person who cannot be convinced that he is understood by any one! Luther again says: "As I was always repeating my absurd accusations, my confessor once said to me: 'You are a fool! God does not will to contend with you, but you with Him. He is not angry with you, but you with Him!'"

"You would wish to be without sin," said Staupitz to Luther, "and yet you have no real sins with which to reproach yourself. Christ pardons the true sinner, patricides, blasphemers, apostates, etc. Take an examination of conscience in your hand: in it sins are clearly defined. Give up your nonsensical and ludicrous notions, and do not make of every trifle a mortal sin." How excellently well suited are these admonitions of Dr. Staupitz to souls that are always occupied with their own anxious conscience! "One can truly say," Cazalès here very justly remarks, "if the sinner acknowledges, confesses, and truly repents, gross sinfulness is more easily cured than the demoniacal proceedings of the scrupulous person who, in the over-estimate of his own strength, aims at freedom from sin, and thus strives to elevate himself to a condition impossible here below."

In order to procure interior peace through his own efforts, Luther led a very austere life in the punctual and constant discharge of the rules of his Order. He himself testifies to this effect: "It is true," he says, "that I was a devout monk, and in my heart attached to my Order; so that I can say, if ever monk gained heaven by the monastic life, I too should reach it. All the brethren of the monastery that knew me can bear witness to this: for if I had persevered in it longer, I should have killed myself with vigils, prayers, reading, and other penitential works." Melancthon, too, informs us that Luther excelled in all pious exercises, such as reading, fasting, and prayer. John Mathesius adds, that Luther had quite exhausted his strength with vigils and fasting. Finally, Seckendorf tells us that Luther, without allowing himself time for meals, would lock himself in his cell to recite the Canonical Office when his studies left him no leisure for this duty. This manner of life so weakened the unfortunate man, that for seven weeks he was unable to sleep, and he almost lost the use of his mental faculties.

General information concerning the state of his health at this period gives evidence of deep-seated hypochondria and disturbance of mind, whose source was secret pride concealed under the mantle of false humility. Journeying to Italy, he was attacked by so violent a vertigo, together with singing and roaring in his ears, that he thought his end had come. His biographers tell us that at this time his terrible fear as to the remission of his sins increased his bodily sufferings. In Rome he was so slow in celebrating Holy Mass, that, during his, seven others could be begun and ended; and if there is no exaggeration in his own assertion, the server called to him: "*Passa! Passa!*"—*Make haste! Make haste!*—at which he was very much vexed.

Such proceedings certainly indicate that one means to damn one's self by main force.

How many religious were at that same time working out their salvation in the same convent by the vow of obedience! Whereas, this unfortunate man, though tormenting himself so frightfully, was hurrying with rapid strides to his own perdition! Why was it that he did not sanctify himself by so austere a life? What was wanting? Nothing but a little humility and obedience. These two virtues would have enriched him in the eyes of the Lord, who requires submission of heart above all else, and who rejected the offerings presented Him by His people with the words: "I have no pleasure in you, and I shall accept no offering from your hand, because your own will is in your fasts."

Ah, like Luther, how many scrupulous persons ruin themselves, soul and body, for a mere nothing! They offer to the Lord a thousand sacrifices that He does not at all require, whilst they obstinately refuse what alone He does exact; namely, their own will and judgment. They refuse to be guided by their spiritual director; in short, they deny to the Lord that humble obedience which is far more pleasing to Him than all other sacrifices. Shall they not finally see at what a price they could have purchased the good pleasure of God, peace and salvation to their soul?

Some of Luther's table-conversations give us an insight into his troubled conscience, and show that whilst still in the monastery his confessor had represented to him his false and erroneous turn of mind. It was his own fault that he wished to save himself by his own efforts, without the help of divine mercy, of which he thought he had no need. His superiors and confessors explained to him the doctrine of the Church as it then was, as it is now, and as it ever shall be—the same in all time. They admonished him to resign himself to the mercy of God, who, for the sake of the merits of Jesus Christ, forgives us our sins, but in whom we must believe and hope. No one nurtured Luther's insane scruples. He was told to be at peace and trust in God; and this, according to the principles of Catholic truth, is the only proper method of treating this malady of the soul. But Luther's self-will baffled every argument; and thus the temptations that constantly exposed him to despair had sooner or later to bring about a definite crisis in his soul. In an attack of melancholy he once locked himself in his cell for several days, and refused to see any one. Then, says an old chronicle, came Luke Enderger with some children playing sweet music at his door, and knocking for admittance; but the door remained closed. Then it was forced open, and Luther was found lying prostrate in a faint. Again the children played, and their music restored him to consciousness. Later, the self-willed monk entertained the thought of suicide, and once declared at table that the sight of a knife conjured up painful pictures before him. His unhappy condition brought about no catastrophe of this nature—events took a different, but not a less lamentable turn. Luther's moral errors passed to the mind and spirit, thus leading to the sad end—formal heresy.

After long efforts to save himself by his own strength, Luther suddenly caught at the contrary extreme, an occurrence by no means rare in such cases. Excessive austerity was followed by slothfulness; exaggerated, passionate, penitential fervor ended in his abandonment of every means of amendment and sanctification. With the passionate violence of his character, he took refuge in the truth of faith, that Jesus Christ by His death on the cross has won for us salvation. It was not sufficient for him to despair of attaining salvation by his own strength, but he went still further. He altogether rejected man's co-operation in the work of salvation, as if he would say to God: "Since I cannot do all, since I am unable to attain my ideal, I will do nothing at all, not even that which is in my power!"

Sad and insane conclusion, to which scruples not unfrequently bring a soul weary of fruitless combats, and conscious at last of her own impotence to carry out her vain theories of perfection!

Let us pause here and leave more detailed consideration of this frightful example to those to whom these lines are addressed, since it speaks more forcibly than any warning that could be adduced. Granting that but few self-willed, scrupulous souls become, like Luther, the authors of heresy; yet many perish, less strikingly indeed, but in a manner not less fearful. They reject religious obligations; and final impenitence or insanity is often the sad outcome of their high-minded self-will. But even should scruples not lead to such extremes, they at least render life useless and

Danger in Self-willed Persistence in Scruples.

unhappy, impede spiritual progress, and subject the soul to continual alarms. There is only one infallible remedy to oppose to this evil; namely, the unconditional renunciation of one's own direction. In this is followed the Gospel counsel of losing one's self in order to find one's self. This sacrifice costs an effort, but it is necessary. Peace, oftentimes indeed eternal salvation, depends upon it. Courage and strength to make this sacrifice is, for the scrupulous soul, the grace of graces. Fail not, therefore, ardently to implore it of the Divine Goodness, through the intercession of the Blessed Virgin and St. Joseph, those two most humble and obedient souls. To their protection also we confidently commend all the efforts contained in the foregoing pages to restore lost peace to unhappy souls.

A. M. D. G.

APPENDIX.

Preparatory Remarks.

ONE often hears pious souls complain that they can neither pray nor meditate nor examine their conscience. They ask what they must do to make these exercises easy and useful. In answer we give them the following method.

We give also a formula for making a one day's retreat profitably. The exercises may be performed every Monday. Souls that have their perfection at heart will gladly subject themselves to it, for it has been sanctioned by the example of the saints, and its advantages have been proved by experience.

General Remarks upon each of the Various Methods of Prayer.

I. Never omit the remote preparation for prayer, which consists in continual interior recollection. Avoid, therefore, as much as possible, every occasion of distraction. A soul habitually dissipated is never fit for good meditation.

II. Endeavor to make the immediate preparation, that is, read before retiring at night the meditation for the next morning. Think upon it before going to sleep; and next morning, as soon as you awake, recall it to mind. Try between these two periods to banish every other thought.

III. The immediate preparation is not less necessary. It comprises the following points:

(1) Recall the presence of God as vividly as possible.

(2) Offer Him all the powers of your soul, your memory,

imagination, and will, and earnestly implore of Him the grace to apply them exclusively to the subject of the meditation.

(3) If you meditate upon sensible objects; for instance, on the birth of Christ, place yourself in spirit where the mystery was accomplished, in the stable at Bethlehem, at the crib. . . . If you consider a purely spiritual truth, for example, the misery into which sin plunged man, you can the more easily fix your attention upon it. Imgaine a soul held fast in the prison of the body, banished to this valley of tears, condemned to the society of animals. . . . This preparation is called preliminary, or the representation of the place. The end of this first preparation is to produce upon the soul an impression similar to that which a faithful picture of the mystery under consideration would make upon the corporal sight, which impression will serve to fix the imagination and render meditation more easy. This preparation should be short, and made without effort. It must not fatigue the mind. If it should prove wearisome to souls or become a hindrance, it would be better to give it up entirely.

(4) Ask God for a grace corresponding to the subject of your meditation, by which you may rightly understand and put it into practice. This is the second preparatory exercise.

IV. If through God's grace you feel particularly impressed by some reflection, pause there without concerning yourself about the other points of your meditation. A gleaner remains in the field as long as he finds anything to glean, and thinks not of pushing on farther. Be less intent upon meditating truth than upon taking it to heart and rightly relishing it.

V. If you make use of a book containing fully prepared and finished meditations, do not read too much at once. Stop at every point or at every sentence in order to reflect, otherwise your exercise will be a reading instead of a meditation.

VI. Be not changeable in the choice of your meditations. Go regularly through the book you have chosen; and when you have finished it, either begin it again or take another.

Prayer of St. Ignatius at the End of Meditation.

Receive, O Lord! my entire liberty, my memory, my understanding, and my whole will. Whatever I have and all that I possess Thou hast bestowed upon me. To Thee I return all and I surrender all, to be governed entirely by Thy will. Grant me only Thy grace and Thy love, and I am rich enough, nor do I desire anything more.

First Method of Prayer.

The Actual Meditation.

REMARK.—We take for granted that the preparation, remote, proximate, and immediate, has been *always punctually performed, as mentioned above.*

Meditation implies the directing of the three powers of the soul to the consideration of some pious subject, as a means of becoming better and of elevating ourselves to God. Meditation is also an exercise of the memory, the understanding, and the will.

Exercise of the Memory.

The exercise of the memory consists in this: First, briefly to recall the subject of the meditation one has prepared, as if he intended to relate the whole to another. After that he returns to the first point, fixes it vividly before him, pauses upon the truth or mystery contained in it, and awakens an act of faith. During the meditation, also, the memory is from time to time active. This happens as often as one recalls anything bearing on the subject, to draw from it new matter for consideration and affections.

Exercise of the Understanding.

The exercise of the understanding consists in consideration and application.

I. Consideration consists in reflections upon what must

First Method of Prayer.

ve believed, practised, or avoided with regard to the truth or mystery of which the meditation treats; the motives for its utility, necessity, justice, facility, etc., that should impel us thereto, and the harm that might arise from the neglect of them. One should ask himself what he should counsel his best friend on this or that point, or what he should wish to have done when on his death-bed. After this he goes on to weigh some of the motives or consequences calculated to move the heart, and says to himself everything that he would say to another, to induce him to put into execution the resolutions suggested by such reflections.

II. The application is twofold: general and particular.

1. The general application is made by reflecting on how most men conduct themselves in regard to this truth, and how we ourselves judge of their conduct. If we find that we too belong to the number of the blind, then this judgment must be turned upon ourselves. But one should not dwell too long on this application; and he should be careful lest it prove an occasion of distraction.

2. In the particular application one reflects how he has hitherto valued the truth considered, whether his conduct in general has been regulated by it, or whether he has neglected it. If the latter proves to be the case, he examines on what points he has failed, and reflects on the harm that has come to him from it. He goes back over the causes, intentions, etc.; he compares his own negligence with the zeal worldlings evince in striving for riches and honors; and, finally, he looks into what, in the future, has to be done or omitted.

Exercise of the Will.

The activity of the will, which is generally regulated by the conviction of the understanding, expresses itself during the meditation in different acts, which form the most excellent and essential part of the whole exercise.

I. The will produces devout affections corresponding to

the subject of the meditation, the present state and feelings of the soul, and the attraction of the Holy Ghost.

The usual affections are: (1) Sorrow and regret; (2) humility; (3) astonishment; (4) gratitude; (5) mistrust of self; (6) patience; (7) total surrender of one's self to God, to do, to suffer, and to sacrifice all without reserve, as it may please Him; (8) confidence in God's goodness and in the merits of Jesus Christ; (9) offering of self; (10) renunciation of all that prevents or retards progress in virtue; (11) acceptance of all anticipated suffering; (12) fervor; (13) love; (14) conformity to the will of God; (15) resignation to the arrangements of Divine Providence. These affections, of course, should be chosen according to the subject of the meditation.

II. The will makes resolutions, which are the outcome of the preceding reflections: (1) A general resolution; (2) one or two particular resolutions which apply the general one to the present needs of the soul; and (3) a very special, practical resolution to embrace this or that means to carry out more securely during the present day the particular resolution.

III. What is understood by the colloquy in meditation is also an exercise of that power of the soul called the will. Colloquies are reverential and confidential conversations with God, in which we praise Him, thank Him, offer ourselves to Him, beg His grace, etc. In these colloquies one speaks to God at one time as a child to its father; at another, as a servant to his master; again, as an invalid to his physician, etc. The colloquies may also be addressed to Jesus Christ, to the Blessed Virgin, or some saint. The meditation is concluded with an *Our Father* and *Hail Mary*.

Concluding Act of the Meditation.

1. Pause for a moment to see whether the meditation has been made well or ill. In the latter case, review the meditation to find the cause, recall the light that was given, the emotions of grace experienced, and the resolutions taken.

2. Offer the resolutions to God, beg pardon for the faults

First Method of Prayer.

committed during prayer, and implore the assistance of the Blessed Virgin and patron saints.

3. The third thing to be done is to make choice of some of the essential reflections or affections by which you have been particularly touched, of which to form a spiritual nosegay. This will, from time to time during the day, remind you of your prayer, and renew in your soul the holy sentiments excited by God's grace during the meditation.

An Example applicable to this Method.

A merchant learns through a friend that in a specified place certain goods are for sale. Now this is the subject of meditation and the preparation.

He reflects upon what he has heard, collecting all the powers of his mind, to concentrate them upon the matter. It seems to him that he sees the whole affair passing before his eyes. (This is the immediate preparation, answering to the preparatory acts, the preludes.)

He then represents to himself very distinctly and in detail the goods, their quality, price, and the city in which they are for sale. (This is the exercise of the memory.)

Next he considers the various uses he can make of them, what motives induce him to purchase these goods, what successful result their purchase may have for him, what gain they will bring him, etc. (This is the exercise of the understanding, the weighing of the matter.)

He sees, moreover, how many other business men have utilized similar favorable opportunities, have reaped much profit from them; and he cannot but approve the project. (This is the general application.)

Now, he sees also how, through his own fault, he has up to the present neglected to learn and to embrace such opportunities, although he either had the money in his possession, or would have been able to procure it. He now reckons the loss his neglect has caused him, and considers how he can indemnify himself for it; what obstacles are to be overcome, what means to be employed. (This is the particular application.)

He regrets his negligence, reproaches himself for it, resolves without delay to atone for it, and concludes that, for a specified amount, he will in this or that way purchase such and such goods. (These are the affections, the general and particular resolutions.)

He now communicates his project to an intimate friend, and this is the colloquy.

He ends by asking himself whether he has well weighed the matter, and thus strengthens his determination. (These are the acts that conclude the meditation.)

Instead of business, take a truth of salvation, a mystery of our holy religion, a virtue, etc. Work it out precisely as did the merchant, after first asking God's assistance, and you will have made a good meditation.

This illustration proves that all can meditate, that the form given above is in perfect harmony with the natural method of thought pursued by the human mind, and that it is much easier than is often imagined.

Second Method of Prayer.

Contemplation.

REMARK.—The second method of prayer is contemplation, and is to be applied in meditation to a mystery of the life of Jesus or Mary, or, in general, to some historical fact. Having most vividly impressed upon the soul the thought of the presence of God, the immediate preparation should be made as follows:

1. Recall the event or mystery to be considered as a whole, without at all entering into particulars. 2. Represent to yourself the place in which the mystery was enacted; for example, the Temple, the Cenacle, Mount Calvary, the seashore, the desert, or the mountains, according to the event or subject selected. 3. The help of God should be asked here, to obtain the grace corresponding with the mystery meditated: for example, humility, patience, compassion of

heart, spiritual joy, according to the subject, as the Birth of Our Lord Jesus Christ, His sufferings, His death, or Resurrection.

This must be done briefly, after which follows the meditation proper, which must certainly prove easy and simple, as well as successful. One has only to consider the persons, their words, and actions. Let us take, for example, the baptism of Jesus Christ.

I. What persons are there present? The Eternal Father, who gives testimony to the Divinity of His Son; Jesus Christ, the Son of God, who, like a sinner, receives the baptism of penance; the Holy Ghost, who descends under the form of a dove; St. John the Baptist preaching penance; a multitude of sinners, male and female, of every condition. Let us ask ourselves who these people are. Who is the Heavenly Father? Who is Jesus Christ? And so of the rest.

II. What do these persons say? St. John says to Jesus: "I ought to be baptized by Thee, and comest Thou to me?" And Jesus answering, said to him: "Suffer it *to be so* now. For so it becometh us to fulfil all justice."[1] Oh, that contest of humility, in which Jesus gains the victory! We can also reflect on the words of the multitude that surround the Precursor of the Lord. Finally, consider the words of the Heavenly Father: "This is My beloved Son, in whom I am well pleased." Solemn words, containing rich matter for reflection!

III. What do these persons do? Jesus draws near, He descends into the Jordan. Behold His interior recollection, His humility. He has no need of the baptism. St. John takes water and pours it over His head; and at the same moment the heavens open, the Holy Ghost descends, the voice of the Heavenly Father is heard. Think of the emotion among the assembled crowd gazing with breathless attention upon this astonishing miracle.

What fruit can one draw from this meditation? It

[1] Matt. iii. 14, 15.

naturally appears to be humility. If, however, through God's inspiration, the soul feels more drawn to another virtue, the attraction of grace must be followed; for "the Holy Spirit breatheth where He will!" The meditation is concluded with a colloquy, the *Our Father*, and the concluding prayers.

REMARKS.—I. One should not begin by considering the persons in the mystery individually, and in the same way take up their words and actions. But the scene should be contemplated in the whole. The different actions should be viewed with the actors concerned. What does this one say? what does that one do?—for it is in this order one would witness the scene if present at it. The natural course of events, therefore, should be followed. The person meditating should endeavor to be present in spirit at the mystery contemplated. When one circumstance has been considered from every point of view, proceed to the next in the same way. The separation of persons, their words and actions, given above, are intended rather to afford material for contemplation. It is not necessary to confine one's self to the order therein observed.

II. In lieu of spoken words, consider the interior sentiments; for example, in the mystery of His Birth the Child Jesus does not speak. But we can easily imagine what sentiments animated Him when He was placed in the manger, when His holy Mother caressed Him, and offered Him her first loving services, when the shepherds and the Wise Men adored Him and offered their gifts.

III. If one person, one word, or one act affords sufficient matter for occupation during the whole time of meditation, stop there without proceeding further.

Third Method of Prayer.

The third method of prayer is in the way of examination of conscience, united with affections of sorrow and resolutions. One can make this examination either upon the Ten Commandments of God; on the Seven Deadly Sins;

Third Method of Prayer.

the three powers of the soul, memory, understanding, and will; or the five senses—sight, hearing, taste, touch, and smell. The method is, as follows:

(1) Before beginning, recollect yourself and ask yourself the question: What am I going to do? I am going to meditate on this or that subject.

(2) Implore God for the grace to know your transgressions against the Ten Commandments, and promise henceforth faithfully to observe these Commandments.

(3) Now begins the examination of conscience, not as for confession, but in the form of a meditation, a short statement of conscience to be made to one's self before God. Ask yourself: How have I sinned against the First Commandment? against faith? against hope? against love? against religion? Examine yourself for one or two minutes, beg God's pardon for having committed the faults remarked, and promise to do better. Then add some pious affection to which you feel interiorly attracted; for instance: "O my God, I believe! But do Thou increase my faith! O my God, pardon me that I have not always had sufficient confidence in Thee! My God, I shall ever love Thee more and more!" After the examination upon the First Commandment, go to the second, observing the same method; and so on to the end of the Commandments.

If the time allotted for meditation is over, finish here for to-day, and conclude with the *Our Father*. On the following day the exercise can be resumed.

If instead of the Commandments of God one chooses for the subject of his meditation the Seven Deadly Sins, the five senses, or the three powers of the soul, the method to be pursued is the same; the matter alone is different. Instead of asking: How have I sinned against faith? say, Have I been guilty of pride, of envy, etc.? . . . or have I sinned with my eyes, tongue, etc.? . . . or have I sinned with my memory, will, or understanding? . . . Conclude, as before, with the *Our Father*.

A very excellent form of prayer is to reflect how Jesus

Christ and His most pure Mother made use of these exterior senses. What modesty in their looks! . . . What retirement! What charity in their words! . . . What strict watchfulness over their ears, in order to hear only edifying things! . . . What moderation at meals! . . . Finally, what precaution and modesty in the use of all their senses! . . . Now ask what use you have, up to the present, made of your senses! . . . Have I been in this respect a true imitator of Jesus and Mary? . . . If you have to reproach yourself on this point, then excite sorrow, make a firm resolution to be more watchful in future, and to keep your senses in more restraint.

Fourth Method of Prayer.

The fourth method of prayer is the easiest and often also the most successful. It consists in taking some vocal prayer, for instance, the *Our Father*, the *Hail Mary*, or any other to which you feel attracted, and meditate upon it word for word, proceeding to the next word only when the former no longer affords matter for pious thoughts and sentiments. Other suitable thoughts and comparisons may here come in with great profit, thus developing the subject. Let us apply this method to the *Hail Mary*.

Before Kneeling Down.

What am I going to do? I am going to meditate upon the *Hail Mary*. O ever-Blessed Virgin! obtain for me the grace to make this meditation well.

Kneel Down.

"Hail!" Who speaks this word? The Archangel Gabriel. To whom? To the ever-Blessed Virgin Mary. Such a word testifies deep reverence. The archangel owed reverence to Mary, for she was to become the Mother of his King, consequently she was to be his queen. What honor for Mary! O Holy Virgin! I congratulate thee on thy happiness! Thy virtues merited this honor. By them thou didst prove thyself worthy of it. I, too, salute thee as my

Fourth Method of Prayer.

Queen, as my Mother, as the Mother of my Saviour! It is meet that I should salute thee with the deepest reverence, since an archangel has humbled himself before thee! When I say *Hail Mary!* I unite with all heaven and earth, for everywhere the sound of this beautiful salutation greets thee!

"Mary!" O beautiful name! Most consoling name! Name most worthy of love! Name everywhere repeated with love! Mary! Mary! This sweet name is the support of the weak, the comfort of the sorrowful, the hope of the sinner, the last help of the dying. Mary! If the whole time of my meditation were passed in repeating it, in tasting its sweetness and rejoicing in it, the time would be profitably employed. The name of Mary signifies Star of the Sea. Behold how she justifies this title by guiding us happily through the dangers of life! Mary signifies Lady and Queen: and is Mary in truth not such? Mary signifies Light: and does not divine light come through her? O Mary, be my star, my queen, my light!

"Full of grace!" A vessel filled is incapable of receiving more. If more be poured into it, it will overflow. Thus it was with Mary. Her soul was full of grace, of light, of knowledge; her heart was full of grace, of love, of holy desires; her virginal body was full of grace, full of purity, full of holiness. "Thou art full of grace!" Therefore there was in her no vacuum; sin could find no room in her. O Immaculate Virgin! All is grace within thee; there is no sin. Thou wast full of grace from the moment of thy Immaculate Conception, and thou didst afterward receive by thy faithful co-operation that full, heaped-up, and overflowing measure of grace of which the Holy Scripture speaks. In the mystery of the holy Incarnation Mary's measure of grace was unspeakable; for she possessed the Source of all grace. "Thou art full of grace!" Mary was inundated with graces, that their superabundance might flow over upon us. Oh yes, I shall often hasten to this holy source, which never ceases to pour out on men the living streams of divine grace.

"The Lord is with thee!" The Lord is in all just souls, but in Mary in a much more perfect manner; since she was the most just and most perfect of all creatures. The Heavenly Father is in her by divine complacency, as in His best-beloved daughter. The Son of God is in her as in His purest tabernacle, which from all eternity He selected and prepared for Himself. The Holy Ghost is in her as in His temple, which He adorned and fitted up with His richest gifts. "The Lord is with thee!" He is always with thee, and He was always with thee, because sin never forced Him to withdraw from thee. O my God, be Thou always with me! Permit not that I should ever be separated from Thee by sin!

"Blessed art thou among women!" Mary herself announces to us, in her canticle of praise, that from henceforth, now, and forever all generations shall call her blessed. And, in effect, her sanctuaries are, everywhere and throughout the length and breadth of the land, the expression of the love and ardent devotion of her children. What woman was ever honored as Mary is? And what woman ever merited to be so honored?

"And blessed is the fruit of thy womb, Jesus!"—Jesus! Divine Name, brought by the archangel from heaven!—Jesus, Saviour of the world; Jesus, Son of the Most High, is also the Son of Mary, the fruit of her chaste womb! O holy Virgin, I congratulate thee that thou art the Mother of Jesus, the Mother of thy God! Blessed be Jesus! Blessed in heaven, blessed on earth! O Jesus, I praise Thee, I love Thee, I adore Thee, I give Thee thanks for Thy great glory!

The *Hail Mary* may be paraphrased differently. This example will suffice for illustration. It is hardly necessary to add that the same method may be applied to other vocal prayers.

If two or three words of the prayer chosen suffice to fill

up the whole time of meditation, pause upon those words, and repeat the rest at the close without dwelling on the particular words. On the following day, resume the meditation where you left off the day before.

Fifth Method of Prayer.

The fifth method of prayer consists in slowly reciting some vocal prayer, and pausing after each word for a space long enough to draw one breath.

Let us apply this method to the prayer "Soul of Christ, sanctify me."

(1) Recollect yourself, and ask yourself this question: What am I about to do?

(2) Implore God's grace to derive great profit from this exercise.

Now begin the prayer: "Soul of Christ, sanctify me! Body of Christ, save me! Blood of Christ, inebriate me!" etc.

While sending forth these sighs laden with saving petitions, think either on the sense of the words, or the dignity of the person to whom they are addressed; or upon your own unworthiness.

This method is suitable to all persons and to all hours of the day. It may be used even during labor. It will be particularly beneficial to those who have the bad habit of saying vocal prayers hurriedly. According to this method, you can go through several prayers one after the other, discontinuing and resuming at pleasure. Conclude, as usual, with the *Our Father* and *Hail Mary*.

Sixth Method of Prayer.

Spiritual Reading in the Form of Consideration.

Should a soul find herself in such a state of mind that, in spite of the five methods given above, meditation is still too difficult for her, then let her have recourse to the sixth method. This at least can always be employed, since, although affording almost the same advantages, it is much easier than the foregoing.

The sixth method of prayer, called also Consideration, is an exercise which takes the middle place between meditation and spiritual reading. In it one makes use of those books of devotion in which much meaning is contained in few words, as the "Following of Christ," "The Spiritual Combat," and other little books recommended by directors of souls according as necessity requires. Having made choice of a book, keep to it and go regularly through it, without lightly changing it, or skipping from one page to another. Beginning the consideration, recollect yourself before God, invoke His assistance, that you may derive advantage from this exercise; and then read attentively a few lines from the book of devotion you have chosen. As soon as a thought containing some useful light, such as an admonition, an interior reproach, or one in any way suited to her wants, strikes the soul, stop reading. Weigh, measure, and digest this thought till the heart is thoroughly penetrated with it, and has received from it a salutary impression. If the imagination strays, lead it back to the thought in question by re-reading the sentence that suggested it, and thus repeat as its greater or less importance may require. In a word, such spiritual nourishment should be masticated until all its flavor is tasted, without the least concern as to whether or not the reading is advancing. Your business is to apply to yourself the truth to which you feel drawn. After completely exhausting it, proceed with your reading. If a second thought offers similar food for the soul, dwell upon it as before, and then proceed to the third, fourth, and fifth; thus continuing till the time prescribed for the exercise has expired. In this way you may possibly read at one time more, at another less. At one time half a page will suffice; or again, you may require a number of pages. But what you read, whether much or little, will always be of immense profit. Of what use to the soul is it to devour the very best books and writings without making reflection? No matter how copious the spring, he that draws from it in a sieve will never get but a few drops of water. Therefore, read slowly. Take time to digest, so to say, what you have read; for spiritual nourishment is like corporal food in this, that it does not produce the good effects it should when taken too hurriedly.

The sixth method of prayer is very like to the fourth, only that a book takes the place of a prayer. The book is before the eyes, and is, therefore, all the better suited not only to furnish new material for thought, but also to fetter the inconstant imagination. This method is particularly recommended to souls that complain of dryness and distraction in prayer. St. Teresa says that she herself used it for a long time, and with great profit. She tells us even that for several years she was quite unable to meditate in any other way.

Method for Examination of Conscience.

In the examination of conscience five points are required: (1) Thanksgiving; (2) Petition for light; (3) Self-examination; (4) Sorrow; (5) Resolution.

(1) THANKSGIVING.—After placing one's self more particularly in the presence of God, recall the innumerable benefits He has bestowed upon you, and compare them with your own ingratitude—a comparison which ought to confound the soul deeply. After this thank our dear Lord for all His gifts and graces, in general and particular, spiritual and temporal, known and unknown, and in particular for those bestowed upon you this day. All this is to be done briefly and fervently.

(2) PETITION FOR LIGHT.—Here one prays for the grace to know and detest his sins. The heart is an impenetrable abyss, in which self-love spreads the deepest darkness. Without light from above, one can never rightly know one's self; therefore, pray for this light.

(3) THE EXAMINATION PROPER.—One may examine himself upon his thoughts, words, and actions: or ask him-

self whether God, his neighbor, and he himself can be satisfied with them; or he goes through his various occupations since his last examination, and probes to find whether he has sinned in motives, intentions, or external actions. Yet this should not, in general, occupy more than three or four minutes.

(4) SORROW.—This and the following point are the most important of the examination of conscience; hence the greatest care ought to be employed in them. This will be rendered much easier to us by some sensible representation, some striking example from real life, or a touching illustration. Among the most applicable we select that of St. Peter, on whom the Saviour, after his denial, cast a tender and reproachful glance; St. Mary Magdalen at the feet of Jesus during the meal at the Pharisee's house; the publican who, in his humility, stood at the door of the Temple. It is good at this time to gaze upon a Crucifix or some other representation of Our Saviour's Passion, or of His holy Mother; for example, the agony in the garden, the scourging of Jesus, one of the Stations, or a picture of the Dolorous Mother. This should be accompanied by reflection on the different motives which could move us to sorrow. Such practices are good, and one should follow in them his particular attraction. In concluding, an act of contrition should be made with all possible fervor; and for some souls it would be well to pronounce the words with the lips.

(5) RESOLUTION.—Here one may use some comparison that will assist his weakness and enkindle holy sentiments in his heart. Let him ask himself, for example: Would not a traitor condemned to death, but who has been magnanimously pardoned by his prince, henceforth serve that prince most faithfully? Would not a captain whose carelessness had almost led to shipwreck be more careful in future?

After these and other short reflections, promise our dear Lord with the assistance of His grace to sin no more. Consider now in advance to what occasions of sin you will be exposed until the next examination, and beg God to strengthen you to pass through them unscathed. Implore also the assistance of the dear Mother of God and the guardian angel, and conclude with the *Our Father* and *Hail Mary*.

Let us now make a practical application of this.

Before Kneeling:

O my God, grant that I may know Thee and know myself! (St. Augustine.) Grant me the grace to make this examination well.

Kneel.

FIRST POINT: THANKSGIVING.—O my God, I thank Thee from my whole heart for all Thy benefits! Thou hast created me, and in Thy infinite mercy preserved me until now. Thou hast granted me in preference to so many others the gift of faith, and after having by the light of the Holy Gospel shown me the way of virtue, Thou dost also lead me therein by Thy holy grace. (Here recall some special benefit you have received from God.) What choice graces have again been bestowed upon you even on this day by the Divine Goodness! (for example, Holy Mass, confession, Communion, a sermon, holy inspirations, good example.) O my God! I acknowledge that Thou willest my salvation, my perfection. Be Thou a thousand times blessed for it!

SECOND POINT: IMPLORE LIGHT.—After all these benefits grant me O Lord, the grace of Thy divine light, that I may know all my sins, particularly those which displease Thee most. O Divine Sun of Justice, enlighten the darkness which distraction, earthly inclinations, and self-love have created in my heart and mind! Let me understand how often and severely the enemy has wounded my soul, that I may seek and apply a remedy before it is too late!

THIRD POINT: EXAMINATION.—How have I performed my usual occupations to-day?

In the morning: Rising, morning prayers, meditation, Holy Mass, breakfast, work, intercourse with others, etc.?

Noon: Dinner, recreation, visits made or received, labor, spiritual reading, prayers, etc.?

Have I in all this offended God or my neighbor? failed in some virtue?

FOURTH POINT: SORROW.—O my God, how deeply confused I should feel when I compare Thy benefits with my ingratitude; Thy love with my indifference; the proofs of Thy loving and preventing grace with my endless delays! Yes, I acknowledge that I have wounded Thy Sacred Heart, and this fills me with sorrow and confusion. Reject not, O Lord, the sorrow of a contrite and humble heart! Give to my eyes a fountain of tears, and day and night I will bewail the misfortune of having offended Thee. Grant me the contrition of St. Peter, the tears of St. Magdalen, the humility of the publican, since like them I am laden with debt. O Eternal Father! look upon Thy only-begotten Son Jesus Christ, who became an atoning Sacrifice for us! Behold His nail-pierced hands and feet, His thorn-crowned head, His wounded Heart! His wounds are so many eloquent tongues imploring grace for me. O my God, forgive me! Upon my knees I implore Thy pardon. Thou wilt surely grant my petition, for Thou hast said: "I will not the death of the sinner, but that he be converted and live."[1]

FIFTH POINT: RESOLUTION.—My God, henceforward no more sin! I shall carefully close against it all the doors of my heart. I will avoid every occasion of sin, yes, even when possible, every thought tending thereto. I have hitherto been so unfaithful to my resolutions that I scarcely venture to renew them; but I hope in future to be more watchful and courageous; and I firmly expect from Thee Thy holy grace, with which assistance I shall faithfully and perseveringly fulfil my good resolution till death. O ever-Blessed Virgin Mary, bless the resolutions that I place

[1] Ezech. xxxiii. 11.

under thy care and protection! *Our Father* and *Hail Mary*.

NOTE.—This method may answer for the particular examen, in which you make it a point to overcome some evil propensity or to acquire some special virtue. One may combine the particular examen with the general by inquiring, at the close of the latter, whether since the last examination one has been guilty of the fault in question, or failed in the virtue.

Directions to render the Exercises of the Monthly Retreat of One Day profitable.

Choose one day in the month on which you will have most leisure, on which you will be less occupied or distracted. On the eve of the retreat say most devoutly the hymn, "Come, Holy Ghost," to implore the light of the Holy Spirit, and one *Hail Mary* to commend your retreat to the protection of the Blessed Virgin Mary. Then make the following meditation, which may serve as a preparation for the retreat:

Meditation for the Eve of the Retreat,

On the Virtues which are Necessary as a Preparation for Retreat.

I. PRELIMINARY PRELUDE.—Represent to yourself the healing of the blind man of Jericho. He casts himself on his knees before Jesus. The Saviour asks him: "What wilt thou that I should do to thee?" "Lord, that I may see!" answered the blind man. And Jesus said to him: "Go thy way, thy faith hath made thee whole."[1] Imagine Jesus putting the same question to you. Answer Him with the blind man: "Lord, that I may see! That in this retreat I may see what is wanting to me and what Thou requirest of me."

II. PRELUDE.—O my God! do Thou Thyself infuse into

[1] Mark x. 49-52.

my soul the disposition in which I should be, to derive great profit from my retreat.

FIRST POINT: FIRST VIRTUE.
The Sincere Desire to know One's Self thoroughly.

Have I this desire? Is it not a secret fear of seeing myself in the true light that alarms me, lest I should have to reproach myself? If I really and honestly desire self-knowledge, I shall have to ask myself seriously: What progress have I until now made in perfection? What profit have I derived from the reception of the holy Sacraments? What victories have I gained over myself, the devil, and the world? What virtues have I practised? What merits have I accumulated? What zeal have I displayed for my eternal welfare? Could I now appear before the judgment-seat of God without fear?

SECOND POINT: SECOND VIRTUE.
Great Confidence in God and Mistrust of Self.

Without God I can do nothing, but with Him all things! His grace is more powerful than all hell—and this grace is already prepared for me. I need only ask for it. God loves me, notwithstanding my past infidelity; and through love He again grants me this retreat as a means of salvation. "Come into solitude," He says to me, "and there I will speak to thy heart."[1] What goodness! And shall I not have confidence in Him? O my God! I can do nothing, but Thou art all-powerful. Assist me with Thy grace.

THIRD POINT: THIRD VIRTUE.
Generosity.

The Lord will during this retreat speak to your heart. Excite in yourself the same dispositions in which St. Paul was when he was struck down on his way to Damascus: "Lord, what wilt Thou have me do?"[2] or say with Samuel: "Speak, Lord; Thy servant heareth;"[3] or with David: "My heart is ready, O Lord; my heart is ready."[4] What offering

[1] Osee ii. 14. [2] Acts ix. 6. [3] I. Kings iii. 9. [4] Ps. lvi. 8.

dost Thou expect of me? I shall bring it to Thee without delay. Speak, O Lord! my heart is ready.

Conclude the meditation as you began it, with the prayer: O Lord, that I may see, that I may see my soul as it is, with its weaknesses, its imperfections, its sins! O Blessed Virgin Mary, obtain for me the grace to know myself thoroughly, and truly to amend! *Our Father, Hail Mary.*

Before retiring to rest, read the points of meditation for the next morning. For this purpose choose some good book, and in it a serious subject; for example, the end of man, the necessity of salvation, the heinousness of sin, the abuse of grace, an eternity of happiness or misery, etc. But if you have no book, ask yourself the following questions:

(1) What has God done for my salvation? Baptism, Christian education, graces, Sacraments, good example, retreats. With fewer graces I should already have become a saint.

(2) What does God require of me? That I should faithfully follow His inspirations, avoid sin, do violence to my passions, particularly to the predominant one; that I should be modest, retiring, humble, fervent, Have I in all this complied with what God requires?

(3) What have I to expect from God? He blesses those that are faithful to Him. But the unfruitful fig-tree He caused to be hewn down, the unfruitful vine uprooted and consigned to the flames. O my God! avert from me this misfortune! I will love and serve Thee. Do Thou strengthen me, and grant me the grace to be faithful to all the resolutions I shall take in this retreat. *Our Father, Hail Mary.*

Exercises for the Day of Retreat.

On rising, offer the day to God and beg His grace to spend it holily.

After the ordinary morning prayers, spend half an hour in meditation, for which you prepared the evening before in the manner above mentioned. Then assist at Holy Mass, at which communicate.

During the whole day observe silence and interior recollection, in so far as your condition, occupations, and surroundings permit. It is well that those of our household should not know that we are in retreat, unless in the case that it would occasion no unpleasant consequence.

In the course of the morning, read attentively the regulations of the day, and the resolutions taken in former retreats; or if you have not written any, recall the advice of your confessor, particularly that which he has most impressed upon you. See how you stand with God, and resolve firmly to banish from your heart all that displeases Him, in order to live henceforth according to His good pleasure. You may make one of the following reflections on the present state of your soul, devoting to this an hour or a half-hour, as circumstances may allow.

If you have time in the afternoon visit the Blessed Sacrament and a chapel of the Mother of God, where you may with great benefit make use of the truly excellent book compiled for this purpose by St. Alphonsus Liguori. Then read some good book of devotion for half an hour, and toward evening prepare yourself for death, as mentioned on page 368.

Reflections on the Present State of the Soul.

After imploring the light of the Holy Ghost, consider in the presence of God how you perform your most important actions, and how you are affected toward God, your neighbor, and the most essential virtues. In this observe the order here given.

I. DEVOTIONS.—Do I value them more highly than anything else? Do I perform them faithfully and punctually? Is my exterior deportment reverential? Am I recollected, retired, modest, keeping exact custody of the eyes? Do I neglect to prepare carefully for my devotional exercises by recollecting myself some moments before, quieting my imagination and senses, recalling the presence of God, and reflecting on what I am about to do? Do I, without anxiety or disturbance, banish distractions when perceived? or, at least, do I deny them deliberate consent, when I cannot at once rid myself of them? In spiritual dryness, am I not vexed, instead of enduring it humbly and patiently in punishment of past negligence? Do I not give way at once to discouragement?

Now go through your essential devotions separately. See how you have performed them, and what profit you have drawn from them:

Meditation.—Preparation for it; the ordinary cause of its not being successful, or of its trifling results; distractions, too great attachment to creatures.

General and Particular Examinations of Conscience.—Do I make them seriously? Are they accompanied with an earnest desire of amendment, or do I go through the work carelessly, or with a cowardly, superficial oversight? For every trivial fault that I commit do I impose upon myself a corresponding penance?

Spiritual Reading.—In this do I indulge my curiosity or satisfy the wants of my soul? Do I read regularly and perseveringly, or am I inconstant, changing at every moment my subject or my book? Do I read with a prayerful spirit? Do I honestly desire to derive profit from my reading? Do I pray to God for this grace? Do I pause to reflect when I come upon something particularly applicable to my state? When the reading is finished, do I think over it, and call again the most striking points, to impress them more deeply on my mind?

Holy Mass—Vocal Prayers—Public Services—Church Devotions.—With what attention, reverence, and devotion do I assist at them? In what sentiments do I hear the Word of God?

Confession.—Do I confess through custom, without purpose, or desire of amendment? without carefully exciting contrition? Is my accusation open, generous, clear, and void of a thousand useless narrations that serve but to perplex? Do I in every confession make a particular resolution?

Communion.—Do I abstain from it through fear? Do I desire to receive often through vanity? Do I prepare myself carefully, especially by offering some small sacrifice every time? How do I make my thanksgiving? What advantage do I derive from Holy Communion? Am I not negligent in making spiritual communions?

II. DEPORTMENT TOWARD GOD.—Do I evince toward Him due reverence, love, resignation, confidence, and gratitude? Do I try to please Him as my Lord, Father, Friend, and Spouse? Do I perform my actions all for God, and do I often renew this intention? Do I recall that I am always under the eyes of God? What care do I bestow on the purity of my conscience? Do I not lightly commit many faults, under the pretext that they are but venial? What is the nature of my love for Jesus? my devotion to the Blessed Sacrament of the Altar? to Mary? to the saints? to my patron saint? my guardian angel?

III. TOWARD THE NEIGHBOR.—Do I wish him well? Am I indulgent in my judgments, gentle and patient? or do I not sin by bitterness, jealousy, aversion, and censoriousness? Whence spring so many other faults against charity—detraction, slanders, rash judgments, slight injuries, desire of revenge, ridicule, little secret rancor, outbursts of ill-humor, emotions of violence? Do I in a spirit of faith regard my neighbor as the representative of Him who said: "As long as you did it to one of these my least brethren, you did it to Me."[1] How easily we would bear with one another if guided by this principle of faith!

IV. Do I care for my salvation and perfection? Do I consider this care as my most important, my only affair? What progress do I make in virtue, in self-denial, in the spirit of penance? Do I love the cross? or do I at least embrace every opportunity to bear my own with resignation

[1] Matt. xxv. 40.

and without murmur? What sacrifices do I impose upon myself to please God and to atone for my sins and faults?

How far have I advanced in the most necessary virtues—in faith, whose spirit should penetrate my whole life; in hope and in confidence; in that interior peace whose foundation rests on confidence, and excludes all anxiety, faintheartedness, and discouragement; in obedience according to my state of life, the renunciation of my own will, and divestment of all earthly goods; in purity, and careful avoidance of dangerous occasions, of curiosity, levity, and a too natural love; in humility and mistrust of my own strength? Do I love or do I at least peaceably endure humiliations, contempt, being forgotten, having others preferred to myself? How do I stand in regard to vanity, self-complacency, the desire to shine and rule? Do I ever despise my neighbor?

V. How do I correspond with the grace of divine inspiration? What victories have I gained over my predominant passion? What pains have I taken to govern my temper, to detach my heart from creatures? Does not some inordinate inclination, some impediment to my perfection, reign in my heart, which I will not sacrifice, although God has long demanded it of me? What is this inclination? What must I do to remove it; for what am I waiting, in order to be able to sacrifice it to God?

In what do I employ my time—in useful things or in trifles; in idle talk, vain fancies, airy castle-building, in dreams that are so often dangerous? Every moment of time can purchase eternity. What would not a damned soul give for a single moment?

VI. Reflect, also, how you comply with the special duties of your state and office, for general duties too often lead us to forget particular ones. And yet these require attention, fervor, assiduity, punctuality, and perseverance, to overcome one's self when at times one experiences such disgust for them as to be tempted to leave them undone.

In a word, do I live by faith, like the just man who considers all earthly things in the light of eternity? or do I live according to my self-love, according to the spirit of the world, which regards all things only in relation to this earthly life?

Upon all these matters examine yourself seriously before God. Then with sincere sorrow blot out the faults you have committed. Think of the occasions in which you may be likely to relapse, renew your resolutions with humility and confidence, and start on the way again with fresh courage, placing all your hope in the Lord, being neither discouraged nor cast down at the sight of your own misery.

Preparation for Death.

Kneel down before a Crucifix, and represent to yourself that your last hour has come; that an angel says to you as once to Ezechias: "Give charge concerning thy house, for thou shalt die, and not live."[1] Implore of God the grace of a happy death.

FIRST POINT.
What does it Mean to Die?

I shall die, that is: (1) I shall leave all, . . . parents, family, friends, house, goods, furniture, everything. . . . To what persons or things do I most cling? These as well as all the rest I shall leave. Terror seizes me at the thought of this all-embracing separation—and yet death is nothing else. And should I attach my heart to earthly things? Should I weary and torment myself in the pursuit of perishable goods? No—a thousand times no!

I shall die, that is: (2) My soul shall separate from my body. This body, a ghastly corpse, will then lie without life or motion, an object of horror or compassion for all; finally, it will be buried, and become the food of worms. Yes, this head, these eyes, this tongue, these feet, these hands, will be consigned to rottenness . . . . And through love of this body of clay, shall I risk my soul, my eternity? No—a thousand times no!

[1] IV. Kings xx. 1.

SECOND POINT.
When and How shall I Die?

I know not. One may die at any age, at all times, and in all places, of any kind of disease. Shall I have time to prepare for death? Shall I be able to receive the holy Sacraments? I hope so, but I do not know. Many have been suddenly surprised by death, and the same may happen to me. When one is ill, and particularly when he is in the last agony, he cannot easily prepare well for death. At that moment he possesses but little memory, but little knowledge, and perhaps but little strength of will; and yet our eternity depends upon that moment!

THIRD POINT.
Am I Ready to Die Now?

Does nothing hold me to the earth? Am I ready to appear before the judgment-seat of God? Does no sin cause me anxiety? Have I nothing to fear for my confessions, for my Communions, for so many graces received? O frightful moment! To be judged . . . by an all-just, ... all-wise, ... all-powerful God, . . . who hates sin above all things! After a serious meditation of these truths, make your resolutions, and recite, kneeling, the following prayers:

Prayer of Absolute Submission to the Law of Death.

O God Almighty, Lord of life and of death, who for the punishment of sin hath in Thy unchangeable decrees appointed for all men once to die, behold me humbly prostrate at Thy feet, prepared to submit to this law of Thy justice! In the bitterness of my heart I bewail my transgressions. As an obstinate sinner, I have deserved death a thousand times; therefore I accept it in obedience to Thy holy will. I accept it as an atonement for my innumerable sins. I accept it in union with the death of my Redeemer.

... I wish to die, O my God! when it pleases Thee, where it pleases Thee, and how it pleases Thee. .... The time Thy divine mercy still grants me shall be employed in divesting myself of a world in which I have only some moments to stay; in loosening the bonds that enchain me to this place of banishment; and in preparing my soul for the hour of Thy fearful judgment. ... I remit myself without reserve to Thy ever fatherly providence. Thy holy will be done in all things forever! Amen.

Prayer To Obtain the Grace of a Happy Death.

O my God! prostrate before the throne of Thy adorable Majesty, I beg of Thee the final grace of a happy death. I have indeed often made a bad use of the life Thou gavest me; but grant that I may end it well, and die in Thy love!

Let me die like the holy patriarchs, leaving without regret this valley of tears, to go and enjoy eternal rest in my true country!

Let me die like blessed St. Joseph, in the arms of Jesus and Mary, calling upon those sweet names, which I hope to love and praise for all eternity!

Let me die like the ever-Blessed Virgin Mary, inflamed with the most pure love, and ardently desiring to be united with the only Object of all my affections!

Let me die like Jesus on the cross, in the most lively sentiments of hatred for sin, love for my Heavenly Father, and resignation in the midst of sufferings!

Heavenly Father! into Thy hands I commend my spirit: have mercy on me!

Jesus, who didst die for love of me, grant me grace to die in Thy love!

Holy Mary, Mother of God, pray for me now and at the hour of my death!

Angel of God, faithful guardian of my soul, and you, great saints, whom God gave me for protectors, do not forsake me at the hour of my death!

Preparation for Death.

St. Joseph, obtain for me, by thy powerful intercession, that I MAY DIE THE DEATH OF THE JUST! **Amen.**

Invocation.

Soul of Christ, sanctify me:
Body of Christ, save me:
Blood of Christ, inebriate me:
Water from the side of Christ, wash me:
Passion of Christ, strengthen me:
O good Jesus! hear me;
Within Thy wounds hide me:
Permit me not to be separated from Thee:
From the malignant enemy defend me:
In the hour of my death call me,
And bid me come to Thee,
That with Thy saints I may praise Thee
Forever and ever! Amen.

Consider other great books and booklets direct from the publisher, or ask for them at your local bookstore. Inquire for price.

Books:
Following of Christ by Thomas A Kempis	N-FOLLOW
Introduction to the Devout Life by St. Francis de Sales	N-INTRO
The Faith of Our Fathers by Rev. James Gibbons, D.D.	N-FAITH
Self Improvement Impr 1939	N-SELF
Spiritual Exercises of St. Ignatius	N-SESI
Mary Help if Christians - Impr 1908	N-HELP
Confessions of St. Augustine - Translated by F.J. Sheed	N-CONFESSION
The Sinner's Guide - Impr 1883	N-SGU
The Spiritual Combat - Impr 1945	N-SPCO
Thoughts for All Times - Impr	N-THOUGHTS
Eternal Punishment - Impr 1928	N-ETERNAL
Visits to the Most Holy Sacrament and to the Blessed Virgin Mary	N-VISITS
Defense of the Catholic Church - Impr 1927	N-DEFENSE
Anecdotes and Examples Illustrating the Catholic Catechism	N-ANC
Fifteen Saturdays of the Most Holy Rosary	N-FSAT
The Summa Abridged, Impr 1950	N-SUMM
Our Lady of the Miraculous Medal	N-LMM
Liturgical Novenas and Triduums for All the Feasts of the Blessed Virgin Mary	N-LN
Mirror of True Womanhood	N-TRUE
Our Spiritual Service to the Sick and Dying	N-SSD
In Love with the Divine Outcast	N-LDO
Confession Made Easy IMPR 1910	N-CME
An Hour with the Little Flower	N-FLOWER
Life of St. Philomena	N-LIFE
Things Catholics are Asked About	N-THINGS
Catholic Ready Answer IMPR 1914	N-CRA
Catechism of the Council of Trent	N-TRENT
Sunday Missal Compiled by Fr. Lasance	N-SM

Booklets:
The Conquest of Fear	N-CONQUEST
Christ and Women Impr 1928	N-CW
Is Your Child Handicapped?	N-HANDICAP
Our Way of Life Must Prevail	N-PREVAIL
How to Stay Young Fr Daniel Lord	N-YOUNG
The Woman in the Home Rev. Hugh Calkins	N-WOMAN
Love is Like That Fr Daniel Lord	N-THAT
Hours Off Impr 1945	N-OFF
Marriage in the Home Rev. Edmond Bernard	N-MARRIAGE
Novena in Honor of St. Patrick Impr 1958	N-PATRICK
Is it a Saint's Name? Impr 1948	N-NAME
Parenthood Fr Daniel Lord	N-PARENTHOOD
Novena in Honor of St. Dymphna	N-DYM
The Secrets of Purgatory	N-SECRETS
In the School of Jesus Introduction to the Interior Life	N-SCHOOL
Our Heavenly Companions Impr 1956	N-OHC
The Catholic Funeral Service Impr 1935	N-CFS
Novena, Hymns, and Prayers for the Holy Souls in Purgatory	N-HSP
All-Souls Novena 22 page booklet	N-ASN
After Death - What? Impr 1927	N-AFTER
The Man Who Really Was Santa Claus	N-SANTA
A Novena for Conversions Impr 1949	N-NC
My Life - What Shall I Make of It?	N-WHAT
Training Your Child From Infancy to Maturity	N-TRYC
In the Footsteps of St. Scholastica	N-FSS
Words of Consolation for the Sick and Afflicted	N-WORDS
Wonders of the Holy Name by Fr O'Sullivan	N-WONDERS
Peace, the Fruit of Justice Impr	N-FRUIT